POSITIVE COACHING

Building Character and Self-Esteem Through Sports

JIM THOMPSON

Director, Public Management Program
Stanford Graduate School of Business

Warde Publishers

Portola Valley, California

Copyright © 1995 by James C. Thompson. Warde Publishers, Inc. publishes *Positive Coaching* under an exclusive worldwide license of the copyright from the copyright holder. All rights reserved. No part of this publication may be reproduced, stored in a retrieval system, or transmitted, in any form or by any means, electronic, photocopying, recording or otherwise without the prior written permission of the Publisher, except in the case of brief excerpts in critical reviews and articles. For permission requests, write to the publisher, addressed "Attention: Permissions," at the address below.

Warde Publishers, Inc.
3000 Alpine Road
Portola Valley, CA 94028
(800) 699–2733

Library of Congress Cataloging-in-Publication Data
Thompson, Jim, 1949–
    Positive coaching: building character and self-esteem through sports / Jim Thompson
ISBN 1-886346-00-3   94-061721
                                                      CIP

Printed in the United States of America
10 9 8   02 01

Warde Publishers, Inc. and the author disclaim responsibility for adverse effects or consequences from the misapplication or injudicious use of the information contained in this book. Mention of resources and associations does not imply endorsement by Warde Publishers, Inc. or the author.

Cover designer: Detta Penna, Penna Design and Production

Contents

Foreword

Jim Thompson is a versatile coach—on the athletic field, in the classrooms of the Stanford Graduate School of Business, wherever his gifts are needed.

Even large corporations are recognizing that coaching is a special and highly creative form of leading. I spoke recently at a meeting of the marketing division of a major company and every one of the hundred or so executives in the room had a name tag with his or her first name preceded by the word coach. I was "Coach John."

So this is really a book for all ages, whether you're a parent, teacher, counselor, manager, leader, or friend. Forget the categories: If you're human and not insanely self-centered, you've had that impulse to help someone learn, grow, perform better, "be what they can be." When I began my job as a cabinet officer in the federal government, I needed a lot of coaching. And luckily I had some great coaches to get me through the shark-infested waters.

Every leader (and every first-grade teacher) knows that explaining (or reaching consensus on) what course of action should be taken is only half the task. The other half is to convince people they have it in them to do it. Confidence! Every athlete understands the importance of it. The best coaches build it. But all too many build the confidence of only their star athletes, sending many a lesser player away with wounds to confidence that will last for years.

There's a better way to do it and Jim Thompson tells what it is. Everyone can't be a star but everyone can grow. Everyone can't make the varsity but everyone can learn important lifelong lessons from sports about determination and mental toughness. And everyone can learn to enjoy sports, regardless of how well he or she performs.

Positive Coaching will be of value in a very practical, down-to-earth way to any coach. But Jim Thompson has a larger goal in mind. He would like to change the way youth sports are conducted in this country. He would like to see a positive coaching movement sweep across Little League America. And he may well succeed. Ideas are powerful, and this book tosses some lively ones into the conversation.

John W. Gardner

Preface
How to Use this
"Letter to a Friend"

In Lloyd Douglas's *Magnificent Obsession*, erstwhile play-boy Bobby Merrick puzzles over Dr. Hudson's secret journal. When finally he succeeds in breaking the code, he discovers: "Reader I consider you my friend."

When my colleague and friend Gene Webb read an early draft of this manuscript, he told me, "It reads like a letter to a friend." I'm not sure he meant it as a compliment but it felt like one to me, and I couldn't get the phrase out of my head.

The title of this book is probably misleading to some people. *Positive Coaching: Building Character and Self-Esteem Through Sports*—it sounds like a detached, impersonal how-to manual. It's true the book contains lots of practical, how-to information. But it is neither detached nor impersonal. I don't know how coaching could be either. My family, friends, fellow coaches, teams, individual players, and I, myself, are all inextricably woven into the fabric of this book.

Coaching is primarily about relationships. You don't coach disembodied "players." You coach individual young persons—persons with problems and hang-ups, ideas of their own (some good, some bad, some hard to tell), character strengths and weaknesses, parents who raised them permissively or strictly or somewhere in between, jokes to tell and sadnesses to bear, and dreams of glory and fears of disappointing.

Nor are these individuals coached by robo-coaches. Coaches have all the same kinds of personal stuff. And when the stuff of coaches interacts with the stuff of players, as Manly Wade Wellman says in his delightful book *Who Fears the Devil?* ". . . you'd best go expecting anything."

Several people who reviewed the manuscript gave me pretty much the same feedback in different words. One person told me he had no idea there was so much *to* coaching, how complicated it is. Another said he felt that he couldn't measure up to the high standard described in this book. Along the same lines, a third said that she felt a little intimidated but was relieved from time to time when I wrote about my shortcomings and blunders throughout the book. When she finally read Chapter 18, she said she felt very empowered. A fourth noted that there were a lot of ideas in the book and suggested I needed a section at the front to give people permission to *not* have to read it from cover to cover.

So . . . I would love to have everyone who picks up *Positive Coaching* read it from cover to cover. I've tried to present a philosophy of coaching with ideas in one chapter often connecting with points in later chapters to (hopefully) build to a grand climax.

But, reader, I *do* consider you my friend. You have my permission to read this book however *you* want to read it. Feel free to browse in the table of contents and the book as a whole. If you are interested in ideas on how to organize practice sessions, go right to Chapter 8. If you have a superstar or a child with a behavior problem on your team, turn to Chapter 15. If you are looking for ways to help kids develop increased self-esteem or positive character traits, check out Chapters 5 and 6, respectively. If you're a perfectionist who never met a mistake you didn't hate, flip to Chapter 7. If you really don't want to let losing tear you up inside so much, try Chapters 11 and 12.

It has been said that sports don't develop character as much as reveal it. If you really care about coaching and the kids you coach, and seek to become good at it, coaching will test you. You will confront parts of yourself that you might just as soon not have to see. If you come to a point where you begin to feel that you are just too neurotic to be an effective coach, Chapter 18 is the ticket.

I've put a lot of myself into this book. I hope it is helpful to you and the children with whom you work. I hope you come away from reading *Positive Coaching* more excited about coaching than you were before. Indeed, I hope you will come to see it as a letter from a friend.

Acknowledgments

A major theme in *Positive Coaching* is the great personal power that can come from being in a supportive network of friends. Throughout the writing of this book I have been enriched and nurtured by an alarmingly large number of people.

It all started with the antics of those precious, disturbed children at the Behavioral Learning Center in St. Paul, Minnesota. I don't know where Kevin, Judy, David, Chuck, Greg, Karry, Laura, Ronald, Ricky, the other Ricky, Chris, Janet, Tim, and Randy are now, but if there is any justice in this world, they will be among friends who appreciate them for the wonders that they are. Many other children in Rock Springs, Wyoming, and Palo Alto and Cupertino, California, have continued to make coaching and teaching exciting and special.

Winston Mathews got me hooked on sports many years ago. Mike Saxenian first pushed me to begin writing seriously. Marisha Chamberlain served as my main muse. When such a talented writer, poet, and playwright believes so strongly in my writing, how can I fail to believe as well? Rich Kelley has reassured me from the perspective of the serious athlete in his many and detailed comments on several versions of the manuscript. Fred Miller, the source of many management ideas adapted to coaching, continues to be the prototype of the manager *par excellence* as well as a mentor and friend. Richard Close has encouraged me with his perspective from the counseling world. Alison Davis helped me become a leaner and meaner writer, continuing a lesson begun years earlier by Bill Sanderson. Alison also graciously applied her friendly critical eye to my ramblings in spite of a total lack of interest in organized sports. Tom Copeland provided me with *pro bono* legal advice to go with his longstanding friendship. I'm convinced he has a future as an agent if he decides to give up his post as tax guru to day-care providers.

Two organizations have played major roles in the development of the ideas in this book. Cupertino Hoops has been a laboratory as well as a source of friends. Paul Solomon, who founded the organization with me, has heard (if not read) and reacted to many of the ideas in the book while running around the De Anza College track. The Stanford Business School has provided an environment as intellectually stimulating as I could imagine. Our MBA students in the Public Management Program, contrary to whatever stereotypes people may have about MBAs, are part of the hope for the future. As my wife has said so often, "They just don't seem like MBAs. They're so nice." If these young people rise to positions of power—in business, government, and the nonprofit world—as I have no doubt they will, our world will be in good hands. Perhaps some of them will even become coaches.

Two giant influences from afar in my earlier life have been John Gardner and Elizabeth O'Connor. It has been a dream come true to have gotten to know them as friends and to discover that they are even more authentic, wise, and generous than they appear from their authentic, wise, and generous writings.

I have been blessed by having benefitted firsthand from many, many wonderful managers, teachers, and coaches: David White (who introduced a fearful freshman at Macalester College to the promise and power of nonattachment to the fruits of one's actions), Ralph Rusley, Polly Ames, David Montplaisir, DeWitt Batterberry, Tom Engh,

George Bender, Marvin Leidel, Shirley Pearl, Don Challman, Gerald Wolfe, Eileen Serr, Walt Pollock, Lynn Frank, Boyd Haight, Gene Webb, Jim Patell, Jim March, Jeff Pfeffer, David Brady, and Jerry Porras, to name just a few.

Many people have encouraged me from far and near: Ralph Hietala, Ivy Hietala, Bobbi Baumgartner, Sib Farrell, Val Floch, Joyce Pharriss, Jim Collins, Rich Kurovsky, Tom Tutko, Jerry Kindall, Stacy Geiken, Mike Dunlap, Larry Gray, Sharon Gray, Bob Reasoner, John King, Rachel King, Pat Baker, Rosa Alvarado, Robert Silvers, Steve Landers, Steve Lehman, Kathy Childers, Carol Colbeck, Jeff Olson, Debbie Wolter, Elizabeth Ozer, Frank Butler, Don McClanen, Tom Cronin, Danny Grossman, David Arfin, Chris Coleman, Sam Won Lee, Leo Redmond, and John Zorn.

Close to home, I am indebted to my first teacher and home court advantage, my mother, Marjory, from whom I got my spunk; my father, Bill, from whom I got my special feeling for the underdog; and my stepfather, Orville, who was there for me.

My son, Gabriel, has blessed and seasoned my life so that I can't imagine what life was like before he was part of it.

And finally, I dedicate this book to my wife, Sandra, my spiritual guide and the light of my life.

Introduction
The Untapped Potential
of Youth Sports

I mean to keep playing games with my son, so long as flesh will per-
mit, as my father played games with me well past his own physical
prime. Now that sports have begun to give me lessons in mortality, I
realize they have also been giving me, all the while, lessons in immortal-
ity. These games, these contests, these conversations of body to body, fa-
ther to son, are not substitutes for some other way of being alive. They
are the sweet and sweaty thing itself.

—Scott Russell Sanders
Secrets of the Universe

It is the greatest moment of my young life. With less than
a minute to go in the game with arch-rival Jamestown
(North Dakota) High School, West Fargo High (my school)
is behind by two points. I drive to the free throw line, pull
up, and shoot. The ball goes in! Tie game. As Jamestown
takes the ball out, we full-court press. My teammate stops
a Jamestown player with the ball near the sidelines close
to midcourt. I circle around behind him while he is distracted and grab for the ball. I get it! I turn and dribble to
the wide open basket, and shoot the underhanded scoop
shot I had recently developed. I score. We win!

1

Eighteen years later, I'm coaching a team of second-graders. We're behind by four points with less than a minute to play. My son steals the ball and dribbles the length of the floor to score; with an opposing player hanging all over him. The other team brings the ball up the court. I can see in Gabby's eyes he's going for the steal again. He does and again dribbles the length of the floor to tie the score. This time the opposing team is more careful. They get off a shot but miss. Gabby gets the rebound and yet again he drives the length of the floor and scores. We win!

Why do grown men (and now, more and more, women) spend literally the better part of their lives coaching young people in sports? More than anything else, it is moments like these that help one understand the incredible power of sports in the lives of adults as well as kids. A person can go for a long time on the psychic energy of memories like these, and lots of us do.

A friend in politics once described to me the rush of standing on a platform with Michael Dukakis during the 1988 presidential campaign. Thousands of people in the audience were cheering wildly. Although the cheers were for Dukakis and not for him, my friend was still swept up in the emotion of the moment. We all want to be cheered for, if not by thousands, at least by a few.

A few years ago I arrived at a Stanford-Cal basketball game at halftime; a late meeting had kept me from seeing the beginning. For a moment I thought I had entered into the Twilight Zone because the scoreboard seemed to suggest that Stanford was 20 points ahead of a very strong Cal team featuring future NBA superstar Kevin Johnson. But, in fact, the scoreboard was correct. Stanford had simply played a terrific half of basketball. The Stanford team eased past me on the way out to the court for the beginning of the second half. The Stanford Band was playing, so the players paused to wait for the band to finish before making their entrance onto the floor.

I looked over the players—Todd Lichti, later to play with the Denver Nuggets; Howard Wright; Terry Taylor; and the rest—and had a profound feeling of sadness and envy that I had never had the chance to be standing where they were, with a packed auditorium watching and cheering *my* every move on the basketball court.

The band finished its song, and the Stanford players ran out onto the court. Maples Pavilion erupted, as would be expected when the home team is ahead of a fierce rival by 20 points. That game ended happily (at least for Stanford), but often the outcome is not as positive, and that can leave lasting scars.

THE LIFELONG IMPACT OF YOUTH SPORTS

The movie *The Best of Times* starring Robin Williams depicted an outwardly successful man who was still burning from dropping a pass that would have won a championship football game 10 years earlier. The movie describes his successful attempt to stage a rematch with the same players from both teams.

Most of us who have played organized sports as youngsters wouldn't go to the extremes that the Williams character does. But I am struck by how many men I know who can tell you in excruciating detail about one or more athletic contests they participated in as youngsters. I sometimes begin coaching workshops by asking the coaches to pair up and tell each other about a time when they made a critical mistake in a game and a time when they made the big play. The conversations are invariably animated and lively, as people travel back in time to an occasion that has lain in memory for years.

My own stories are of Greg Lokken and Bob Green. Greg Lokken was *the* athlete in the Fargo-Moorhead area when I was in junior high and high school. Greg played football for South Moorhead Junior High, and he had blazing speed. Our West Fargo Junior High football team had little chance against South, and we lost convincingly; but the moment I will always remember was the time I could have tackled Greg Lokken. Moorhead South was inside our 20-yard line, and I was playing linebacker. Lokken got the ball and slipped through our line without much problem. He came toward me and I froze. He sped past me on his way to a touchdown—one of many for him that day if my memory serves me.

It was only later that I realized that I *could* have made the tackle. He was not a big person. And while he was faster than me, I had a perfect angle on him. He shook his hip at me a little bit but mostly I just didn't believe that I could do it—and so I didn't.

Two years later, as a junior, I attended Boy's State at North Dakota State University. The activities included sporting events, such as basketball. I was on a team that didn't have many good athletes, so I tried to make some things happen. Several times I went past the player guarding me to score on drives to the basket. Then, when he slacked off, I made some outside shots. I was hot and it felt good, but the big surprise was to come. After the game, we shook hands and I asked who he was and where he was from. You could have knocked me down with a feather when he said that he was Bob Green from Mandan. Mandan had won the state Class A Boys Championship that year, and Bob Green and Scott Howe, both juniors, were the stars of the tournament. I had just gone one-on-one with Bob Green and had done quite well.

Thinking back on both episodes, I believe that one reason I did so well against Bob Green was that I didn't know who he was. If I had, my lack of self-confidence at the time probably would have kept me focusing more on how great he was—as I had with Greg Lokken—than on doing what I could.

4

But it is not just "we few, we happy few, we band of brothers" (and sisters) who have played the games, for whom sports have long-lasting importance, but the larger society as well.

THE SYMBOLIC IMPORTANCE OF SPORTS

Sports are highly valued in this culture. We could argue long and hard about whether they *should* be so important to us, but the evidence is everywhere that they are. In this country, Michael Jordan is a hero to children, all races and classes, who often go to extremes to find the money necessary to buy sneakers with his name on them. In 1990, nine people were killed during the celebratory frenzy in Detroit after the Pistons won their second NBA championship in a row. Closer to home, parents of 13-year-olds playing a Little League baseball game in my hometown almost came to blows over an umpire's call. In May 1992, a Little League coach in North Carolina took his frustration considerably further when he slashed the throat of a rival coach before a game.

Washington Post sportswriter Thomas Boswell has argued that sport "has become central to what remains of our American sense of identity" and even has become "the meeting ground where we discuss our values." Competitive athletic contests carry with them immense pressure and symbolic meaning in this culture. Many observers argue that organized youth sports are destructive to most children, and as they often are played out, there is some merit to that viewpoint.

But the silver lining is that it is exactly *because of* the symbolic meaning inherent in youth sports, and the pressures that children choose or are coerced to face on the playing field or in the gymnasium, that an incredible opportunity arises to teach positive lessons about life.

Our culture seems to have lost any sort of rite of passage for young people moving from childhood to adulthood. I recently attended a bar mitzvah for one of the players on my basketball team. I was struck by what an important event it was for him. He was required to perform adult chores—leading parts of the service and reciting vast amounts of memorized scripture. It was a very big deal, and it symbolized his entrance unto the cusp of manhood in a way that my family's Protestant Christian tradition failed to provide for me.

In some ways organized sports may fill this need at least for some youth in our society. There is a lot of pressure on kids in sport. For the most part I think this is not healthy and, in fact, much of this book is about trying to reduce the pressure on children so they can become who *they* need and want to become. But the positive side of pressure is that thoughtful coaches can use it to build up players by helping them to prepare for and succeed in dealing with it (which may have little or nothing to do with who actually wins a particular game or season title).

Like the Native American youths who went out alone into the wilderness for their "vision quest," our young people can experience stirring challenges on the fields and courts of organized competitive sports. And like ancient rites of passage, physical transformation or disfigurement can sometimes be involved. Young athletes build up their bodies with exercise and weightlifting. Some even risk ultimate disfigurement by use of steroids. Reading *Friday Night Lights* by H. G. Bissinger, I was taken aback by how often the young men of Permian High School in Odessa, Texas, vomited before, during, and after games and even practices.

Clearly, there is a lot going on below the surface of every athletic contest. Any activity that carries that much symbolic meaning deserves a thoughtful approach to helping our children get the most from it.

THE CORRELATION BETWEEN SUCCESS IN SPORTS AND IN LIFE

My friend Stacy Geiken told me about his experience at the National Outdoor Leadership School (NOLS) in Wyoming when he was a teen-ager. He saw a TV program about NOLS and, although he felt afraid, he knew he wanted to try it. For the final activity Stacy was appointed the leader of a group of four teens who were given the challenge of negotiating their way out of the wilderness while living off the land. Stacy, who is an outgoing, confident fellow, tells me that he was quite shy and introverted before this experience. After successfully leading his group to their goal, he says he felt a sense of self-confidence that has stayed with him throughout his life. I believe he came away from that experience with a reformulated sense of what psychologist Albert Bandura calls "self-efficacy," or, translated into sports terminology, the ability to make things happen, to act rather than be acted upon.

The potential exists in sports for most children, whether great athletes or not, to rise to the occasion, to give their best in a moment of symbolic meaning, and to take a greater sense of self into the rest of their life. A few years ago on my baseball team, I coached Kirby, a player who tried hard but had not been blessed with great strength, speed, or coordination.

When the final game of the season came around, Kirby had still not gotten a hit. Since our team had no chance for the playoffs, I decided to have Kirby play the entire game at third base *and* to bat leadoff. I will never forget the look on his face when I announced that he would bat first to give him as many chances at bat as possible. Mixed in with the fear and shock, I believe, was the glint of a joyful smile.

I would like to be able to report that Kirby got his first hit of the season, but I can't. He did, however, crank his level of play up a notch. He didn't strike out and he made a nice play at third base on a pop fly. We won the game and he scored two of our six runs, after hanging tough and getting a walk both times. After the game it was clear that he was proud of himself. As my assistant coach said, "He knew we were counting on him and he came through."

While it is not an open-and-shut certainty that success in sports leads to success elsewhere in life, I believe that it can certainly help. But a lot of that depends on the lessons that a young athlete takes away from his or her sporting experience.

LEARNING FROM EXPERIENCE: MARK TWAIN'S CAT AND BENCHLEY'S DOG

It is not at all clear to me that adults, let alone children, always draw appropriate lessons from their experiences. As Mark Twain noted, "We should be careful to get out of an experience only the wisdom that is in it—and stop there; lest we be like the cat that sits down on a hot stove-lid. She will never sit down on a hot stove-lid again—and that is well; but also she will never sit down on a cold one anymore."

John Gardner recalls another pet analogy: "Experience, thought to be the best teacher, is sometimes a confusing teacher. Robert Benchley said that having a dog teaches a boy fidelity, perseverance, and to turn around three times before lying down."

I believe that one reason so many kids quit playing competitive sports before their time is that they learn the wrong lesson from the experience. I am reminded of my son's first competitive athletic experience. We had recently moved from Oregon to California, and he had come to his first soccer game never having been to a practice. He met his coach and teammates, got his uniform, went into the car to change clothes, and soon found himself playing goalie without a clue as to what soccer was all about.

The other team scored several goals, and I was in severe pain seeing the look of confusion on his six-year-old face. By the next week's game he had attended his team's practices and knew quite a bit more about soccer. He also knew he didn't want to play goalie and, with one exception, never played the position again. Perhaps he learned an inappropriate lesson about goalkeeping from that traumatic experience. What may have been lost became apparent two years later when he played his one and only complete game at goalie.

His team's only loss that season was to a powerful team that had won every game by at least three goals. Gabby's team had lost to them 6-0 the first time they played. This was the last game of the season and would determine the league champion. Gabby's coach decided to play him at goalie. He spent the week before the game studying a video on how to play goalie. In the first period, the opposing team scored a goal, and it looked very much like a rerun of the first game.

But it wasn't. Much to the parents' surprise, our team scored a goal, the first they'd managed against this team all year. Shortly after that our team had a chance for a penalty kick in front of the other team's goal. The coach pulled Gabby out of the goal to kick the penalty kick, in spite of the fact that he would have to run the length of the field to return to his own unguarded goal if he missed the kick and the ball remained in play. But on this day Gabby could do no wrong, and he nailed the penalty kick, putting the other team behind for the first time all season.

The rest of the game was spent in front of our team's goal with the opposing team taking thunderous boots and Gabby somehow deflecting each one, including a couple of carbon copies of the blocks demonstrated in the video. At one point he dived through the legs of an opposing player to grab a ball that was squirming around in front of the goal. Another time he got the very ends of his fingertips on a ball and managed to deflect it just over the goal. Yet another time he came charging out of the goal to narrow the angle on a player who had a one-on-one breakaway. Had he stayed in the goal and waited, it would have been almost impossible for the opponent to miss the shot. But by charging he covered up a bigger portion of the net and the kick went off to the side. At the game's end, his teammates picked Gabby up and carried him around as if they had just won the World Cup.

That was the last game of the season. The next year the coaches from the opposing team moved their team up to a more competitive league and asked Gabby to join them to play goalie. He did join the team and played with them for several years before dropping soccer. However, he didn't play goalie for them, or ever again.

Gabby said he didn't want to play goalie because it was so boring most of the time, which reminds me of how my policeman cousin describes police work: "99 percent boredom and 1 percent sheer terror." But I can't help but wonder if that first experience of playing goalie wasn't a hot stove-lid that left him with the lesson that he could very easily do without the threat of the public embarrassment of having people score against him. And his triumphant second experience at goalie may have convinced him that he now had to live up to such a high level of expectations from his coaches, teammates, and perhaps even, alas, his father, that he could live a very satisfying life without that aggravation as well.

One reason I wrote this book is because too often I have seen young athletes diminished by their experience with sports. They seem less willing to embrace life than before they got involved with sports. I want kids to come away from sports with a heightened sense of themselves as people who can strive for great things . . . who learn that they can fail and get up and try again, and even fail again

. . . who are less afraid, or perhaps more willing to act in spite of their fear, and more willing to take the risk that achievement and excellence require of all of us . . . who are willing to set goals for themselves and then make the commitment to achieve those goals. But like Mark Twain's cat, I see too many children who get burned by their encounters with organized sports, and choose not to take any further chances with stove-lids, hot or cold.

THE ACCIDENTAL COACH AND THE REPETITION COMPULSION

Many coaches get into coaching the way that I did, almost by chance. I attended the innocent sounding "parents meeting" at the beginning of the soccer season in which the league director informs the parents who have obediently assembled at his home that "your children's team has no coach." You then find out that if someone in the room doesn't volunteer to do it, your children will not be able to play soccer this year.

I first got involved with my son's baseball team by accident (although these many years later I realize that it was an accident waiting to happen). I went to the games to watch, but all too often there was no one who was willing to be the umpire. I didn't want to be the umpire, but here was a group of six- and seven-year-olds wanting to play tee-ball and how difficult could it be? (Tougher than I'd have thought, actually.) That gave me a taste of sports again, after many years of abstinence.

What I saw troubled me. As I watched usually well-meaning, often kindhearted adults working with young athletes in self-defeating ways, the glimmer of an idea that eventually turned into this book first appeared. I saw parents and coaches who interacted with kids in ways that were virtually guaranteed to have bad results. As my wife says, parents tend to treat their children the way they have been treated. Child abusers tend to be people who were themselves abused as children. I recently heard Michael Lerner, the editor and publisher of *Tikkun* magazine, describe it as the "repetition compulsion": we act out what we have experienced—whether we liked it or not—in some cases consciously, many times subconsciously. Coaches tend to act the way they think a coach should act. And that is often based upon how their coaches treated them and their teammates. Absent some other model of how to coach in a positive way, amateur youth sports coaches can often slide into a negative, snarling kind of coaching that they may believe is "how to coach," based on what they see on television from college and professional coaches.

The next winter I decided to give coaching a shot. I was in my second year of business school at Stanford, which is not nearly as life-threatening as the first year, so I felt confident I could devote enough time to it to do a decent job and have some fun. The next thing I knew, I was coaching basketball and baseball, and keeping statistics for a soccer team. Fortunately I didn't know enough about soccer to coach, but I even considered coaching soccer with a friend who did before I came to my senses.

In the meantime I read lots of books on coaching, almost all of which focused on teaching the technical skills of the sport. The questions I had didn't seem to be addressed. I wondered how one organized a practice session with 14 squirming kids on a baseball field so that they would go home afterwards excited about coming to the next practice. I wondered how you dealt with parents who were on their children constantly, to the point that if the child had killed the parent, any reasonable court of law would have found it justifiable homicide. I wondered how you worked with other adults who offered to help you coach the team, when they had quite different ideas about how to handle the job. I wondered about how you kept a strong team from becoming arrogant and ungracious with the teams they easily defeated. And, conversely, how you kept a weak team from getting so down in the dumps after a long losing streak that they quit coming to practice. I wondered how you conveyed the joy and love of a game like baseball to kids who seemed to be under too much pressure. I wondered how . . . well, you get the idea.

This book is an initial response to those wonderings in the hope that others can learn from my mistakes and successes. It has been said that anyone can learn from their own mistakes (although even that is optimistic). The wise learn from the experience, and mistakes, of *others*. In my experience, volunteer youth sports coaches are rarely prepared to help their players capture all the meaning in the sports experience. Most of us learned about coaching the hard way, in the school of hard knocks. And since I didn't find a book like this one in bookstores, I decided to write the book I wanted to read. Which leads to the issue of what gave me the crazy idea that I have the qualifications needed to write such a book.

WHO DO YOU THINK YOU ARE?

It was polite, but stinging nonetheless. I had just been introduced to the spouse of an old college friend at a college reunion. He was a Ph.D. student and heard me mention that I was writing a book on coaching: "On what basis are you writing it? Do you have an academic background in sports psychology?" Well, no, not exactly . . .

(Having spent quite a few years now in an academic setting, I am very aware of what it means to be an expert in a subject matter, and the appropriate disdain that the academic world has for people who bill themselves as experts when they really aren't. So . . . let's get it straight from the beginning: I am not considered an expert in sports psychology, nor human development, nor athletic performance, nor coaching in general, nor in basketball, baseball, or any other team sport in particular. So if you are looking for some great books on those subjects, check out the bibliography at the back of this book.)

. . . but I do have some things to say, some insights to share, and some experience that I am convinced will be of benefit to amateur youth sports coaches. What then are my qualifications for writing this book?

First, I was an enthusiastic athlete as a child. Following my parents' divorce, my mother and I moved to Wyndmere, North Dakota, when I was four. We rented an apartment from another single parent, Margaret Mathews, the high school principal. Her junior high-age son, Winston, was a sports fanatic—in particular, about baseball. Winston and I made a great pair. He knew a lot about sports, and liked to explain. I was a sponge, trying to learn as much as I could about baseball, and I hung on his every word. By the time we left Wyndmere to move to San Diego, California, four years later, I lived for baseball and intended to become a major league ballplayer when I grew up.

We moved to West Fargo, North Dakota, as I began junior high school. I had become quite a good athlete. I was big, strong, and fast for my age. I played on the eighth-grade team as a seventh-grader and the ninth-grade team as an eighth-grader. However, as I got older, I stopped growing. I was five feet eight inches as a seventh-grader and then grew only about another inch and a half. During my high school years I went from being an outstanding athlete to a pretty good one. I made the freshman team at Macalester College in St. Paul, Minnesota, but my heart wasn't in it anymore.

It was the 1960s and I became disillusioned with sports. I lost interest both in participating in sports and in following professional or college teams. My son's interest in sports reawakened my own. We moved to California in 1984 as

Gabby was starting first grade and beginning to play soccer, basketball, and baseball.

In the meantime, I had acquired some highly specialized training in working with children. When I dropped out of Macalester after my junior year, I began working in St. Paul as a teacher's aide at the Behavioral Learning Center (BLC). The BLC was a new school that was about to open to address the educational needs of emotionally disturbed grade school children. The disruptive behavior of these kids made it impossible for them to be contained (let alone educated) in a regular classroom. As part of the staff, I was trained in the "natural and logical consequences" of Rudolf Dreikurs and the "reality therapy" of William Glasser. I also got to see firsthand how some talented professionals implemented these powerful ideas with extremely disturbed and difficult children. Dr. Shirley Pearl, the school principal, Don Challman, the school social worker, and Art Lovering, the crisis room teacher, as well as many other teachers at the BLC, gave me daily lessons in how to handle situations well beyond what most classroom teachers have to face. I discovered that positive reinforcement works amazingly well, even with severely disturbed children. And daily I saw people successfully implementing a positive approach to discipline and learning.

I know lots of people who believe *theoretically* that a positive approach works better than a negative one, but few of them get the opportunity that I had to *see* difficult kids open up and begin to learn and grow in a positive, safe environment. I became a believer, and it was natural that I would try to implement, years later, the same kind of approach on the baseball field and the basketball court.

After working at the BLC for two years, and meeting my wife there, we both went back to school. At the University of North Dakota's Center for Teaching and Learning, we learned the latest in "open classroom" techniques for getting children involved with their own learning. I then taught for three years at Yellowstone School in Rock Springs, Wyoming. My first year there was in a self-contained third-grade classroom of 32 children. The last two years were in a team teaching situation in an "open classroom" of second- and third-graders.

I began coaching shortly after my son started playing basketball, soccer, and baseball as a first-grader. I had recently gotten involved with the Parent Education Program of the San Jose YWCA. I became familiar with a wide array of positive skills and methods available to parents to develop strong relationships with their children.

At the same time I saw many negative interactions between coaches and players (and parents and players) around a game that should have been the source of great joy. A mental connection was made between the positive parenting approach and what seemed a great lack of similar kinds of techniques and philosophy in youth sports. Two other influences also bear mention.

Alice Miller and Self-Esteem

When I first learned about Alice Miller, I felt like a blindfold had been removed from my eyes. I read several of her books on children and childraising (*The Drama of the Gifted Child, Thou Shalt Not Be Aware, For Your Own Good*). In her description of how adults have used children through the ages for their own ends, I detected parallels with what I saw happening on athletic fields and gymnasiums. Grown-ups use children to meet their own unfulfilled needs in sports perhaps as much as anywhere else in our society. Many youth sports organizations are structured for the entertainment of the coaches (and, to a lesser degree, the parents) much like a giant game of rotisserie baseball except with live players. Since many coaches are frustrated jocks, we can easily slip into the trap of trying to live out unrealized dreams of *ours* through the lives of our children. Alice Miller's work inspired me to examine my own unrealized dreams around sports and to try to develop a child-centered approach to coaching kids.

In 1987 I was appointed to the Santa Clara County Task Force on Self-Esteem and Personal and Social Responsibility. I read avidly about self-esteem and attended, and even organized, lectures, conferences, and workshops. Occasionally I would run across some specific, practical tips on building self-esteem in kids. But more often I was disappointed in the vagueness of the material. In particular, I rarely found anything directly relevant to the coach's role.

Later I became familiar with Albert Bandura's work on self-efficacy and became determined to try to translate what has been discovered about self-esteem and self-efficacy into practical "how-to's" for youth sports coaches. In Chapter 5 ("The Coach's Role in Increasing Self-Esteem"), Chapter 6 ("The Opportunity to Build Character"), and Chapter 13 ("Nurturing Outstanding Individual Competitors"), I directly address the questions that I initially began examining five or more years ago.

The Bottom Line: Every Child a Winner

But the most important reason why I wrote this book is because thousands of kids every year have bad sports experiences which cause them to quit. A recent study indicated that the highest rates of participation in sports occur at age 10! Too many kids quit sports early because they didn't find the joy in sports that some kids do. A sport like basketball should be the source of a lifelong love affair, not constant agonizing over what might have been.

This book is dedicated to the proposition that *every* child can be a winner. Some kids will be outstanding athletes, most won't. Some teams will have winning records, about half won't. But in the bigger picture, every child can develop a stronger sense of herself through participation as a member of a team. Every child can learn important lessons about life by making great efforts, enjoying the taste of victory, and returning to try again after a loss. I have often thought the motto of youth sports organizations should be "More, Better, Longer": *more* kids having a *better* experience with sports and staying with it *longer*. If this book makes even a small contribution toward that end, all the time spent writing and rewriting will have been worth it.

1

Living in a Fishbowl: Why Coaching Kids is So Difficult

Managing is like holding a dove in your hand. Squeeze too hard and you kill it; not hard enough and it flies away.

—Tommy Lasorda

Coaching kids is difficult.

If you don't believe me you haven't done it. Or you've been doing it so long that you've forgotten how hard it was when you started.

There are a number of perfectly good reasons why coaching is hard. For one thing, everything you do (and fail to do) is exposed for everyone to see. Before I started coaching, I would go to my son's games and watch. I remember feeling that I could do it so much better than his coaches were doing it. Once I tried it, I realized my arrogance, because it wasn't nearly as easy as it seemed from the sidelines.

When I started coaching, I constantly worried about what parents were thinking about my coaching moves. As the years have gone by, I worry less and less, but moments of anxiety still occur, typically when an unfamiliar situation comes up and I don't know what to do.

There is an exercise that management trainers sometimes use called the "fishbowl." It involves one group of people sitting in a circle and role-playing or interacting to try to solve some concocted problem or other. Around them is another group of people who are watching everything they do and making notes. If you haven't been on the inside of the circle, you probably can't imagine what it is like the first time when you realize you are supposed to "carry on normally" while people behind you are watching (and no doubt criticizing) your every move.

Coaching is like that. Many parents have played the sport you are coaching. They have not made the commitment to coach as you have, but they wouldn't be human if they didn't occasionally conclude that they could do a better job than you. Your mistakes often are obvious to everyone, while your genius moves can be invisible. The players look like stars for doing what you taught them to do, while all the parents can think about is how the kid is a chip off the old block.

I remember watching a Little League all-star baseball game in which the opposing team's best hitter (who had already gotten a couple of smash hits in this game) was to be intentionally walked with the tying run at third base. Since this was the first time this had occurred that season, the pitcher and catcher weren't experienced with the procedure. The first pitch was thrown wide of the catcher, allowing the runner on third to score the tying run. The parents in the stands were irate: "A clear case of overcoaching. The manager should have let Freddy throw his best stuff against their best stuff."

Now, of course, if the manager had opted for that strategy and their "best stuff" had hit the ball out of the park, you might have heard those same parents tittering: "Dumb move. The manager should have walked that guy. He'd already hit a couple of hard ones."

20

It seems to have been written into the Bill of Rights that Americans have the inalienable right to be Monday morning quarterbacks. One of the great joys in life is to watch a professional sports contest and then argue into the night with friends about the dumb moves that the coach or manager made that lost the game. And if we are used to doing it for professional contests, why not also for college or even high school games? And for that matter, why stop there? It's natural to second-guess the coach when he or she makes a bonehead move, especially if it involves removing *our* kid from the game. So it often appears that a coach can't win, which may be why many people with the potential to be great coaches and developers of young people are reluctant to even try.

BRINGING OUT THE WORST IN PARENTS

It's bad enough that almost everything a coach does is subject to public scrutiny by people with little reason to be objective (i.e., parents of players), but competitive sports also tend to exacerbate the situation by bringing out the worst in the parents of young athletes. This is especially true in all-star situations where players who have been stars on their own teams are suddenly not playing as much, or playing lower-status positions. As a coach, you are generally expected to win, *and* to win in such a way that gives every player equal playing time, results in every player feeling great about himself, improves the skill level of each player during the year, etc., etc., etc.

I have known parents who are sincere, gentle human beings who have become positively monstrous in their behavior towards coaches when they perceive something (real or imagined) that violates their image of how their child should be treated. I have been astounded at the transformation of these kindly, decent people into roaring engines of vengeance, all because we (for I have been among them) care so much about our children and our image as parents. And coaches, as well, are the owners of self-images that can get in the way.

THE COACH'S IMAGINARY SELF-PORTRAIT

I once started a coaching workshop by asserting that every coach had one objective whether he knew it or not. I asked the group what that might be and got all sorts of replies, many of which were plausible. When I told them my belief—that every coach wants to look good (or conversely, at least not look bad)—one coach became distraught: "That's not true. I'm in this to help the kids. I don't care how I look or what other people think about me."

I didn't argue the point because I couldn't see inside of him, but I'm skeptical. I know that in my head I have an imaginary self-portrait of myself. It consists of me as the greatest coach (or parent, or teacher, or writer, or whatever) in the world! This imaginary portrait doesn't usually let itself be seen, even by me. But whenever something happens that rumples the portrait, I begin to get irritable. When the portrait starts to tear, I become a *much* less pleasant person.

When I find myself doing something that violates my principles, it is usually because my imaginary self-portrait is disturbed. And I believe most people have some image of themselves that they work very hard to maintain. A particular coach may not have the same fantasy picture of himself that I have of me. But I am quite confident that he has *some* mental picture of himself that, if disturbed, would tempt him to act in a way that he would later regret.

Because coaching is such a public event, with the whole world (it seems) watching, the typical coach is constantly at risk of seeing that portrait take a beating. When the portrait gets scratched, something's got to give. And that can result in a lot of erratic and seemingly irrational behavior on the part of the coach.

THE COACH'S CONFLICT OF INTEREST

The coach's imaginary self-portrait collides directly with his higher aspirations, leading to a conflict of interest inherent in the coach's task. On the one hand I want to develop character and self-esteem in my players while helping them become better athletes. But if I want to keep my self-portrait intact, I also want to be recognized as a good coach. So I need to look good. To look good, my team also needs to look good, and the surest way to look good is to win. Often the easiest way to win is to not play your weaker players, focus most of your attention on the stars, and do whatever else it takes to win. And don't kid yourself: it is the rare parent or observer who can recognize good coaching in a losing effort.

One year I was coaching a Little League minor team. My goals were to make sure that every kid had a positive experience, got to play multiple positions, and developed a stronger sense of self-esteem. One of my coaches, who had been around longer than I, was frustrated. He saw that with our talent, if utilized properly, we could win the league title.

Our toughest competition tended to play their strongest players at the most important positions for the entire game. My philosophy was that everyone (who wasn't a threat to get themselves beaned) should get to play the infield and even, within reason, to pitch. We rotated weaker players through third base and often the really weak players through second base. I'm sure this frustrated our pitchers, because all too often a routine groundball to second base would end up in the outfield.

Finally, in our last game against this team, I decided to "coach to win." When my assistant came to the game and saw my lineup, he said immediately, "Now that's more like it." We had our strongest players at the most important positions and we kept them there the entire game. Everybody still got to play, but the weaker players played the minimum required by the league rules and they played the outfield only.

The result was never in doubt. We trounced them.

Feeling I had proven something, the next week, we went back to our regular rotation. Once again, everyone played about an equal amount. Now that we (adults) had proven (to other adults) that we were the best team, we could go back to coaching for the benefit of all the kids.

But, being new to Little League, I didn't realize that "there was something at stake" here. It turned out that at the end of the season, the winning team got to represent the league in the Tournament of Champions, or TOC. Now for minor league teams, this is a limited event that doesn't go beyond the local county. It is different for major league teams which can go all the way to the Little League World Series in Williamsport. Still, it bothered me that my team, which "coulda won" the league title was unable to play in the TOC.

My naivete was further thrown in my face when I applied to coach a major team the next year. I was told that there were several people in line for the job already, including the coach of the rival minor team, and that he had the inside track "because, after all, his team won the league title last year."

This ultimately was not a tragedy since he was a great coach and has since become a good friend. But the point is that no one, in my humble opinion, had taken the trouble to look beyond the standings to see how good a coach I was. They looked at who had won.

America is like that about sports. Professional coaches can get away with almost any atrocity as long as they win. Coaches that put the benefit and development of their players first are generally not revered, unless they also win. America loves a winner and tends to disdain a loser, even a loser who puts the welfare of his players above winning.

THE COACH'S OWN HANG-UPS

Yet another set of reasons why it is often difficult to enjoy coaching revolves around the set of expectations and hang-ups that typical coaches bring with them to the field or gymnasium. Three that come readily to mind are a yearning for lost youth, problems of scale, and the need to be in control.

1. **Lost youth:** One prevalent reason many people get into coaching is a longing for their own lost youth. I certainly can tell you that when baseball season comes around, I remember what it was like to be young and strong and fast and just chomping at the bit to get a swing at a pitch I could hit.

   Many coaches have experienced some moments of greatness on the athletic fields. They are remembered vividly and the desire to relive them is like a drug you just can't get enough of. Even if coaches haven't experienced the thrill of making the big play, they certainly have seen others do it enough times to be able to imagine how great it must feel. Either way, there can be a problem with trying to live through players what you had or never had as an athlete yourself.

2. **Problems of scale:** There is a great line in the movie *Hook* when the grown-up Peter Pan is battling Captain Hook. Peter says, "You seemed so much bigger before." Hook, played by moderate-size Dustin Hoffman, responds, "To a 10-year-old, I'm huge."

   Which reminds me of the terror of batting against Bernie Graner when I was a junior high school baseball player. Bernie was a left-handed pitcher in Fargo, North Dakota, with mind-boggling speed and, just to add insult to injury, a wicked curve. Getting a piece of the bat on the ball for even a foul ball against Bernie was a real accomplishment. None of us ever expected anyone to get a hit off Bernie, because on our scale he was virtually unhittable.

But now that we, like Peter Pan, have grown up, we forget what life is like for a 10-year-old. I look out at the baseball field with my 40-year-old eyes and see a pitcher who doesn't seem that overpowering. I become frustrated when my batters bail out of the batters box even before the pitch leaves the pitcher's hand. "Why can't those kids be as brave as I am? Why can't they hang in there and put the bat on the ball the way I could?" These internal conversations are a hazard of the job for a youth sports coach. But a more reasonable question might rather be, "Why can't they be as successful as I was against Bernie Graner?" And the answer is obvious. Every one of them already is. They can't help but be: I don't remember *ever* getting a hit against Bernie Graner.

We grown-ups forget how Captain Hook looks to a kid. We aren't kids anymore, and we tend to forget to look through the eyes of the child. Sports psychologist Tom Tutko recently gave a talk to parents of Cupertino Hoops, the basketball league that some friends and I started (see Chapter 17). He asked us all to imagine what a soccer field looks like when you are only three feet tall. From that vantage point, it can look like it stretches on forever.

Coaching is difficult because we coaches often forget that we are working with children. And children typically don't have the same ability level that adults do. So we look at a fat, slow pitch coming over the plate and we can't understand why our players can't hit the darn ball!

3. **The need to be in control:** My wife breeds dogs. We have two pugs, named Puggins (I admit it's not very original) and Lucy. We bought Puggins first and then put in an order for a female. When we went to pick up our female puppy, we walked through a house that seemed to have litters of pugs and rottweilers at different stages of growth all over the place. We walked out to a porch in back where the breeder opened up a gate allowing seven (eight? nine?) pug puppies onto the porch. There were so many of them and they moved so fast that I literally could not focus on any single puppy. It was all a blur of movement with one pug melting into another.

The breeder knew we wanted a female so she started by removing the males, leaving four females. Now I could almost pick out individual pugs, but it still wasn't easy. She then removed puppies one by one until we were left with our lovely Lucy, the pick of the litter.

Well, coaching kids is a bit like trying to control that bunch of puppies. If you are getting into coaching with the idea that you intend to be in control of the situation, forget it. A list of things that a coach can't control would never end, but here's a start. As a coach you usually can't control which players will be on your team. You can't guarantee that your players will show up for practice, *especially* when you're prepared to work on a skill that the no-shows really need work on. You can't know or control whether key players will get sick right before a crucial game. And you certainly should not go into coaching with the idea that you will be able to control the outcome of the games themselves. A coach's life is a ready-made heart attack for a Type A personality. And since many coaches openly or secretly want to exert control the way they believe Vince Lombardi or Bill Walsh or Red Auerbach did, it can be a humbling experience. The reality is more like a blur of pug puppies totally out of focus, let alone control, at times.

INAPPROPRIATE ROLE MODELS

Another problem many coaches bring with them is a lack of positive role models. I was impressed by the demeanor of Phil Jackson, coach of the on-their-way-to-becoming World Champion Chicago Bulls, as I watched the 1991 NBA playoffs. He never seemed to lose his cool, never seemed to berate his players in front of the fans or cameras, never panicked during or after a loss.

This behavior caught my attention because it seemed so different from much of what we see of major college and professional coaches on television. I acknowledge that I may be influenced by the fact that Phil Jackson grew up playing basketball in North Dakota, as I did, but it is certainly true that the behavior of many, many coaches leaves much to be desired.

We've seen coaches yell verbal abuse at players, punch players during a game, even attack cheerleaders from the other team. We've seen them violate contracts (often shortly after promising their players that they would stay at that university) to go to another job. We've heard them whine and complain about calls and even occasionally attack officials. We've read about them almost coming to blows with each other after hard-fought games. And we've read about them promising young athletes the moon if they would only come to their university and play for them, then reneging when it suited their purpose.

As long as they win, the media and the fans condone it. And that seems to be the bottom line. If you win, you can get away with acting like a jerk. If you lose, you are often treated as the lowest form of life.

I once read of a former professional football player who wouldn't let his son play youth football. He had known Vince Lombardi and believed that too many youth football coaches picked up the yelling and screaming that they see from professional and college coaches without also developing the teaching ability and commitment to their players that he said Lombardi had. The yelling and screaming comes through while the teaching and the strong relationships that many of the greatest coaches establish with their players are invisible.

COMMITMENT FRUSTRATIONS

Another reason why coaches get gray is because they have players who don't have a commitment to the game that they did when they were young. Kids today in northern California, where I live, have many more things to occupy their time than I did as a child. In addition to baseball, which was pretty much the only organized sport in rural North Dakota during my youth, there is competition from organized soccer (including spring soccer which cuts into baseball season). Many kids also have music lessons. In our area there are a lot of Asian Americans, so a coach can be faced with his star shortstop missing big games on Saturday morning to go to Japanese school, or a key playmaker going to Chinese school and regularly missing Friday night basketball practice. Last season, one of my best basketball players missed one practice a week to take drawing lessons. Then there are music lessons, karate lessons, swim club, television, hanging out at the mall, skateboarding down to the corner convenience store to get a slurpee, video games (often right in the kid's own home), and the ever-present homework.

On the other side of the equation is a coach who loves baseball (or soccer or basketball or . . .) as much as life itself. Often he is someone who didn't benefit from sophisticated coaching as a kid. He may spend a lot of time learning how to be a better coach and be dedicated to his players' improvement. He would sacrifice a lot to be able to have had a coach like himself. He might have gotten to play in a mere handful of "real" games each year. So when players

29

(and their parents) groan about 24 baseball games in a season being too many, the coach throws up his hands.

In this disparity of commitment are the ingredients for an explosive situation, with coaches feeling underappreciated and resentful that their dedication is not matched by their players. The players, for their part, may come to feel bewildered by a coach who becomes disgusted when a piano recital takes precedence over a ball game.

Now, often I'm skeptical about the coach's own memory. Sometimes I am just a bit unwilling to believe that baseball was the *only* thing that we lived for back in the good old days. But whether our memories are reliable or not, they *seem* very real and can cause a great deal of unneccesary gnashing of teeth when young athletes demonstrate a different level of commitment.

A friend who coaches baseball recently lamented to me, "When my parents or teachers told me something, it went in one ear and out the other. But when my coach told me to do something, I did it!" He went on to complain about how one of his best athletes, who had the potential to become a really outstanding player, just wouldn't put in the extra time needed to master the intricacies of the game. He ended with, "If I had had just a fraction of his ability . . ."

And that drives a lot of us as coaches and as human beings. *We coulda been somebody!* But we didn't have all the advantages that ballplayers nowadays have. And again we mourn for our lost youth and what we coulda done if only . . . if only.

ADDING TO THE WOODPILE

This feels like a depressing chapter, dwelling on the negative aspects of coaching. But coaching also can be among life's greatest pleasures. A few years ago I had a basketball team of enormous energy but little talent. Most of the kids were hyper much of the time, and I had the hardest time getting them to settle down long enough to run even one play. I worked with them throughout the season and finally in the last couple of games some small headway was made. A mother of one of my players missed the last game but called the next day. Her husband had been to the game, his first of the season. He had heard horror stories about the team and how they didn't play together or take direction. He thought his wife must have been watching another team because he thought they looked "pretty good." She knew that the season had been a hard one for me, and thought that I would appreciate her husband's positive comments, which I certainly did.

Yes, coaching is difficult. But it can be incredibly rewarding. So much of what we are required to do as adults in this society is not particularly interesting, let alone exciting. But coaching can be both.

Paul Harvey, the radio commentator, once talked on the air about the joy of cutting wood and seeing the stack of firewood get bigger the longer you cut. He noted that he wanted to be able to say when he died that he had left society's woodpile a little bit bigger than when he had arrived. In our increasingly complex society it's getting harder and harder to find "woodpile-like" activities to devote our time to. But coaching is one activity where we can actually see what we've accomplished at the end of the season. So let's get on with it. Let's chop that wood, and coach those kids, and see if there aren't some ways to make it one of life's great joys.

2

Teachable Moments I: Relentless Positivity

See everything.
Overlook a great deal.
Improve a little.
—Pope John XXIII

O_{ver} the years I have acquired quite a large collection of books on coaching. Most of them are concerned primarily with how properly to teach certain skills or concepts. The unspoken assumption is that, if only taught properly, the athlete will learn. My experience tells me that this is not the case—that proper teaching of skills is less than half of it. The hidden part of the iceberg is the receptivity of the learner.

People do not have the same capacity to learn at any given moment. Imagine that you have just come to a language class from work after having been told by your boss that you will lose your job shortly. How receptive are you to what your language teacher is teaching you (regardless of how perfectly it may be taught)?

The concept of learner receptivity is captured beautifully in the phrase "teachable moments," those timeless times when an athlete is focused on what she needs to do to learn, to change, and to improve. How do you, as a coach, produce the highest number of teachable moments for each of your athletes over the course of a season?

This chapter is the first of three dealing with principles and techniques that I have developed, stumbled upon, or borrowed from others. These principles and techniques have one thing in common: more often than not, their use helps create a teachable moment where young athletes are receptive to what you are trying to teach them.

Chapter 3 addresses how coaches can use ideas to inspire young athletes to greater effort to learn and improve even in difficult situations. Chapter 4 discusses how to get players engaged in taking responsibility for their own learning.

This chapter begins at the beginning, with relentless positivity, the cornerstone of great teaching because it leads to teachable moments. It ends with practical ways to infuse your coaching style with the positivity that brings teachable moments again and again and again.

THE CASE FOR POSITIVE COACHING

The case for practicing the discipline of positive coaching is simple. It works better than negative coaching. It also works better than so-called "balanced" coaching where criticism and praise are dished out about equally. There are several reasons why positive coaching works better.

1. **The greatest coaching principle in the world:** Awhile ago I ran across a little book by Michael Leboeuf with the intriguing title of *The Greatest Management Principle in the World*. I paged to the payoff and came to this insight:

   The things that get rewarded get done.

   Is that profound or simpleminded? Or both? When

you think about it, it seems pretty obvious, but I've noticed that time and again parents, teachers, managers, and coaches ignore this principle. There is a famous organizational behavior article on this very topic called "On the Folly of Rewarding A, While Hoping for B." It happens all the time in the corporate world, and it happens all the time in youth sports.

When a coach is trying to get a group of kids to pay attention, who gets rewarded (in this case with attention)? Usually it is the kids who are dawdling or talking. Those who come right away, ready to learn, are ignored and made to wait while the noncooperating kids are the center of attention. Toward the end of this chapter I discuss how to use "positive charting" to reinforce kids for learning what you are trying to teach them.

2. **The futility of punishment:** Punishment leaves bad feelings that eat away at motivation. Excelling in sports requires emotional energy. When kids are punished, yelled at, or criticized, their emotional energy is used up being angry, feeling sorry for themselves, thinking up reasons why the coach is wrong, etc.

An exercise from a positive parenting class illustrates the point. A volunteer leaves the room and returns to try to complete an unknown task (i.e., she must discover what the task is by the "feedback" given). She is told that when she does the wrong thing, she will be hit (gently) on the head with a rolled up piece of paper. When she does something that moves her closer to accomplishing the task, the hitting will stop. Rarely does the volunteer figure out the task and accomplish it. Often the "mature" adult gets so frustrated with being whapped that she can't even complete the task. Occasionally she will take a whap back at the other person out of sheer frustration. So far I've not heard of any "whappers" getting disfigured by "whappees," but the potential is certainly there.

Later the exercise is repeated with positive reinforcement. When a correct move is made, a friendly sounding bell is tinkled. When she moves in the wrong direction, the tinkling stops. Each effort is timed. You probably can guess the results. Invariably the positive approach works much more quickly (often as much as 10 times as fast).

Punishment does carry with it some information value and it can stop a behavior, but it rarely can teach new ones. It takes positive reinforcement and recognition to get a child to try something new, such as fielding bad hops without turning his head.

I was interested to read recently that dolphin trainers rely exclusively on positive reinforcement. Punishment simply doesn't work with dolphins. They withdraw and refuse to perform. Kids are a lot like dolphins. Positive works better.

3. **Pretending to work:** Kids use passive-aggressive tactics against adults who dominate them. In totalitarian countries, passive resistance is sometimes the only option available to people to express their disdain for those who hold power over them. It has been said that the former Soviet government pretended to pay workers who in turn got back at the government by only pretending to work. Kids (and adults too for that matter) have a great ability to fight back against adults who are down on them by such methods as coming to practice late, not trying, not concentrating during a drill, misunderstanding instructions, etc. They may even go through the motions and "pretend to work" but they won't be motivated to become their best.

4. **Responding to a challenge:** For most kids (and adults too!), responding successfully to a challenge requires emotional support. When people are facing a challenge that requires them to change their behavior, they need all the physical and emotional energy they can get. With-

out support, the child's energy goes into defending himself against real and perceived criticisms from others, *not* into trying to accomplish the task. When a child is secure in knowing that he will be valued and accepted by the coach, parents, or someone, *no matter how he performs*, more of his energy can go to responding to the challenge.

It may not be obvious from our adult perspective, but a child who is trying to learn to bat against a fast pitcher without "bailing out" of the batter's box *is* responding to a challenge.

When my son was drafted to a Little League major team as a 10-year-old, I noticed that he seemed tense a lot of the time. Since he is usually a pretty loosely strung person, I watched more closely. It seemed that he was reacting to the stress of advancing to a tougher level of competition. He had been a star as a nine-year-old in the minors. Now he seemed to be silently comparing himself to the 11- and 12-year-olds on his new team and worrying about whether he would match up.

He was fortunate to have coaches, John McCallion, Tom Braucht, and Steve Culver, who gave him a lot of positive reinforcement. His mother and I also tried to give him lots of positive support and encouragement. We did *not* criticize him or give him any reason to believe he would not succeed. By the middle of the season he had become the starting second baseman. His energy was free to go into learning what he needed to be successful at a higher performance level.

WHY *RELENTLESS* POSITIVITY?

I began my education career working with emotionally disturbed children whose behavior problems were so severe that they could not be contained within a normal classroom. The rules of the school I worked in were simple: reinforce positive behavior; ignore negative behavior as much as possible; and, when negative behavior can no longer be ignored, intervene in a way that extinguishes the behavior rather than reinforces it.

The results with very troubled children were remarkable. The extent to which the school's staff was able to follow these guidelines largely determined how well the children behaved. We had a weekly "goody-guy" awards ceremony in which children who had met their behavioral goals for the week received recognition in a public forum. These were children whose parents and previous teachers had given up trying to use positive reinforcement because, they said, ". . . with this kid, it doesn't work . . ."

Why did it work with our school and not in the original situation? One reason was that we were relentless about being positive. We kept being positive in the face of behavior that *seemed* to be telling us that positivity wasn't working.

We found ourselves from time to time saying, ". . . being positive with Kevin just isn't working" or ". . . no one could be positive with Judy." But our system wouldn't let us follow through on those discouraged thoughts. Dr. Shirley Pearl, our principal, reinforced us for being positive and ignored our negative behavior, and pretty soon we were back to being positive again. And then we were surprised, because over time Kevin and Judy responded. The key was our being relentlessly positive, not just positive at first.

I have talked with many, many parents, coaches, and teachers, who say, "But I've tried being positive . . ." My advice is to be *relentlessly* positive. It is the relentless commitment to positive coaching that brings the biggest successes and has the most impact. It's when things go wrong that you can have the most impact. It's also the time when it is the hardest to be positive. But it does work.

Positive Charting

Earlier in this chapter I referred to the "greatest man-agement principle" (what gets rewarded gets done). Well, there is a corollary from the same book:

People do what gets measured.

To maximize the amount of time I can get my players to practice what I am trying to teach them, I have developed a simple technique, called "positive charting," that takes advantage of this corollary. Here's how it works.

Each game I carry a clipboard or notebook with a listing of each player's name followed by blank space for my no-tations. Whenever I notice a player doing something I want to reinforce, I note it. For example, if I am trying to teach Ellie to stride toward the pitcher without bailing out, I will remind her before the game that I will be watching her front foot. Every time she strides forward I note it.

At the beginning of the next practice, I take about 10 minutes and share with the team the good things I've noted about each of them. I also keep track of the regular statistics (hits, great fielding plays, etc.) and share them as well. But there are always several significant positive things I have marked down about *each* kid, so the weaker players are recognized and reinforced as well as the superstars.

This activity usually sets a positive tone for the practice and helps motivate each kid to continue trying to improve since they know any improvement will be noted and called to the attention of the entire group.

This is a powerful technique, especially with younger kids. One time I went to pick up my then seven-year-old son at a friend's birthday party. One of the kids on my basketball team was also there. As soon as he saw me he asked if I had brought my clipboard! Older athletes often feel they have to be cool, so the impact of positive charting on them is not as obvious, although I am convinced that it works with them as well. It's not hard to see why kids respond so well to it. Most of the average kid's life is spent being corrected, criticized, yelled at, punished, or in some way being made aware of shortcomings. Here is a moment where the child can do no wrong. Kids love it, and they respond by trying harder to improve.

Over the years, I've developed some guidelines to making the most of positive charting.

1. Each kid should have about the same amount of things noted and shared for each game. The tendency will be to have lots of things to say about the superstars and often nothing at all about the weakest kids. This is bad for both sets of kids. The superstars need to be pushed and taught more advanced things (see Chapter 15 for more on this). The weaker kids need to be taught the basics and reinforced when they master *any* part of the lesson.

2. Recognize kids for great things they have done on their own, as well as on what you are teaching. The whole point of coaching is to create teachable moments. Be on the constant look for kids doing what you have instructed them to do as well as other useful things you'd like to reinforce. There is nothing that will get them to be more receptive to your instruction than having their efforts noticed and recognized.

3. Include "character" items when appropriate (more on this in Chapter 6). For example, a child may have trouble controlling her temper when an opposing basketball player elbows her. If so, make that one of the things she is working on and note it and share it with the group when she makes progress.

4. Give recognition for effort, not just results. A catcher who has trouble remembering to call out cuts on throws from the outfield so they can be heard by the infielders can be singled out when he finally trumpets. Even if he

is only slightly louder than before, mark it down and share it. Most improvements come about little by little. Note and reinforce the little victories on the way to the play that wins the championship game.

5. Do note negative things during the game but don't share them with the kids at this time. My rule on criticism is clear and inviolate: *praise in public, criticize in private.* Charting notes on things needing improvement are grist for the next practice at which time I will schedule drills that deal with the problem without mentioning who screwed up in the last game. I may discuss the problem with the player in question but I will try to never embarrass a player in front of her teammates.

   One exception is when a player makes an obvious-to-everyone mistake that loses the game for us. In this case I may talk about it during the positive charting session to give credit to the kid for trying, for being a good sport about it (assuming he was), or for coming to practice ready to go at it again. I may talk about mental toughness (see Chapter 6 for more on this) being the ability to spring back after a disappointment and how this particular kid is demonstrating this quality.

6. Ask kids to help you observe good things that other kids are doing. Tell them (truthfully) that you aren't able to catch every good thing that happens and that you need their help. This will contribute to a home court advantage and a stronger team (see Chapter 14), with kids feeling appreciated by their peers as well as by their coaches. It also will help prepare these kids to be positive coaches, parents, managers, or teachers when they grow up.

7. After the last practice before a game, get together with your coaches and note what things you want to watch for with each kid during the next game. While positive charting will have a tremendous impact on your team, your teaching will be even more effective if you are primed to notice kids when they implement what you

have been teaching. If you have delegated certain teaching tasks to others, this will help get you up to speed on what they have been stressing in the last few practices. Although there are times when I don't want to make the effort to note and record the positive things that happen in a game, I always regret it when I don't. I am almost always glad when I make the effort to positive-chart because it leads to more teachable moments and better performance.

CONSTRUCTIVE CRITICISM AND THE PLUS/MINUS RATIO

The paradoxical beauty of relentlessly positive coaching is that it makes criticism easier for you to give and easier for the player to accept. When feeling appreciated and valued by you, a player will be more open to hearing your criticisms.

Fred Miller, director of the Oregon Executive Department, who so beautifully demonstrates the effective practice of recognition, once said that his rule of thumb is four to one. If he gets much below four positive feedbacks for each criticism with the people he manages, he feels things are deteriorating. I have strived to maintain that ratio over the years and it has worked for me as well. Kaoru Yamamoto, in *The Child and His Image*, concludes that an even higher ratio is better: ". . . a reward to punishment (R-P) ratio of five rewards for every one punishment is about optimal in guiding and directing a child's behavior. However, when the R-P ratio falls down to only two rewards for every one punishment, neurotic symptoms begin to develop, especially those of inferiority and inadequacy and a generalized fear of failure. When the R-P ratio drops further to one-to-one or even below, the child begins to despair of ever winning the adult's approval, and hostile, angry (sic) feelings arise. Predelinquent acts are often observed in children who chronically experience this R-P level."

It is hard to imagine a child reaching her potential as an athlete when the dominant emotion is despair. And given the punishment-oriented styles of many college and professional coaches, is it really surprising that we see so many talented athletes engaging in predelinquent (or worse) behaviors?

I am aware of the "sandwich" criticism, where a criticism is sandwiched between two compliments. I have never felt good about using that approach. It seems artificial and gimmicky. It also seems likely over time to result in people devaluing the positives as in, "He just said those things to soften me up for what he really wanted me to hear." I prefer to try to create a climate of positivity that surrounds the team, so that a well-placed criticism here or there falls softly among children who feel so secure and accepted that they can hear and apply it, rather than tune it out.

Fred Miller notes that a management job is similar to coaching in that it's all too easy to fall into spending most of your time correcting things done improperly while taking things done well for granted. To combat this tendency, Fred monitors his plus/minus ratio periodically. He will mark on the side of his desk blotter a "+" for every positive comment he writes or says in response to the work of subordinates. A "−" is marked for every criticism. After a couple of days this technique gets him back into the habit of looking for good things and reinforcing them.

During a practice I record +'s and −'s on my hand with a pen if I don't have a clipboard handy. I have found that focusing on my plus/minus ratio during practices and using positive charting during games keeps me in a positive mood. Since we often don't even notice the times we are correcting kids, you might find it useful to have another adult monitor you at a practice session for a half hour or so. If you are like me, you will be surprised at how many criticisms you hand out without being aware of them.

My wife is invaluable to my remaining positive. Anytime during a game that I get carried away with yelling at my players, Sandra will wander over to the dugout or sidelines and quietly say to me in her cheerful singsong way, "Jim, you're getting just a littttttle bit negative."

SOME MOMENTS ARE JUST NOT TEACHABLE

As positive as you might be, there are some moments that are just not, and cannot be made to be, teachable moments.

1. **Games:** In general, games are not filled with teachable moments. Games *can* provide a setting in which lessons previously introduced to the players are driven home (see Chapter 9). But there is so much tension in any game that is closely contested, or that means a lot to the kids, that there isn't a lot of extra energy to go around to learn something *new*. Games are for implementing skills that have already been taught and practiced. This may be difficult for many coaches and parents to accept at first, but it is a rare child, with the psychology of a top competitor (see Chapter 13), who is able to process new things during the pressure of a game. Lessons from games should be noted and part of the next practice can be used to cover skills that address the lessons.

2. **Mistakes:** When a child makes a mistake that costs the team a game, he knows it better than anyone. The last thing in the world he needs is someone yelling at him that he screwed up. He has already gotten that feedback. He is not going to be in a receptive mood, so don't try to teach him what he did wrong just then. Even if the mistake is made in a practice, he is probably feeling

frustrated. To the extent possible, give the child as much privacy as possible and wait for a teachable moment to roll around later.

Someone once told me what happens to a bleeding chicken in a farmyard. Other chickens peck at the blood and, if not stopped, can kill the bleeding chicken even if the original wound was quite minor. This is how I see what often happens when a kid makes a mistake. Adults and other kids start peck, peck, pecking and it doesn't help the kid learn. The best response to a mistake is support (see Chapter 7). If you are emotionally caught up in the mistake and can't be positive at that moment, then be silent. There is no more appropriate time for practicing the maxim "if you can't say something nice, don't say anything at all" than when a kid makes a big mistake that costs your team the game.

3. **When you are angry:** I firmly believe that it is okay, even desirable, to be able to get angry at kids. It's not okay to hurt them, but it is an unavoidable part of life, if you are connected with people, to get angry from time to time.

   However, do not confuse this with the idea that you can teach much of anything to a kid when you are mad. Kids sense anger and are unlikely to respond to the teaching at that time. Anger kills teachable moments. Call a break, have your assistant take over for a while, work with another kid, or whatever. But wait for the anger to subside before you try to instruct again.

4. **Factors beyond your control:** Sad as it may be, bad things happen to kids. A child whose parents have recently divorced or whose father has recently died is probably not going to have as many teachable moments as he otherwise would have, no matter how positive you are. In those situations, all you can do is try to be even more positive than normal.

ACCEPTANCE TIME AND NONOBVIOUS TEACHABLE MOMENTS

The concept of "acceptance time" has been a valuable tool for me as a coach. This is the time it takes an individual to process a suggestion or criticism and embrace it as her own. Some things take time because the physical skill is difficult to master. Some attitude and behavior changes take time to occur because the person just isn't ready to immediately drop an attitude or behavior that has become habitual.

Often I am struck by how my son is able to process messages from me without the slightest indication that he has heard me. If I watch carefully over a few days or weeks, I see that often he *has* adjusted his behavior, based on my feedback, without advertising it. And he can easily resent it if I try to point out to him that he has finally come around to the "correct" (i.e., *my*) point of view.

Kids don't always say, "Why, thank you, Sir, for pointing that out to me, Sir, I didn't realize that before, Sir," even though they may actually be processing your message and learning from it. I have found this particularly true with teens, where there is a large element of face-saving involved. In some cases, kids need time to be able to "forget" that the idea wasn't theirs in the first place so they can embrace it as their own. Sometimes, simply doing what one is told to do can seem pretty slave-like to the adolescent athlete. Often the most talented and robust personalities, the children with the drive to accomplish great things in their lives, are the ones who have the most need for acceptance time, and for making an idea their own.

In situations like this, the enlightened coach will derive satisfaction from the learning he has inspired and not try to force the player to acknowledge the source of the new skill.

So . . . you can't always tell when you have struck a

teachable moment by the immediate and obvious feedback. Teachable moments are not always discrete, teary-eyed flashes of breakthrough. Often what makes the difference is an accumulation of many seemingly ordinary interactions that create an atmosphere in which learning, growth, and change take place. Continuing to coach in a positive manner and giving people the right to process in their own way and time will pay off whether or not it seems to be working right away.

PRIVACY AND TEACHABLE MOMENTS

I once had a terrific karate teacher named Larry Seiberlich. In trying to understand why he was such an effective teacher, I noted that I appreciated the privacy he gave me to work on the skills he had taught me. He would circulate among the students while we were practicing a maneuver, watching how we were doing from a distance. From time to time he would approach an individual and make further suggestions. Then he would again withdraw to let the person try (and often initially fail) to implement his suggestion. It took a great deal of pressure off his students since we knew he would let us try several times before he came back to us again.

WATCH OUT FOR GRUDGING POSITIVITY

During a recent baseball season I noticed that I was going through the motions. I'm sure that people watching me thought I was still being positive, but I knew that it was a grudging sort of positivity that left me unsatisfied.

I was disappointed because my son had decided not to play baseball and without him our team did not win many games. I was pouting for much of the season, constantly thinking about what it would have been like if he'd played.

I also deeply missed sharing the experience with him as I had in previous years.

When players made crucial mistakes, I would express my disgust under my breath to one of my fellow coaches. To the players I would put on a happy (tight, but happy) face and tell them it was okay to make a mistake. But inside myself I didn't believe it. I was being grudgingly positive and it was neither fun nor effective.

Instead of remembering that my goal was to encourage and develop kids, and that losing is a part of life, I had gotten seduced by the desire to win. I wanted to win the league championship. I wanted to demonstrate my superior coaching ability, winning with players that weren't as talented as those on some other teams. When my players refused to cooperate and made the typical kinds of mistakes inexperienced players make, I got frustrated.

Now sometimes the best you can do *is* to be "grudgingly positive." But don't mistake the one for the other. When you are able to be relentlessly positive rather than grudgingly positive, wonderful things happen. You experience sports and your players the way they were meant to be experienced, with great joy and enthusiasm. So if things are tough, and grudgingly positive is as good as it's going to get for awhile, keep at it. But if you can recognize the difference and break through to a higher level of positivity, you'll be able to see the difference.

THE DISCIPLINE OF POSITIVE COACHING

At the beginning of this chapter, I used the phrase the "discipline of positive coaching." This was not an accidental choice of words. There are few activities as difficult as maintaining a positive attitude when things go wrong—as they will from time to time.

There are two hilarious scenes in Penny Marshall's movie, *A League of Their Own*, that illustrate how difficult (and important) it can be for a coach to be positive. Tom Hanks plays a manager who chews out a player for missing the cutoff on a throw from the outfield. She begins to cry and he gets angrier and angrier, saying, "There's no crying in baseball!" Later in the season, the player again makes the same mistake but the Hanks character has learned a lot. At great physical effort, he remains calm (for him) and suggests she continue to work on the skill. She responds well to his disciplined, positive approach and comes through with a big play in the final game.

I am always bemused by commentators who talk about so-and-so, a major college coach, who is so "tough" and shows it by yelling at his players. There's nothing tough about getting negative when things don't go your way. Any three-year-old throwing a temper tantrum is tough in that sense. A truly disciplined coach is one who can provide emotional support to a kid who just blew an "easy" play (easy from the sidelines) that cost a game. He can remain cool while analyzing the situation that contributed to the mistake. Then, at a future practice, he can introduce drills to help the player reduce the likelihood that the same mistake will be repeated. True mental toughness is exhibited by remaining positive in the face of adversity.

3

Teachable Moments II:
Ideas and Inspiration

*An invasion of armies can be resisted, but
not an idea whose time has come.*
—Victor Hugo

Ideas are the great motivator. Human energy is released
by the right idea at the right moment. History tells us that
it is not when times are terrible that oppressed people become motivated to revolt. It is typically when times are
getting better, in a time of rising expectations, that revolts
occur.

It is when people get the *idea* that things could be better
that they get excited, sometimes inspired enough to do
brave things.

The power of ideas can be used by coaches. The best
coaches have always known this and carefully incorporate
the use of ideas to motivate and create teachable moments.
But the best idea can't inspire until it is properly communicated. I use three effective ways to communicate ideas
that motivate: *stories*, *metaphors*, and *vision*.

THE COACH AS STORYTELLER

Coaches should tell stories. Moreover, they should be collectors and cataloguers of great stories that they can tell to their players on the bench, on the sidelines, and in the dugout.

Humans respond to stories. As Anthony de Mello has written, "It is common to oppose a truth, but impossible to resist a story." Ronald Reagan may owe much of his success as a politician to his ability to convey his ideas in crisp, often humorous, anecdotes that capture people's attention and communicate. The "Win One for the Gipper" story about Notre Dame coach Knute Rockne is famous as an example of a coach using a story to motivate his players. Sheldon Kopp notes that "it is the compelling power of the storytelling that distinguishes men from beasts."

The simple fact is that stories motivate and part of why they do so is because of the seemingly random nature of the world around us.

The Random World

There is a memorable scene in *Out of the Silent Planet* by C.S. Lewis in which the hero lands on a distant planet and finds that he is effectively blind, even though there is nothing wrong with his sight. Since *nothing* looks familiar, he has no base from which to recognize any individual thing. It seems like a random pattern (or rather nonpattern) of colors. After he has spent some time on the unfamiliar planet, he begins to be able to see where one "thing" begins and another leaves off, and gradually he is able to become part of the life of this new planet.

To most kids, a baseball or soccer game seems like a series of random events. There's no big picture. There's no logic or structure to what's happening. It's either "we're winning" (not sure why, *we* must be better) or "we're losing" (not sure why, *they* must be better).

One of the coach's most important roles is to help the players impose a framework on events that can help them gain some measure of control. For example, it is a game late in the season against a team with the best pitcher in the league. He is throwing nothing but darts and we are behind 4-0 at the end of the second inning. The players are depressed, the coaches are depressed and the fans are quiet (because they're depressed).

But wait . . . there's a structure to this game that can give us hope if we can just see it. In our league each pitcher can only pitch three innings per (six-inning) game. That means that we will soon see a new pitcher, one who will not be as good as the one now pitching. However, if we get too far behind it won't matter how the next pitcher pitches. I call the discouraged group of boys together before they go out onto the field for the top of the third inning. I tell them that even though it looks bad for us, we do have hope: "A new pitcher has to come in next inning. Eric will pitch the last three innings for us (I don't have to tell them that he's our best pitcher). All we have to do is keep it close and we can win this game."

I literally can see the players' attitudes change, and their "Go Giants" cheer sounds strangely out of place to our fans who are still depressed. They don't all charge out onto the field, but some of them do. Our left fielder, Cary, makes an incredible twirling catch of a towering fly deep near the fence, and we emerge at the end of three innings still down only 4-0.

In the fourth we fail to score but we load the bases (I tell the kids, "See, we're improving already"). In the fifth we score two runs but still enter the last inning down 4-2. In the bottom of the sixth we score three more to win the game.

Now it doesn't always happen this way. Sometimes I introduce the same kind of ideas (for how we might be able to win) and we lose anyway. But I am convinced that Cary would not have believed that he could make that incredible catch in the fourth inning before the pep talk, nor would he have tried as hard as he did.

What the introduction of that idea (*their best pitcher will stop pitching soon*) and short-term goal (*just keep it close until then*) does is give hope which inspires kids to make efforts. In some sense, whether we win or lose the game is irrelevant. People who can make valiant efforts against great odds in a worthy cause are winners regardless of the outcome.

Stories that Give Perspective

Awhile back a baseball team I was helping coach was in a playoff game against the team that had won the second half championship. We had won the first half championship but hadn't done so well since then. It was a *very* hot day in late June in northern California. Everyone seemed low on energy, even sluggish. There were complaints about having to play in such hot weather. I could almost hear the inner dialogue of some of the players: "We shouldn't have to play in such hot weather. No one can expect us to play very well on a day like this."

I was reminded of a high school basketball game I had played in while growing up in North Dakota. It was late in a game and we were neck and neck with an arch rival, Valley City. I felt exhausted as I was running up the floor after Valley City had scored. However, I noticed that the player guarding me was breathing heavily and it inspired me. He was tired, too! In fact he might be even *more* tired than I was. In fact—*in fact*—I might take advantage of his tiredness and go even harder. All of a sudden, I was inspired to put more effort into my playing and I sped by him in time to get a pass and score.

I shared the story with the players, including the point

(just so they wouldn't misinterpret it): "Today is hot for *both* teams. But if you guys can put even more effort into your play, it will demoralize the other team since they will be thinking about how hot it is, while you will be thinking about how much more miserable they will be in the heat when you outhustle them." I have no hard evidence that this story had anything to do with the fact that we soundly defeated the other team, but I like to think it helped get our guys out of their doldrums and focused on playing well rather than on how miserably hot they were.

Practice, Practice, Practice

As the famous story goes, when Isaac Stern was asked by someone on the street in New York City how to get to Carnegie Hall, he replied, "Practice, practice, practice." In John McPhee's wonderful biography of Bill Bradley, *A Sense of Where You Are*, there is a passage about how Bradley became such a great shooter. As a Princeton basketball player, Bradley would stay after practice every day until he made 10 of 13 from every one of the spots on the floor that he might shoot from in a game.

I tell my players that one reason Bill Bradley was a basketball hero of mine was because unlike so many outstanding players he didn't have overpowering strength, speed, or leaping ability. But in spite of some physical limitations, he became an All-American player and professional star because he worked and worked to improve those parts of his game that he could control.

Years after Bill Bradley last played professional basketball, this story is still powerful because it gives young athletes a tool to use to improve their shooting and a way of structuring their individual practice regimens. Ten for 13 is an ambitious undertaking for many kids, but it is guaranteed that if you do it consistently, you will eventually be able to shoot the lights out on a basketball court.

CUTTING THROUGH THE NOISE WITH METAPHORS

Kids have lots of what we adults think of as distractions or "noise" competing for a share of their attention. They have fantasies. They wonder what other kids think of them. They hear the traffic passing by on the streets next to the baseball field. They see birds fly overhead. They get hungry and wonder what's for dinner. They get thirsty and wish for a soda. They get tired and begin to wonder when, if ever, this practice or game is going to be over. They remember things they were supposed to do but didn't. So it's not surprising that our players don't always (or even often) get what we're trying to teach them the first time.

I sometimes think the best subtitle for a youth coaching book would be, "Why It's a Wonder Kids Ever Hear Anything We Say." Given the noisy battle raging for our young athletes' attention, or mindshare, as advertising people call it, it's not surprising that coaches need to find memorable ways to communicate. That's where metaphors can help.

Although I had certainly heard of the word, I didn't really understand metaphors until I had to teach a lesson in metaphors and similes to my third-grade students at Yellowstone School in Rock Springs, Wyoming, many years ago. Until then I didn't realize how much fun metaphors are for children (of all ages), nor what a wonderful teaching tool metaphors can be. A metaphor can cut through the noise and make what you are trying to teach your players accessible and understandable for them.

The Webster dictionary defines metaphor as "a figure of speech in which one thing is likened to another, different thing by being spoken of as if it *were* that other" (emphasis added). A simile is a metaphor that makes the comparison between two unlike things explicit by using the word "like," as in "move like a monkey."

1. **Move like a monkey:** For weeks I had been trying to get my young basketball players to shuffle their feet when guarding an opponent. When the opponent would change directions, most of my players would try to change directions with them by running. Now running is a faster way of getting to one place than shuffling, but it's harder to change directions quickly when running. The opposing player would try a crossover dribble and leave my players behind while they were going through the elaborate and slow process of trying to stop running in this direction and begin running in another direction.

   I had been trying all kinds of ways to get the message across, but nothing worked. Finally, in desperation (the source of many great ideas), I began scratching under my arms as I demonstrated for the hundredth time. It was kind of fun so I began to make monkey noises as well. The kids thought it was both funny and fun, and they began to mimic my mimicking the way a monkey moves.

   Then it hit me. They were doing what I wanted them to do. They were shuffling their feet. They were moving like a monkey. From that point on, whenever I would see someone running when they should have been shuffling, I would yell out "Move like a monkey" or simply "Monkey!" That would be enough to remind them how much fun it was to move like a monkey, and never again did they have to think about the boring concept of shuffling.

2. **Watering the tomato plants:** A friend who is a community college president once told me about a management seminar he and his management team attended together. The goal was to develop a common vocabulary that would allow them to easily communicate with each other and avoid falling into common traps that reduce productivity and effectiveness. One of the sayings

they came away with was "Don't put out more tomato plants than you can water." This was a group of people who had trouble saying no to additional responsibilities with the result that some critical things didn't get done well because everyone was trying to do too much. So "tomato plants" became a shorthand metaphor for "don't take on more responsibility than you can handle."

As I began to work with older kids, it became clear that they simply could not become outstanding athletes without practicing outside of regular practice times. There just is not enough time in practice to learn to dribble behind your back, or develop a left-handed hook shot, or become a 90 percent free throw shooter. Remembering the tomato plant metaphor, I adapted it to this situation. I tell players that if they want to improve dramatically, they will need to practice on their own.

What we do in practice is planting tomato plants; but plants that are only watered during practice won't get enough water to bloom. If you want to become a great ballplayer, you need to water the tomato plants that you want to make sure will come up and bear fruit.

As with the monkey metaphor, after awhile, all I have to do is ask the players, "Have you been watering the tomatoes?"

As a side note, I often use the tomato plant metaphor in exactly the opposite way from which it was originally intended. I *like* to put out more tomato plants than can be watered because I'm never sure at the beginning which ones will come up (i.e., which ones will capture the imagination of the people who will have to make the commitment to water them). When I work with young people, I want to encourage them to try many different things and not get hung up when any given one doesn't turn out. By putting out lots of tomato plants for them to see, touch, and try out, it is likely that more of them will end up being watered and flowering than if I limited it to only what I thought they could handle.

3. **Ropes and little steps:** A few days before a recent Little League game, I participated in a ropes course. A ropes course is a set of ropes, logs, planks, platforms, cables, and pipes constructed high in a forest. The theory of a ropes course is that one can gain self-confidence from having to face up to the fear of being high above the ground. That self-confidence presumably then can be applied to real-world situations like the classroom or workplace.

In spite of the fact that you are hooked to a cable system from which it would be virtually impossible to accidently disengage, it can be a frightening experience. You are 30-60 feet above the ground, and to get to the next place you need to go, you have to walk across a log about 10 inches wide. While you are in no actual danger, the perceived danger is sometimes so overwhelming that people are literally frozen in place, unable to take a step.

Late in the day, as we were approaching the last part of the course, I heard Laurie, one of the instructors, whisper to one of the more athletic people in our group that this would be the most difficult event on the course. She wasn't kidding. It was a tree-pole about 30 feet high with a revolving metal platform about 12 inches in diameter at the top. Some feet above the platform was a steel ring. We were supposed to climb the pole, get both feet on top of the metal platform, stand straight up, and jump out and up into the air and grab the ring.

We were belayed by rope by an instructor on the ground so the danger was only in our heads. However, one is not necessarily rational in such a situation. Oh, yes, and just to make it more interesting, the tree-pole wobbled when you got near the top.

My stomach was upset from the previous event (a

"cat walk" across a narrow log also about 30 feet above the ground). We had been coached by our instructors that we could choose to not participate in any event and we would be supported by the group. I decided I would choose to *not* try this last event. However, several other people in the group dealt with their fear and gave it their best shot, which inspired me to go as far as I could, even though I knew I wouldn't be able to get to the top of the platform with both feet, let alone grab the ring.

I climbed the pole, got near the top, and looked up at the ring. It seemed so far away that I became discouraged. I was unable to keep my discouragement from my friends below. Kristin, one of the instructors, yelled up that I didn't need to catch the ring yet. What I needed to do *now* was get my right foot up on the platform. What happened next was the stuff of a peak experience testimonial. Calmness came to me. I breathed deeply and spent some time looking at the beautiful forest around me. Then I put my right foot up on the platform, paused, and breathed. I brought my right foot up, paused, breathed, and then let go of the platform with my hands. I slowly straightened up and stretched out my arms. Amazingly, the platform was not shaking. The clear thought came into my head, "Hey, I can reach that sucker!" I leaped up and grabbed the ring with my right hand to the roar of my friends below who had been silently urging me on each step of the way.

Apart from this being a peak experience that I will always remember, Kristin's "little steps" advice has stuck with me whenever I am confronted with a scary or complicated problem or situation. In my head, I often jump ahead of the next step (which I usually can do quite easily) and panic about grabbing a ring that seems so impossible to reach. And it would be impossible without first getting my feet up on the platform. But the view changes with each step, and what seems impossible from further away can come into reach with enough little steps.

At our next Little League game, I told the story of the tree-pole and the little steps. We were playing the first game of the second half of the season. Although we had not won many games the first half, now we could start over. But that in itself made the players nervous. They knew that this game meant more than the most recent games toward the end of the first half, when we no longer had a chance to compete for the championship.

I used the little steps metaphor from that point on to encourage players to concentrate on the next little step facing them. They couldn't win the second half or even the game all at once. What they could do was focus on making the next play, or maybe even only the first part of the next play. Often our fielders would get so concerned about the throw to first base that they would forget to *catch* the grounder in the first place.

And, no, we didn't win the second half. In fact we didn't even win that particular game. But for the rest of that season, "little steps" became effective shorthand for focusing on the task at hand, which is something most young athletes need constant reminders and encouragement to do.

4. **The more outrageous the better:** I used to study books that promised to improve your memory. One of the techniques for remembering a list of items is to link in your mind each item to be remembered with an item on a familiar list in some outrageous way. For example, I use the nursery rhyme, "One is a bun, two is a shoe, three is a tree, etc." as my familiar list. If the first thing that I am trying to remember is to go to the bank to get some cash, I might imagine a huge bun-man bank robber with a nylon stocking over its puffy head, brandishing a huge butter knife, coming into a bank, and robbing it of its cash.

Later when I try to remember the first thing on my list, I think first of "One is a bun," and then, if the link is memorable (or outrageous) enough, it is easy to recall the picture of that huge bun-man, which reminds me that I need to go to the bank to get cash.

The same principle, "the more outrageous the better," should guide you in looking for metaphors to bring to life what you are trying to get across to your easily distracted players. Not only are outrageous metaphors more memorable, they're also more fun.

VISION: SEEING THE OPPORTUNITY

My colleagues at the Stanford Business School, Jerry Porras and Jim Collins, have studied the role of vision in motivating people to attempt great things. One way of thinking about vision is that it is the ability to see the opportunity in a situation. And when that opportunity is articulated clearly to a group of people it has the ability to generate enthusiasm . . . that can lead to great efforts . . . that can lead to surprising successes.

When Steve Jobs first toured Xerox laboratories and saw Xerox's "smalltalk" technology in action, it took him "one microsecond" to realize the commercial possibilities in such a technology. Xerox had developed the technology but wasn't able to see the possibility of bringing that technology to market in a way that could make a profit. Jobs' vision led to the amazing success of Apple Computers.

Using the principle of vision to see the possibility in a situation and clearly articulate it to players has relevance to every coach. There is *always* the possibility of something better occurring in a situation, no matter how bleak it appears. Let me share some examples from my coaching experience.

1. The all-star trouncing: A couple of years ago the Little

League all-star team that I was helping to coach was having a hard time in its first game. Our best pitcher was on the mound and the other team was hitting everything he threw. Their pitcher seemed unhittable. Our fielders were demoralized, missing easy chances. Their hitters looked (and hit) like high school kids. We were behind 12-0 in the second inning. The mood in the dugout needed to improve a great deal before you could say it was somber.

Observers, along about the fifth inning, must have been quite confused. Our dugout was cheering wildly, our batters were aggressively going after the opposing pitcher (the same one), the fielders were rallying behind our second pitcher who was pitching with confidence, and our team spirit was high, even though we ultimately lost 17-3.

What happened? Knowing that victory was beyond reach, I gave the team a more achievable goal by asking them to "tie or win *this* inning." Behind 15-0, even that may not have seemed possible, but in the fourth inning, we did tie: 0-0. The fifth inning was a decisive victory: 2-1; and we also tied the sixth inning 1-1. Our team went on to win the next two games before being eliminated on a bad hop grounder in an extra inning game against a more talented team. I believe that the momentum for that surge was generated in the last three innings of the first game.

As an ironic footnote, the team that finally eliminated us then went on to play the team that had trounced us so badly in the first game, and they lost 1-0 in three extra innings. Perhaps it's just as well that we didn't get to find out but I've always wondered how a rematch with the first team would have turned out if we had gotten to play them again.

2. **The expansion team:** Recently our Little League expanded to add a fifth team. Since the team had only one player with previous major league experience, there was

no way it could expect to have a winning season. And it didn't. But it did have a positive season even though it won only a handful of games.

The reason the players were upbeat and trying hard even though they usually lost was because their coach articulated a vision for them by seeing the opportunity that would motivate them when winning a lot of games was not an option. He told them that no expansion team in our league history had ever won more than a couple of games in their first season. He told them that they could be the best expansion team ever if they won four games. They now had a goal that was achievable, although still challenging.

Then he went further and told them that if they worked hard this year, they had a good chance to win the league championship the following year after getting a year of experience under their belts. Since more than half the players would be returning the next year, this was very plausible.

They surpassed their goal with five victories and, sure enough, they went on to win the league championship in their second year and to establish a winning tradition that all started with a season in which they won only five games and lost 19.

3. **The outfield rules:** I was working with a baseball team that should have locked up the league championship weeks earlier, but for one thing—the outfield. Our outfielders mishandled as many balls as they handled, particularly in pressure situations with men on base. With the final, crucial weeks of the season coming up, things didn't look good. Everyone on the team knew that the outfield was weak, including the outfielders themselves.

In the weeks that followed, the outfielders made the crucial plays that made the difference. Time and again the best hitters on opposing teams would drive balls deep into the outfield and more times than not, the same outfielders as before would make the play. The outfield ceased being the weak link on a team that went on to win the league title.

The opportunity in this situation revolved around the way the outfielders saw themselves. They *knew* they were the weak link. They knew that the other (better) players on the team resented them for always screwing up. They were frustrated with themselves and discouraged about having to play the "crummy old outfield." They were down and disheartened and needed to be pumped up. Articulating the vision started with special practices "just for the outfielders." My initial motivational speech dealt with how our outfield could become a competitive advantage for our team.

> The other teams have kids playing the outfield who don't want to be there. They don't realize that outfield is the key to winning the big games. All the teams have pretty good players playing in the infield. But we can be the only team that also has a great outfield. And what happens when you play against better teams? They hit more balls to the outfield! In the big games, the outfield is the key to winning.

Over the course of the next few weeks, our outfielders began playing with pride. They began to feel like an important part of the team, which they had become. They improved more than even I, with my nearly limitless optimism, would have dared hope for. At one point in a tight game, Jeff, our center fielder, backed up toward the fence under a towering drive. As one parent mentioned later, under the pressure of the situation, he looked like "a prizefighter who was staggering under a few too many blows to the head." But he staggered on and made the catch right up against the fence. Given that there were runners on first and second at the time and the batter was the other team's best hitter, we ended up getting out of the inning without giving up a run. And that was the game. We won.

Another time our left fielder, Brian, ran from left-center field all the way into foul territory to catch a fly behind third base. And another outfielder, Matt, ended up catching three flyballs in a row, more than he had caught the entire season up to that point. They still missed an occasional flyball, but the improvement was dramatic. A group of nonsuperstar kids turned into a tough group of fielders. And it all started with seeing the possibility and communicating it to them in a way they could understand. It gave them what they had been lacking, the feeling that they could make an important contribution to the team.

I've used this same technique to good effect with all-star teams. As anyone who has dealt with all-star teams knows, they are a challenge. Each player has been one of the top players on his or her team. But there are only so many kids who can pitch and play shortstop. So somebody has to play the outfield and typically the all-star players who end up in the outfield haven't played there before and don't like it one bit. But they tend to respond to the idea that the outfield becomes more critical in an all-star tournament because the other team will hit more balls into the outfield.

I am firmly convinced that there is vision to be found in every situation if coaches will begin to look for it. It may not be a vision that will take your team to the Little League World Series, but if your goal is to encourage kids to make greater efforts, the opportunity will be there.

WHERE ENERGY COMES FROM

Many years ago my wife and I signed up to run in the Oregon Governor's Half Marathon which took place in

January. I wasn't in good enough shape to run 13 plus miles, but when I signed up I thought I would train hard and be in shape by the time the race came around. For a variety of reasons, I never did get beyond running about three or four miles at a time in preparation.

However, I decided to go through with it anyway and take it easy, using the half-marathon as a training run. I began running with my wife and another friend. At the six-mile mark I felt tremendous. I felt so good that I said "see ya" to my wife and took off. By the time I got to the 10-mile mark, the tide had turned and I was hurting. By the 12-mile mark I was barely moving.

I will never forget what happened next. At a little bridge that spans Mill Creek less than a mile from the capitol building, I felt a little pat on my butt and an annoying chuckle as my wife passed me by. All of a sudden, I had energy enough to catch up with her and stay with her to the point where we were able to finish together as we passed the capitol steps. My wife says, and I believe her, that she eased up at the end to allow us to cross the finish line together.

What's the point? That almost always we have an untapped reservoir of energy available to us if the right combination of ideas can evoke the emotions that will tap into the reservoir. Before my wife's surprise appearance on the Mill Creek Bridge, I truly believed there was no way in the world that I would have been able to have run hard for the last mile of that half-marathon.

I was able to find additional energy because my emotions and pride were evoked by the idea of seeing her go gliding past me while I was stumbling in. While I am not exactly proud of an ego that would be threatened by my wife's beating me, it did kick in an afterburner of energy that allowed me to finish the race much more strongly than seemed possible.

Human energy *can* be created. It comes from emotions. And emotions are released by ideas. The coach who wants to increase the number of teachable moments will become a student of the power of ideas, in the form of stories, metaphors, and vision, to help players become motivated to make more effort than they think is possible.

4

Teachable Moments III: Engagement

*Great teachers don't teach. They help
students learn. Students teach themselves.*
—Jacob Neusner

Few things are as boring as passively sitting in a classroom listening to a teacher drone on and on about something for which you have little interest. Even in situations
in which one is interested in the material, being in a passive, receptive mode can be agonizing, particularly for kids.

Baseball can be incredibly boring. The sport has more
down moments than almost any activity I can think of.
Watch virtually any Little League baseball game and you'll
see outfielders sitting down, facing away from home plate,
staring up at a passing airplane. And although baseball
moves more slowly than most sports, every sport can become "like school" at times.

Ted Sizer, dean of the Education School at Brown University, notes that we learn best and most when we are *engaged* in the learning process. In one sense this is obvious,
but it amazes me the number of "learning" situations I
find myself in where there is no thought given to increasing the engagement of the "students." A coach can increase

the number of teachable moments by increasing a player's engagement with learning the skills and strategies of the sport, as kids become actively involved with and direct their own learning.

This chapter presents a number of ways to increase players' engagement in their own development and learning. You'll learn how coaches can use questions (rather than simply giving directions), ways to get kids teaching each other skills, and how to help kids set their own goals as well as buy into goals you have for them. The chapter begins, however, with getting players to think.

GETTING KIDS TO THINK

Many coaches seem to want their players to function as highly responsive robots. The coach barks out an order and the player responds without hesitation. I was struck by this repeated message in several recent books about major college basketball coaches and teams. Again and again coaches address their own players or are invited to speak to the players on a fellow coach's team. The message is consistent: just do what your coach tells you and you'll be successful. While this may lead to more victories in the short term, it hardly prepares the athlete to deal with situations where there is no coach to tell him what to do. Even more disturbing, this approach builds in passivity, encouraging players to wait to hear and then follow orders, with the objective of conforming to someone else's standards rather than developing their own.

If we want to help kids develop the ability *and* the self-confidence (two related, but very different, things) to deal with problems and chart a life of their own choosing, we should be looking at sports as an opportunity to develop thinking skills. This means moving away from the coach as a string-pulling puppeteer.

Roland Ortmayer, football coach at the University of La

Verne in southern California, goes so far as to refuse to have a playbook or to put coaches in the stands sending down plays. "If you do this, the coaches are just moving pawns and a few knights and castles. I want the game played by the people the game is for. We have 55 brains on the field. Think how foolish it would be not to use them all."

If all we are concerned about is winning in the short run, it may actually be smarter to train players to be automatons, assuming the coach knows what she is doing. But if we want kids to think, we can start by *expecting* them to do so on a regular basis.

Expecting Kids to Think

Kids are usually told explicitly and implicitly that they are not supposed to think. They are supposed to do what they are told. "Practice this play over and over again and then do it exactly *as* I tell you *when* I tell you," is often the message from the coach.

The first step in getting kids to think is to set the expectation by telling them again and again that you expect them to use their heads on the court or field. The message needs to be repeated because kids won't believe you at first, and because game situations are confusing. I was reminded of this recently when, after an absence of more than 10 years from any kind of participation as a player in a competitive sport, I started playing slow pitch softball. I was amazed at how many things there were to do at the same time and how long it took me to adjust. The first game I played, I almost got run over by a baserunner while playing first base, as I watched the outfielder field the ball. Then insult was added to embarrassment when I was called for interfering with the runner, who was awarded an extra base.

The place where kids will begin to believe you when you say you want them to think is when they make a mistake. I won't go into that in detail here since Chapter 7 is all about the opportunities that mistakes provide a coach. But if you tell kids you want them to learn to think and they take your word, they *will* make mistakes. And you need to respond in a supportive, encouraging way so they won't be afraid to try to think the next time. This is not necessarily easy, especially when the mistake hurts.

Fred Miller told me about an Oregon Department of Transportation employee who wrote a press release informing the public about road construction problems in downtown Salem, Oregon. The press release encouraged motorists to avoid driving in downtown Salem, if possible, until the construction was completed. This press release was not well received by the downtown merchants, who feared it would scare business away. Several merchants complained to the Governor, who called Fred, then the director of the department. Fred didn't like being on the wrong end of the complaint line from the Governor's Office. But he also recognized that the writer of the press release had done what Fred encouraged people to do. He had taken responsibility for his work, had thought about a problem, and done what he had thought was right. Fred wanted to reinforce him for that so he wrote the employee a note saying, in effect, "It didn't work out quite the way you wanted it to, but nice try and don't let that keep you from taking responsibility in the future." As coaches, we need to be able to tell our players that we want them to think. And then when they take us seriously and it doesn't work out (as it often won't), we need to support them so they will continue to think in the future.

Thanks for *Not* Listening to Me!

One of my favorite memories from my first years of coaching baseball involves a second-grader named Dikla who played third base. Dikla, the only girl on the team, held her own with the boys. In one game the batter hit a hard grounder to third with runners on first and third bases. It is very difficult to get the lead runner at this age since so many things can go wrong. The third baseman's throw could be hard to handle or even over the head of the second baseman. The second baseman might forget to cover second. The shortstop and the second baseman might run into each other.

So there I was screaming at Dikla to throw to first base while she calmly fielded the grounder, turned toward second, waited until the second baseman was in position to take the catch, and then threw a perfect strike, which the second baseman caught to get the lead runner. The players and the parents, knowing how seldom this happens at this level of play, erupted in cheers. After a moment of stunned silence at what had happened, I too joined the cheering.

Now, years later, I try not to yell directions at players when the play is going on, but often I get carried away and do it against my best intentions. Every once in awhile, some independent young athlete will go his own way, as Dikla did, and it will work. At times like those, I use the phrase that I tried out on Dikla for the first time that day: "Thank you for *not* listening to me."

ASKING RATHER THAN TELLING

Coaches have thousands of opportunities to tell players what to do. For example, if there are runners on first and third with one out, the infield may expect the coach to tell them whether to go home to try to stop the run from scoring, or to try for the out at second or first.

Now sometimes the game situation is a new one to the players, or the stakes are so high that the coach may feel compelled to tell the players what to do. Often the players can figure out what to do on their own, but *they rarely have to.* The coach, if not the parents as well, is always there telling them what to do so they don't have to think.

The coach who looks for opportunities to *ask* the players what they should be doing next will easily find opportunities. For example, in the situation above, the coach might yell out, "Where are you going to go with the ball if it's hit to you?"

If the players make the "wrong" decision, the coach can go over it with them after the inning or set up a special practice time later to drill on what the appropriate play is given different situations.

During basketball games I ask players on the bench to help me with charting ("Who got the assist when Laurel scored?" "Who got those two rebounds before Howie finally made the basket?"). This involves them in the game and reinforces the areas that I'm wanting all my players to concentrate on.

Questioning the players on the sidelines or bench is also a good way to teach by other players' examples. "What did Kristin do on that play that made it work?" With baseball in particular, there are great opportunities for engaging players on the bench because there usually is plenty of time between plays. "Where did Steven (the pitcher) go after that ball was hit into the outfield? Why?"

Interestingly, I have discovered that my top players, especially, respond better when I stop yelling directions at them and allow them to engage their brains to figure out what to do next on their own, occasionally prompted by my questioning.

The coach who is looking for chances to ask questions will find an inexhaustible source in the moment-by-moment activity of the game. Kids will be forced to think, and, if they are not punished or humiliated for making poor choices, they will improve their decision-making over time. Another pro-thinking approach is to get kids teaching each other.

GETTING KIDS TEACHING EACH OTHER

Have you ever thought you understood something until you tried to explain it to someone else, and then discovered it wasn't as clear as you thought it was?

Our mind plays tricks on us all the time, perhaps out of laziness. I find myself often lulling myself into believing I understand what's being taught when I really don't. I don't want to have to face the fact that I need to do some more *work* to understand this concept or skill so I act as if I got it the first time.

Kids are no different. They will think they understand something they really don't. They may be looking as if they are taking in every word you are saying, but if they can't explain or demonstrate it to someone else, they don't understand it enough to retain it. It is when I am placed in the role of having to teach something to someone else that I really buckle down and learn it. So help your players buckle down by expecting them to teach each other.

Incorporate Kid-Teaching Into Your Teaching

There are a couple of ways to get kids teaching each other. One is simply to incorporate it into your normal teaching process and have kids demonstrate to others how to perform a certain skill every time they are taught it. Too often we teach a skill, but we don't require the student to demonstrate to us that they have heard and understood what we are asking them to do.

If you are teaching a new skill (e.g., sliding), simply add a step to the teaching process. Where you ordinarily

1. explain how you want them to slide,
2. demonstrate the slide for them,
3. have them try to replicate your performance, and
4. give them feedback,

you add some steps. Before you have your players try it, have them tell you how to slide and then demonstrate it to each other. In pairs, each player critiques and offers encouragement to the other. The steps now would be

1. explain how to slide;
2. demonstrate the slide;
3. ask each of them, in their own words, to describe how to slide;
4. in pairs, have them demonstrate sliding to each other; and
5. still in pairs, have them critique and encourage each other.

This frees you up to wander and watch how each person slides in the pairs and offer suggestions, if appropriate. The players having problems are more likely to hear your feedback since it is done in private rather than in front of the entire team. When you believe most of the players have mastered sliding, bring them together for the final steps:

6. have each player demonstrate a slide for the entire group; and
7. give them your feedback.

Notice that your final feedback is likely to be much more positive since they are more likely to have mastered the skill with the extra steps or at least to have shown great improvement over previous attempts. Any time you can praise players in public and correct them privately, they are more likely to accept your feedback. This approach may also encourage players to observe each other's sliding during a game and offer encouragement and suggestions to each other, since they have all learned how to teach sliding as well as how to slide. A more advanced way to incorporate kids teaching kids into your program is a "train-the-trainers" approach.

Train the Trainers

Training the trainers requires that you meet outside of the regular practice time with the player(s) you have selected to be the trainer(s) for a particular skill. If you have a multi-age baseball team (e.g., 11- and 12-year olds), you might pick three "veteran" 12-year-olds to be the designated trainers for a variety of individual skills, such as:

- how to make the pivot at second base
- how to place your feet at first and when to make the stretch
- how to turn and run back for flyballs without losing sight of the ball

It is important to begin this with more than one player. You want to send the message that the process of kids training each other is simply part of how *this* team functions. If you begin with a single player it may be read by the other players as something special that only the "star" player is allowed to do. Even worse it can be seen as something only the coach's favorite is expected to do. Ideally, over time, you will get players asking for the opportunity to become a trainer and learn a skill they can then teach the rest of the team.

Most likely, your players will initially feel a bit funny about the process, and some silliness should be expected. But after the approach becomes integrated into your practices, you will find yourself moving toward having a team of coaches who know a skill not just well enough to perform it but to teach it effectively as well.

Recently, after hearing Stanford Education Professor Henry Levin talk about his ideas on accelerated (rather than remedial) teaching for disadvantaged kids, I asked one of my players who could dribble behind the back and between the legs with great fluidity if he would be willing to teach the other players how to do it. These moves, which were forbidden as showboat moves when I played basketball, have become standard accessories for any ball handler from high school on up. I decided I wanted all my players to learn them. We divided into three groups with my assistant and I each taking a group and the athlete-teacher taking the other group. He worked with each of the other kids on dribbling behind the back. At our next game, a couple of our kids were being hounded by opposing players as they brought the ball up the floor. I asked each of them to try the behind-the-back dribble they had learned in practice the next time they were closely guarded. I told them that I really didn't care if they lost the ball. I just wanted them to try it and see how it went. Both kids executed the maneuver successfully and left their defenders behind. By the end of the season, we would routinely see two or three different players in any given game using one of these dribbles to avoid a defender. I then became a believer in having kids teach each other advanced skills, not just the basics.

An additional step toward engagement revolves around goals and whose goals are preeminent.

WHOSE GOALS?

I will work incredibly hard on something when the motivation comes from me. When the goal is someone else's goal for me, I may work at it, but often only to the degree that I think is necessary to satisfy someone else, not to the point of achieving excellence.

Typically a coach will impose a goal with little or no buy-in by the player. If it concerns a skill that can be learned quite easily without work outside regular practice sessions, this can be effective. If it is a more complex skill, player buy-in is critical to mastery.

Some coaches will impose or suggest a goal and then work to get the player to enthusiastically endorse the goal and make it her own. This is better and more effective than simply laying down the law, but ideally the player establishes her own goals with the coach providing support.

I began this past baseball season by asking each player privately what they hoped to accomplish during the year. Often the answers were not terribly helpful. Many children said things like they wanted to bat .400 or win 10 games as a pitcher, or be selected for the all-star team. The problem with goals like these is that they need to be fleshed out. For example, what specifically does a player need to work on to be able to bat .400?

This can lead to an effective outcome if the conversation begins to make connections in the player's mind between the overall goal and the individual skills and daily commitments needed to master that goal.

You may not be able to get every player to take responsibility for their own goal-setting. But in most cases it results in increased engagement in the learning and development process. For players that just aren't able to come up with their own goals, it can be useful to suggest potential goals to them. Then you can try to get their buy-in to those goals so they are not just going through the motions doing what they think some adult thinks they should be doing. To get this kind of buy-in you need to have a conversation with the player.

For example, if I suggest a goal of learning to shoot a reverse lay-up, I won't leave it at simply suggesting it. I will ask the player if that is a goal that he is willing to work on. Even if the player isn't sure about that, his verbal response can help make him committed to it. Once he says "Yes, I would like to be able to learn to shoot like that," he is on the way to making it his own goal, unless he feels he is being browbeaten into saying it. Then if he will agree to work on the specific skill components needed to achieve the goal, the chances of mastery are much greater.

I am pretty forgiving when players don't follow through on commitments they make to practice a certain skill. This is a voluntary activity designed to give them some enjoyment and make them better, happier people. What I don't want is for them to think about sports the way they would about a job they hate (I can see the bumper sticker now: "The worst day fishing is better than the best day at baseball practice"). So I will encourage them to do what they say they are going to do, and I will ask them about how it went practicing the skill outside of practice. But if they don't follow through, I will not dwell on the failed commitment, but rather try to get them to recommit to practicing it the next time.

Then, when and if they do follow through on their commitment, I will reinforce them for it. But I always try to remember that their commitment is primarily to themselves to improve, not to me. So I avoid trying to make them feel guilty about it or harassing them into doing it just to satisfy me and get me off their backs. People usually become great at something when the motivation is internal, coming from themselves. External motivation can take one only so far and often leaves bitter residues that color other parts of one's life.

Goals, Practice, and Excellence

One of the characteristics of many outstanding athletes is how much they love the sport. They practice and practice and practice. I used to marvel at my son's ability to play baseball hour after hour with no letup. I would pick him up after a two or three hour practice and he would want to play catch for a while longer. He now shoots baskets for hours on end, year round. He loves playing basketball, and he sets his own goals.

It's hard to say how good a basketball player he'll end up being, but he'll be better because he wants to be, not because he is harassed into practicing. Great athletes, perhaps great anythings, are great partly because they themselves are driving the process of goal-setting, commitment to the goals, and then practicing until mastery is achieved (see Chapter 13).

Unrealistic Goals?

Often coaches find they have trouble with the idea of players developing their own goals because they have seen players who take on highly unrealistic goals. When they are unable to accomplish the goals, they get discouraged and give up.

I have no problem with a coach talking reality to a player who thinks he is going to become Michael Jordan overnight. Coaches should help kids select goals that are realistic while still stretching the child. But if the kid still insists that he is going to do what you believe is impossible, at some point you need to trust the process and let him take a shot at it. If and when it doesn't work out, you can be there to help the player reformulate a goal that is still challenging but within reach with a stretch.

WORKERS RATHER THAN PRODUCTS

This all gets back to the heart of the issue which is what you are trying to do. If you are trying to produce victories right now, then the ideas in this chapter may initially set you back. If you are trying to develop a love of learning and a willingness to apply effort to become better at something that children themselves find valuable, then increasing engagement in the learning process is helpful.

Ted Sizer notes that in schools where children get excited about learning, the "central metaphor is student as worker rather than student as product." This means less directive behavior by the teacher (coach) and more work produced and directed by the student (athlete).

The best teachers and coaches are developers of people as lifelong learners. They help their pupils embrace the act of becoming better at whatever *they* choose to do or be. And a big part of this is being able to surrender control of the process to the player rather than trying to direct everything from the coach's perch.

5

The Coach's Role in Increasing Self-Esteem

. . . if your child has high self-esteem, he has it made . . . self-esteem is the mainspring that slates every child for success or failure as a human being.

—Dorothy Corkille Briggs
Your Child's Self-Esteem

Self-esteem is one's internal judgment of oneself. Often it is not a conscious statement as much as a feeling about oneself.

One night several years ago in our living room while reading a book on parenting and self-esteem, I decided to try out the book's suggestion on how to tell whether a child had a high level of self-esteem. I asked my son, who was reading on the couch, "If you could be anyone in your school, who would you like to be?" He immediately said, "Me!" This must have seemed so obvious that he began to wonder if I meant something else. "Or did you mean *besides* myself?"

But he had gotten it right the first time. He had passed the test. It *isn't* obvious that most children would choose to be themselves if they had the chance. A person with high self-esteem is glad to be who they are. They might envy some element of another's life, but they are comfortable in their own skin.

SELF-ESTEEM AND PERFORMANCE

While conventional wisdom says that increasing a child's self-esteem will improve that same child's performance in school, in athletics, and in life, it isn't that clear. The evidence on whether higher self-esteem necessarily leads to higher performance is not straightforward. However, I am convinced that, other things being equal, higher self-esteem does lead to higher performance. Notice I am saying *higher* rather than *high* performance, because high performance is also dependent upon natural ability and the quality of coaching received, things that usually are not equally distributed among children.

However, it is also possible that improved self-esteem may lead one to turn one's energy in another direction, like Conrad, in the movie *Ordinary People*, who drops off the swimming team when he realizes that he is swimming competitively only because his parents expect him to follow in the footsteps of his dead brother. As he begins to become psychologically stronger, he chooses to pursue what is of interest to him, without an overly high regard for what others want him to do.

At the risk of blurring the distinction between self-esteem and self-confidence (or self-efficacy—see Chapter 13), I believe it is acceptable and useful to assume that high self-esteem involves two things:

1. the belief that one is worthy of life's blessings
2. the belief that one is competent to master life's challenges

For the purposes of this book I believe that these two beliefs can be treated as different sides of the same coin. A belief that one is competent can be strengthened (or undermined) by a belief in one's intrinsic worth. Similarly, a child who is raised to believe he is worthy will find that belief undermined if he is unable to accomplish tasks that our culture values highly, such as being able to read. Since much of this book is about increasing competency at skills that are highly valued by this society, I spend most of this chapter discussing self-esteem and worthiness, but let me begin by saying a few words about self-esteem and competency.

SELF-ESTEEM AND COMPETENCY

Athletic ability is highly valued in America. We could debate whether it should be so, but there is no doubt that it is. Youth sports are such a great opportunity to build self-esteem precisely *because* sports are highly valued in this society, and athletic ability is highly valued by young athletes and their peers. Helping young athletes develop skills in sports promotes increased self-esteem because they feel better about themselves as they see themselves develop valued skills that they didn't have before.

This is not to say that success in sports is a panacea for children who receive no positive support anywhere else in their lives. But there is something intrinsically satisfying about sports. It *feels* good to bounce a basketball (which incidently is why it's so hard to get kids to stop bouncing the ball when you want to talk with them). My son and I used to play catch with a baseball for hours on end, occasionally conversing, but mostly just enjoying the feel of the body moving to throw, and the sound of the ball hitting the glove. There is tactile as well as emotional satisfaction in the physical acts of playing games.

Sports also provide a great opportunity, one of the few in this society, for children to learn to work together as a team. Team sports offer the chance to learn to deal with differences in each other. These skills, if truly learned, are transferable to other settings in life.

The Language of Self-Esteem

A child that believes he just isn't any good at baseball, but learns to improve, can make the same leap of imagination in other areas. "Speaking Chinese is hard but I can learn to do it!" In fact the language of self-esteem is encompassed in two phrases:

I can *do* this
and
I can *learn* to do this.

A coach who builds in his players the tendency to use this vocabulary, by *showing* them that they *can* do and *learn* to do, is giving a great and lasting gift to them, the belief that they are strong enough and smart enough to handle whatever life throws at them. Let me now turn to the focus of this chapter, the belief that one is worthy of life's blessings.

SELF-WORTH AND IMPORTANT OTHERS

When I was 21, I was a summer counselor at Camp Owendigo for Neighborhood House in St. Paul, Minnesota. Don Challman, a social worker who helped train the new camp counselors, led off his presentation by saying, "It's not your job to be liked by the kids. Your job is to like them."

I once read an interview with a popular actor. He was asked why he was attracted to his wife. He said, "Because she liked me." He may have meant it as a joke, but I took it as seriously as Don Challman's admonition. I want to be around people who like me because they make it easier for me to like myself and to take the kinds of risks and make the kinds of efforts that are necessary for growth.

Except perhaps in rare cases, most of us can't develop a healthy sense of self-worth by ourselves, simply by willing it to be so. We are social creatures, and we derive much of our feelings about ourselves from how our various social groups (family, friends, classmates, teammates, etc.) treat us. Our sense of self-worth depends to a crucial degree on our perception of how important others value us.

Notice it isn't simply based upon how others value us, but upon our perceptions. If someone thinks highly of me but never communicates it, I do not benefit. As a coach, you can improve the self-esteem of your athletes in a number of ways, but the key is to *communicate* that you accept and value them in ways that they can't mistake, that you like them, and that you endorse them.

Endorsement: The Key to Self-Worth

As a child growing up in North Dakota, I remember regularly choosing sides for various playground games. The captains, typically the oldest and most talented athletes, would alternate picks with the "best" kids chosen early and the rest later. What a thrill it was to be selected early! What a disappointment to be among the last chosen.

What was going on was "endorsement" (or lack of it). Endorsement, being *chosen* for important positions and being *supported* by important others, is ultimately what drives our own feelings of self-worth.

And for young athletes, a coach is a very important adult in their lives. Don Challman's advice was sound. The youth sports coach's first job is to like his players and *show* that he does; to *endorse* them and let them know he chooses them and supports them.

Breaking the Transaction Analogy

The belief that one is worthy comes from feeling appreciated and valued by important adults in a child's life. And for a child who loves sports, the coach *is* an important adult. But how exactly do you show a kid you appreciate and value him—and not just for what he can do for you (i.e., win a game and make you look good as a coach)—but just because of who he is?

I remember attending an awards ceremony at my son's elementary school a few years ago. The children were recognizing the custodian for all the help he had given them during the year. They sang a song that went something like this:

> We love you Dah-a-on, oh yes we do-oo
> We love you Dah-a-on, for what you do-oo
> When you are gah-ha-hon, we're blue
> Oh, Dah-a-on, we love you.

The song really hit a sour note for me. As I tried to understand why I didn't like it, I realized that it was a description of a business transaction. "If you, Don, will do things for us that we want or need to have done, we will appreciate you." At one level it is not that different from a bank saying that if you can demonstrate that you have the ability to manage a loan, and agree to repay the money with interest, it will grant you one.

You may be very happy to get the loan from the bank, but you are kidding yourself if you think that the bank is loaning you the money because you are one special person. And it is very, very unlikely that your self-esteem will be increased because you got that loan, unless it is because of having a sense of accomplishment for having demonstrated that you are creditworthy.

The kind of relationships between adults and children (or adults and adults for that matter) that build self-esteem are ones that are *not* business relationships. As Stanford political scientist and renaissance man Jim March says, "Anyone can love me if I am lovable. What's remarkable is when someone loves me when I am not lovable." What many children who are hard to love need more than anything else is to have someone who loves them not because of anything the child can do for the adult, but *just because.*

After talking it over with my son, we came up with a new version of the "Don Song":

> We love you Dah-a-on, oh yes we do-oo
> We love you Dah-a-on, for being you-oo
> It doesn't matter what you do
> Oh, Dah-a-on, we love you.

Too often the message given young athletes is that their value as human beings corresponds to how well they perform on the field. Talented players are more valued than weaker players. Even talented players can go into the doghouse if they make bonehead plays. This is deadly to the development of strong self-esteem. And it is deadly to the development of great competitors, those who enjoy the challenge of achievement without a paralyzing fear of failure (see Chapter 13).

Among Friends: A Tale of Two Speeches

A couple of years ago I gave two speeches back to back. The contrast was so unusual that I gave a great deal of thought to what had made the difference. The first presentation was on leadership to a group of Stanford MBA students. I was comfortable and relaxed and the presentation almost gave itself. I felt like I was on top of the material, and the response of the audience to what I was saying was gratifying. The second presentation, to a group of youth coaches on positive coaching, was something else again. I felt very uncomfortable, my delivery was tentative, and the presentation seemed flat and unimaginative. I was pretty sure that I had not made much of an impact on the audience.

In trying to understand the difference between the two events, I came to believe that the major factor was how I felt about what I was doing. In the first instance I felt confident. In the second I didn't. It wasn't that I was more in command of the material of the first session. There was a great deal of overlap in the material I was covering, and, if anything, I felt more comfortable with the positive coaching content. Nonetheless, my feeling about my own ability differed greatly in the two sessions.

I tried to revisualize the audience in each case. Suddenly I had an insight. I remembered seeing heads nod approvingly and hearing chuckles in response to my attempts at humor with the business students. I had the feeling that I was among friends in that group. In the second situation, I remembered seeing some crusty longtime coaches peering at me through narrowed eyes. I didn't remember many smiles or laughs. I seemed to be talking to a group of people that didn't particularly like the message or the messenger (me).

Over time I came to believe that the phrase "among friends" could serve as a powerful shorthand way of characterizing my fluctuating feeling about myself. In the first situation, I not only felt witty and eloquent and persuasive, but I *was*. In the second case, I didn't feel that way and I was *not*.

This reminded me of Ross Campbell's little gem of a book, *How to Really Love Your Child*, which first introduced me to the idea of the "emotional tank" that each of us has. The level in the tank varies from time to time, depending on how we are treated by the people in our world around us. When we are on the receiving end of treatment that makes us feel valued, our tank fills. Conversely, receiving negative stuff, or even being ignored, causes the level of the tank to decrease.

Children are much more willing to try new things, and to make efforts, when their tanks are full and they are among friends. When their emotional tanks run down, they tend to withdraw, or in some cases "act out" and become behavior problems that disrupt your well-laid plans for practice or games (see Chapter 15 for methods for dealing with behavior-problem children).

I have found the emotional tank to be a useful metaphor for self-esteem. Actions by important others in our lives that increase the level in that tank are ones that build self-esteem. What are some of those actions?

How to Increase Self-Esteem in Your Players

If my self-esteem is highest (and my emotional tank is at its highest) when I am among friends who like and endorse me, couldn't I increase self-esteem in others by helping them to feel that they are also among friends? I've approached the question of how coaches can increase self-esteem in their players by asking two questions:

Who are the people I enjoy being with?
and
What is it that they *do* that causes me to feel accepted
and valued by them?

These questions have led me to a variety of actions my friends and family members take which help me feel great about myself. A youth sports coach can increase the self-esteem of players by the same means.

1. **Names:** There is an old saying that what most people want to see in a newspaper is their own name. When I had playground duty as an elementary teacher, one of my first insights was the importance of quickly learning the names of the more mischievous kids. It was virtually impossible to maintain any semblance of order

on the playground if I was not on a first-name basis with each of them. Kids respond to adults who take the time to learn their names and call them by name often.

It is also important to get your players in the habit of using each other's names. I once started the first baseball practice of the year with a variation on an ice-breaking exercise I learned at Outward Bound called the Name Game. Everyone gets into a big circle and I start it by saying, "My name is Coach Thompson and my favorite baseball player is Roger Maris." The next person must introduce me to the rest of the group saying, "This is Coach Thompson and his favorite baseball player is Roger Maris. My name is Jason and my favorite baseball player is Will Clark." Each person in turn must try to remember the name and favorite ballplayer for everyone introduced before. This can be done with favorite foods, TV shows, musical groups, etc., in place of baseball players.

Every kid should be greeted by name when he arrives at a practice or game. Whenever a player leaves a game or practice, she should be bid farewell by name. Players should hear their names spoken in a friendly tone of voice often. It's music to their ears.

2. **Smiling:** My friends smile at me often. Many coaches act as if too much smiling is unsportsmanlike. Coaches can communicate that they like a player perhaps more easily by smiling than any other way.

3. **Joking:** Humor that does not make fun of someone is something that typically only goes on between people that like and care about each other. Friendly humor causes people to enjoy each other's company, something that can be important in a stressful setting such as an athletic team.

4. **Eye contact:** Again, it was Ross Campbell's book, *How to Really Love Your Child*, that first alerted me to the importance of eye contact between parent and child. "The more parents make eye contact with their child as a

means of expressing their love, the more a child is nourished with love and the fuller is his emotional tank."

I was initially skeptical but having intentionally tried increasing eye contact with my son and other children, I am now convinced he is right. Eye contact of a friendly nature communicates caring.

5. **Appropriate touching:** Touching kids can be a controversial issue in a time when so much sexual abuse of kids is being uncovered. But a coach who tousles the hair of her players, who appropriately puts her arm around kids' shoulders during a huddle, who pats players on the back, who exchanges "high fives," and who shakes hands with players after good efforts is communicating that she likes and values her players. People simply do not choose to touch people they don't like. Kids know this at some level and respond to an adult who knows how to communicate through touch.

6. **Influence-ability:** One way that I know I am valuable in a relationship or an organization is if I have influence with the other person or people. One of the tragedies of the military chain-of-command model of coaching is that coaches who try to emulate General Patton can end up communicating to their players that they are simply cannon fodder with all major decisions being made by the general-coach.

There is a beautiful scene in the movie *Hoosiers* in which the coach calls the last second play in the championship game. His players, who have been bludgeoned into blind obedience by his overbearing style all season, are glumly silent. They have learned that they have no influence with the coach. However this time, the coach's decision goes against the grain so much that, as a unit, they react in a way that even *this* coach can't mistake. To his credit, the coach asks them what's wrong. To their credit, they tell him. He changes the play with interesting results (if you haven't seen the movie, I'm not going to give away the ending).

A coach who can be influenced by his players is communicating that he cares about them and values their ideas. Nowhere is a lack of influence-ability more a problem than with playing positions. I cannot count the number of times I have heard parents and athletes complain about their coach because he wouldn't let the kids try positions they wanted to play. Often there may be solid reasons why a particular child should not play a particular position. For example, a weak fielder might get hurt at first base if the shortstop has a powerful arm. In cases like this it helps a lot if the coach simply communicates the reason to the player and gives the player an idea of what he can do to get to the point of being able to play his favorite position (e.g., lots of practice catching hard throws from shortstop).

Another reason why a coach may not want a child to play a particular position is because it will hurt the team's chances of winning. But very few teams go through a season without some "laughers," games in which they are either way behind or way ahead virtually from the beginning. These are great opportunities to give weaker kids a chance to play their favorite positions, and to let them know that they have influence with their coach.

Stanford's women's basketball coach, Tara VanDerveer, recently spoke at a coaching clinic I attended. She said that running was the heart of her approach to basketball, and it bothered her to use running as a punishment. She wanted her players to enjoy running, as well as see it as the key to victory over perhaps more talented teams that may not be in as good shape. But in some situations, she just wasn't getting the results she wanted. She finally consulted with Jennifer Azzi, later chosen as the 1990 NCAA player of the year, about what to do. Jennifer said, "Make us run, Coach." So they ran.

What is so terrific about this story was that VanDerveer didn't treat Azzi as a robot to be programmed. She empowered her by asking her advice on a troubling issue. Now granted, Jennifer Azzi is not your typical basketball player, but the same principle can be applied to players and teams at all levels. As a coach, you can ask your player's advice about what to do in a given situation and whether or not they have any ideas (and they will more often than you might believe). When you do ask, a message is transmitted that you care about them enough to get their advice.

7. **Listening:** Implicit in influence-ability is being heard. There are times when a coach simply has to make a decision that the athlete is not going to like or agree with. But it can make an incredible difference if the coach will give the child a chance to say his piece. Just listening without interruption can communicate caring to the player, whether or not the decision goes his way.

In my first full-fledged teaching job in Rock Springs, Wyoming, I learned the value of simply listening. I was on recess duty when several of my third-graders came running to complain that the sixth-graders were bullying them. I investigated and yelled at the sixth-graders. Before I knew it, I had a near rebellion on my hands as the sixth-graders came forward with tons of grievances against my third-graders who were disrupting their kickball game. After recess I asked the sixth-grade teacher if I could talk with her students, but really didn't have a good idea what I was going to say. As it turned out, not having anything specific to say was my best idea.

I opened the discussion by saying that we had some problems on the playground, and I wanted to hear the sixth-graders' side of it. Out poured a litany of frustrations. Since I knew my kids, I was only too aware that the older kids may have had a point. I intentionally showed that I was listening, and several times paraphrased back to them what I heard them saying their problems were. At one point I started to propose a solution. I was about to say that I was willing to tell my kids that they were not to go onto the kickball field if the sixth-graders were playing a game there, when the most vocal of the sixth-grade boys interrupted me: "No, that's not necessary. If the third-graders come onto the field, we'll just ask them politely to not get in the way of our game."

I was flabbergasted. I would never have considered asking for such a radical response from the sixth-graders. However, I looked around the room and most of the kids were nodding their heads. So I asked them if they all agreed with the suggestion. They pretty much all said yes, and I walked out of there scratching my head. I immediately went back to my class and told them of the sixth-graders' response and asked them if they would respect the boundaries of the kickball field. They all agreed and the incident was closed with no further problems that entire year.

In the years since then, I have gained a great appreciation for the power of simply listening in an obvious way to what people have to say when they are upset. It communicates that you take them seriously and that is worth a lot. Sometimes that is more important to a kid than the specific problem he is upset about in the first place.

8. **Apologies:** There are few things in life I find as difficult as apologizing when I make a mistake that hurts someone. I don't like to do it, largely because I don't like to admit that I might have been wrong. But every time I do apologize I feel better, usually the other person feels better, and our relationship is strengthened.

I recently snapped at one of my basketball players in practice. He was a player who was playing on a basketball team for the first time and he was very enthusiastic, to the point of asking if we might practice a third night a week rather than just twice. However, on this particular night I was in a foul mood. At one point I singled him out for not paying attention when I was talking. He immediately said something like "I *was* listening," and then clammed up and mentally withdrew. I realized that it was mostly my crabby temperament that was the problem rather than his behavior. I also was embarrassed to realize that I had broken my own rule of not criticizing a player in public. I called a break and sought him out to apologize. Once I did, he immediately brightened back up and once again threw himself into practice.

Coaches make mistakes. Young athletes are sometimes hurt by those mistakes. A grown-up who finds the humility to apologize to a player is communicating in a direct and clear way that he values the player.

9. **Forgiving:** The flip side of apologizing is forgiving children when they hurt us. Often coaches, myself included, have a tendency to take it personally when a child fails to come to practice regularly, or fails to properly execute a play that had been worked on for weeks. One of the things that gets my blood boiling the quickest is when one of my players shows poor sportsmanship, largely because I too often take my players' behavior as a personal reflection of my coaching. But it's important to remember that these are just children, no matter how talented they may be with a soccer ball or a baseball bat. Being able to forgive and move on to dealing better with each other in the future is an advanced skill, for a coach and for adults in all relationships.

   Once again, the message communicated is that the player has value to the coach irrespective of the player's ability to shoot a ball into a hoop. We forgive people because we care about them and recognize that people make mistakes that hurt each other.

10. **Asking for help:** When I was a new hire at the Oregon Department of Energy, Fred Miller (the director) came by my desk one day and asked if I could do him a favor. His wife's car—like mine, a Volkswagen bug—

97

was in the shop and she needed to drive to Portland (about an hour's drive) for a doctor's appointment. She was in the last days of her pregnancy and he thought she would be more comfortable if she could drive a car like the one she was used to driving. Would I mind lending it to her for a few hours the next day?

Not only wouldn't I mind, I was thrilled. His asking me for help did two useful things. It signaled that I was a "keeper." It was not at all clear to *me* at this point that I had what it took to be a contributing member of what was a very high-performing and entrepreneurial state agency. But he was, in effect, telling me that I was a member of the club, or once again "among friends." The second thing it accomplished was to reduce the distance between us. Even though he was (trumpet flourish here) THE DIRECTOR, and I was a lowly trench worker, he was treating me as an equal. And it is no secret that I, and many others after me, derived a great deal of pleasure from feeling like I was working "with" (rather than "for") him.

A coach can build young athletes' self-esteem by simply asking them to help. When we were in India recently, my wife and I visited the Loreto Day School in the Sealdah section of Calcutta. There we met Sister Cyril, the principal of the school, which is run by the Sisters of Loreto, the group Mother Teresa came from and was supported by when she started the Missionaries of Charity 40 some years ago. Sister Cyril told us that the school serves about thirteen hundred Calcutta girls, including a large number of street children. She believes that middle and upper class children benefit from sharing with children less economically fortunate than they.

When the Loreto Day School receives a donation that allows it to admit a new nonpaying child, Sister Cyril gives a current student the chance to help. She will ask a girl in the school if she would be willing to help make it possible for the school to take in this new student. She explains that they have received a donation and that they need to respond and thank the donor before they can admit the new student. This is quite different than the typical procedure, which would have the child benefitting from the donation thank the donor for herself. Sister Cyril uses a two-bird stone. The donor is thanked and a child's self-esteem is boosted by being asked to help.

Sometimes the player on your team that is the least likely candidate to be a star player may be the one who will benefit the most from being asked for help. Which, come to think of it, may be why Fred Miller asked me for the use of my car in the first place.

11. **Expressing appreciation and recognition:** When someone notices what I have done or an effort I have made, I feel great and am more inclined to make additional efforts. In Chapter 2, the techniques of positive charting and the plus-minus ratio, which systematize the expression of appreciation and recognition, were described in some detail.

Over the years, I've developed some guidelines for recognizing and appreciating my players (and people in general). These include being accurate, being behavior-specific, tying recognition to the goals of the group, putting it in writing, and avoiding the temptation to try to be humorous while recognizing people.

a. *Accuracy:* First and foremost, recognition should be true. You may have to search for something to say about your weakest player, but don't make up something that isn't true just to make him feel better. If the only positive thing you can come up with is that once or twice during a game the player didn't travel when he got the ball, emphasize that. But if you lose your credibility and become a "happy talk" coach, your effectiveness as a teacher and leader will diminish.

b. *Behavior-specific:* The extent to which you can tie recognition to specific behaviors, the more power it will have. There is a *New Yorker* cartoon that shows a manager walking among the workers, saying, "You're doing a great job, whatever it is, whoever you are."

It's easy to just say "Great job!" It's harder, but much more powerful, to say, "You really blocked out strongly for that rebound you got at the end of the game." Positive charting (see Chapter 2) gives you lots of raw material on specific behaviors with which to recognize your players.

c. *Tied to the goals of the team:* If you can tie the efforts of each individual to the overall success of the group, you can help build a real team. The rebounding example above could be amended to tie it to the overall goal of the team by saying, "When you blocked out and got that rebound at the end of the game, you really helped the team protect its lead" (if you won). If you lost anyway, you might end it by saying ". . . that rebound helped keep us in the game right up to the end."

I've found that emphasizing assists in basketball is a perfect way of recognizing team-oriented behavior. I tell my teams that an assist is the "ultimate basketball play." Assists are usually overshadowed by scoring, so I make a special effort to recognize assists as a contribution to the team's success.

d. *Written is better than spoken:* One way a coach can communicate appreciation for efforts made is to *write* a note to a player. Written appreciation or recognition has several advantages over oral. It takes more thought and effort to think through and write down a note of appreciation. People recognize that and often value a written note more because of it. The written word has staying power whereas a spoken statement fades over time.

I still have a note of appreciation written to me by Lynn Frank, who succeeded Fred Miller as director of the Oregon Department of Energy. I was stepping in to manage a highly volatile, politically charged, Governor-appointed solar and energy conservation task force that wasn't getting its work done. There was limited time (set in law by the Oregon Legislature) for the task force to finish its work, and it hadn't even really gotten going yet. Lynn's note to me ended by affirming his confidence in me, by saying that he was glad that I was the one who had this responsibility rather than him and that if I needed any kind of support all I had to do was ask.

My staff and I were able to get the task force on track and it resulted in a widely praised report and the most comprehensive state energy conservation legislation in the nation. These many years later, I still pull this note out and read it once in awhile. And I still get a positive hit from it. The power of the written word is one that coaches can use to great advantage with their players.

e. *Avoiding the temptation to try to be humorous:* I love to joke around with people, and in particular, with kids on my teams. However, I have learned the hard way over the years that it is best not to try to be funny when recognizing players for their contributions to the team. People take recognition of themselves quite seriously. Most people believe that they are so underrecognized compared to what they deserve, that humor often can end up tarnishing the recognition moment. When I am recognizing a player, for example, at an end-of-the-season party, I try to clearly separate the joking from the recognizing. I may joke with a player while she is coming up to the front of the room, but once I begin to talk about the contributions she has made, I stay serious so there is no chance that I will diminish the experience. I want the players and their families to know that I am totally serious when I am thanking them for what they have done.

12. **Bragging:** I like to brag about my son. I am proud of my wife and the exciting work she does, and I enjoy telling people about her. Bragging about someone conveys pride in who that person is and his or her accomplishments. New parents openly brag about their baby and often brag less as the kid gets older, perhaps from fear of the child getting a "swelled head." I take the opposite position: kids need to be bragged about by important adults in their lives. As a coach I try to tell parents something good about their kid's play every time I see them.

When the California Task Force on Self-Esteem and Personal and Social Responsibility was created, the local newspaper carried stories about each of the appointed members. In the section about Lynn Silton, she mentioned a survey she conducted as part of her masters program in organizational development. "In a survey of highly successful people, Silton found that in response to the question 'What did your parents think of you?' she consistently got answers such as 'They thought I was great,' 'Everything I did was right,' 'My parents were really excited about me.' The interviewees' perceptions were that they were frequently praised, even bragged about to the point of embarrassment." Silton then added, "So, if you're bragging about your teen-ager and he tells you to stop—don't believe him."

13. **Individual teaching time:** Typically people do not make the effort to teach something to someone they don't

care about. When people are in a role of teacher or coach, they are expected to teach their students or athletes. Thus, going beyond the group instruction setting to single out a player for special instruction time communicates valuing above the expected level. One way to structure this is to have a different player or players come early or leave late for each practice. When I notice a player having a problem with a skill during practice, I may ask him if he can stay after practice to work on it for awhile. Or I may suggest that he come early to the next practice so we can focus on it before the rest of the team arrives.

Related to this is giving players individualized "homework" assignments. I often have baseball players who are afraid of catching the ball. I bring tennis balls to practice and ask each player to spend some time every day bouncing a ball off their garage door so they can learn to gauge how and where the ball would land and thus overcome the fear of being hurt by the ball.

14. **Negative feedback *gently* delivered:** This commercial sticks in my mind: "Only your best friend would tell you" (that you have body odor, bad breath, dandruff, etc.). And while we may not want to hear negative feedback from anyone, it is true that a gentle word about how we might improve ourselves is a sign that someone cares about us. Failing to give someone negative feedback about something that is hurting them is not kindness. I recently had a player on my team who liked to joke around with me. I enjoyed it also but occasionally became annoyed when it would get out of hand in an inopportune moment. When he kidded me about a serious statement I was making to the team in the heat of a hard-fought baseball game, I called him aside out of the earshot of the other players. I told him that I liked him and enjoyed joking around with him but that it embarrassed me when he did it when I was trying to get a serious message

across to the team. He nodded his head and there was no further problem during the rest of the season. By not allowing my annoyance to muddy the water or disturb our positive relationship, I was able to get my message through to him. Coaches need to intervene to eliminate or reduce inappropriate behaviors by their players in a way that actually helps the child change, rather than come across as simply one more grown-up dumping on a kid who already may feel like she is being picked on.

15. **Helping see one's potential:** When I was in seventh grade, I was part of a gang of boys who took some delight in making life miserable for our French teacher, Mrs. Jarvis. One day Mrs. Jarvis asked me to stay after class to talk with her. In a matter-of-fact and caring way, she told me that I was wasting my potential. At one point she told me that I could do anything I wanted to with my life, even become president of the United States (years later it seems a little overblown, but that's what she said). I was into being cool so I didn't respond much (or at least tried not to), but her words had a big impact on me, and I gradually (so no one would think it had any connection with her keeping me after class) began to shape up my behavior in that class. I disconnected from the boys who screwed around in class and began to put significant effort into learning French and, in fact, into all my classes.

I have heard many, many stories from grown athletes who describe similar lectures from teachers or coaches who cared enough to help them see the potential that they somehow were unaware of. Ted Sizer uses the phrase "unanxious expectation ('I won't threaten you but I expect much of you')" to describe this. With many young athletes a coach is often in a better position than teachers or parents to credibly communicate the Mrs. Jarvis message. And the fact that she may have gone overboard concerning my potential didn't diminish the impact of what she said. In fact it probably helped me set higher goals than I otherwise would have.

Sometimes it is as simple as just telling a kid what you are thinking. Stacy Geiken mentioned that he became highly motivated to train harder when his track coach told him that he could see him making it to the state tournament. Another friend, Mike Chase, once told me that he loved hockey more than anything when he was in high school. He made the hockey team but failed to rise above third line as a freshman and sophomore. He finally quit hockey and took up wrestling, where he made the varsity immediately. He finished out his high school athletic career as a wrestler. At high school graduation his hockey coach said to him in an offhanded way, "It's too bad you didn't stick with hockey. You'd have been in my first line this year as a senior." Mike was devastated. He disliked wrestling even though he was pretty good at it, and only tried it because he saw no future for himself in hockey. "Why didn't he tell me that when I was a sophomore?! I would have worked so hard for him." Isn't that the truth? Most of us would work so hard for someone who helps us see our potential and cares enough to share his perception with us.

16. **Photographs:** I make a point of having pictures taken of my players. The very act of someone asking you to stand still or pose for a picture sends a message of caring. At the end of the year pictures can be put into a booklet commemorating the accomplishments of the season. Or the photos can be given to the kids to take home and show their parents after a practice.

Last year, we engaged a professional sports photographer to take action shots of Cupertino Hoops players during one Saturday's games. The action shots were then shown in a slide presentation at the end-of-the-season potluck dinner. Parents were also given the opportunity to purchase any shots of their kids that they liked. It was a big hit and reinforced a central idea of Cupertino Hoops, that we thought our kids are terrific and wanted everyone to see them in action.

17. **You pick the rest:** The above practices resulted from my attempts to understand how various treatments from my friends and family caused me to feel great about myself and my ability to handle the challenges in my life. All of these practices might not feel right for you. Even more importantly, there are probably others that you can discover by looking at your own experience. I encourage you to do so and then incorporate those methods into your coaching style.

SELF-ENDORSEMENT: THE ULTIMATE IN SELF-ESTEEM

None of us can always be in a supportive environment, with people treating us in ways that make us feel among friends. Some situations, particularly sports as athletes get older, are highly competitive, even cutthroat.

I believe that children who are treated as suggested in this book are more likely to develop the mental toughness to successfully handle difficult situations. But children must also be given the tools to endorse themselves when they find themselves needing to succeed or even survive in an unfriendly environment.

One way I learned (from taking, and later teaching, a course in Systematic Training for Effective Parenting) to help children move toward endorsing themselves in non-supportive situations is to move from telling them your evaluation of their performance to asking them to examine their own feelings about how they've done. For example, when a third baseman makes a great stop on a hard smash but then throws the ball over the head of the first baseman, my natural tendency would be to focus on the positive and say, "Nice grab!" If I am trying to encourage him to look to himself for endorsement I might rather ask, "How did you feel about that play?" If he responded that he felt terrible about throwing the ball away, I might ask," But how about the catch, how did you feel about that?"

Being able to endorse oneself in situations in which others are critical, perhaps even publicly so as in the media, is a sign of advanced character. The youth sports coach clearly has limited influence in this area. But encouraging athletes to look to their own evaluation of their performance and worth can only be helpful to their success as people and citizens. And that is what sports should be all about.

6

The Opportunity to Build Character

*Where does the power come from to see
the race through to the end? From within.*
—Eric Liddell
in the film *Chariots of Fire*

It is often said that sports build character. But there is all too much evidence that young people learn lessons from sports that most of us would rather they not learn. And the character traits demonstrated by many celebrity athletes and coaches are certainly not ones that I want my players to emulate.

As sports psychologist Tom Tutko has pointed out, there is no guarantee that sports will build character. Clearly sports do offer the potential to build character, but it doesn't just happen. We wouldn't expect young basketball players to learn an intricate trapping zone press without a coach who has given a lot of thought to how to teach it. Even then it will require working on it again and again in practice until the team gets it right. However, we seem to expect kids to pick up positive character traits by osmosis.

This chapter discusses how a coach can teach positive character traits to players using normal, stressful, day-today situations to reinforce those traits. Each coach needs to decide precisely what is meant by positive character traits and which traits are important to teach. But first, let's look at the *coach's* most important character trait.

THE COACH'S MOST IMPORTANT CHARACTER TRAIT

One can routinely read of abusive coaches trying to convince the outside world that abuse is part of a sophisticated strategy for teaching discipline. Unfortunately, people are only too ready to believe it as long as the coach has a winning record. In contrast, I believe that the number one character trait of an effective coach is the ability to demonstrate unqualified support for one's players.

It's important to keep your players' needs foremost in your head because it is so easy to let winning or looking good to others cause you to do something harmful to the development of one or more of your players. No matter what happens during a practice session or a game or an entire season, no matter how badly things go, no matter how out of control the situation seems to be getting, you have the opportunity to support your players and help them draw useful conclusions from what happens to them.

I believe it is possible for coaches at any level to demonstrate unqualified support for their players. However, I recognize that it is more difficult for professional coaches to model this character trait. The purpose of professional sports is to entertain and the surest way to entertain is to win. So it gets complicated for a professional coach to be able to support his players when from a business point of view they can no longer "help" him win and entertain.

However, there is no excuse for coaches working with children (and even high school athletes are still children in many ways) to adopt a so-called "professional," meat-market approach to players. The coach's number one priority is to support her players, and it is the key positive character trait of a great coach.

"IT'S CHARACTER BUILDING TIME"

Lynn Frank, my old boss at the Oregon Department of Energy, used to say whenever things got stressful that "this is the fire that tempers the steel." He was right and I often think back to previous difficult times whenever I find myself in tough situations now. Lynn's point was that there is more at stake than simply extracting oneself from a difficult situation. In adversity lies the potential for development of mental toughness and other positive character traits.

While there is more at stake, in a sense, there is also *less* at stake if the opportunity for growth can be seen as more important than whether or not one is successful in the short-term. As time passes, the stressful nature of the challenges fades but the character lessons live on. Although I remember Lynn using the tempered steel metaphor quite often, I now realize that I can't remember what it was that seemed so stressful at the time.

A sense of perspective can help young athletes respond to challenges and grow in their ability to deal with adversity. One way to help players develop character is to acknowledge when someone is facing a difficult situation, either privately to the person or in front of the entire team. For example, I know of no sporting activity more stressful than pitching in baseball. Every play begins with the pitcher whose every action is immediately graded for the entire world to hear. When the pitcher misses the strike zone, it's a "ball." When he finally gets the ball over, it may well be hit.

I tell every potential pitcher at the beginning of every season that pitching is a character building experience. "If you aren't interested in dealing with difficult situations on a regular basis, then don't try pitching."

When bad things happen, as they *always* do to pitchers sooner or later, I remind them that this is a moment in which they can work on building character. When the bases are loaded with nobody out with the opposing team's best hitter at the plate, "it's character building time."

By calling attention to the fact that they are indeed in a stressful situation, you can help them minimize worry about fear of failure. You can help them begin to see the presence of stress as an opportunity to work on playing under pressure without letting it bother them unduly. In fact I often say to my players when they're under stress, "I'm glad you got into that jam. That's the only way you'll ever learn to work yourself out of one."

This works as well for positions other than pitcher and sports other than baseball. The basketball player who has a one-and-one free throw with no time left and his team behind by one point also has the opportunity to work on building character. So does the tennis player who has to make the next serve or lose the match, soccer players participating in a sudden death shoot-out, and on and on.

WHAT TRAITS ARE WE TALKING ABOUT?

I once observed a coach whose favorite saying was "never let up." He would yell it over and over again at his players. He apparently believed that never letting up is a positive character trait, and he reinforced it. In the privacy of my own mind I took issue with him on the use of the word "never." I could think of all kinds of situations in which "letting up" made sense and was not a character flaw. You may disagree with me, which is fine. The point is that each of us needs to decide for ourselves what character traits are important for us to teach and reinforce with our players.

The following is a list of positive character traits that I

think are important. I offer them here as suggestions and encouragement to you to get you started thinking about your own list.

1. **Mental toughness:** Someone once said to me, "Successful people do what unsuccessful people aren't willing to do." Mental toughness is sticking to something that is really important rather than telling yourself that it's too difficult. It means being willing to suffer discomfort for the sake of accomplishing something that is important to you. Kurt Hahn started Outward Bound after it was discovered that strong, healthy, young British sailors in World War II died more quickly than older, presumably weaker sailors while waiting in the water to be rescued after their ship had been sunk. Hahn came to believe that the older, crustier sailors were mentally tougher. They had survived enough hardship that they simply hung in there longer and often got rescued. The younger sailors didn't believe they had the capacity to survive, and simply gave up.

   The Outward Bound creed is "To serve, to strive and not to yield." After having taken a 10-day Outward Bound sailing course at Hurricane Island off the coast of Maine, I am convinced that mental toughness can be taught and strengthened. I encourage any parents in a position to do so to give their child the opportunity to experience an Outward Bound course. Not everyone can participate in an Outward Bound-like experience, but sports offer the opportunity to teach and reinforce the quality of mental toughness in many players.

   In a 1990 speech, author Parker Palmer related his experience at an Outward Bound course. He had started rappelling down a cliff 110 feet high, banging against the side of the wall a few times, when:

   > Wonder of wonders, I began to get it. I leaned back, and sure enough, I was moving down that rock face,

113

eyes on the heavens, making tiny, tiny, tiny movements with my feet, but gaining confidence with every step.

When I got about half way down, a second instructor called up from below. She said, "Parker, I think you better stop and look at what's happening beneath your feet."

So I lowered my eyes (very slowly, so that I wouldn't change my center of gravity), and there beneath my feet a large hole was opening up in the rock—which meant that I was going to have to change directions.

I froze. I have never been so paralyzed in my life, so full of physical fear. I knew I could do it if I could just keep going straight, but I could *not* change directions. I just froze in sheer terror.

The teacher let me hang there for what seemed like a very long time, and finally she shouted up, "Parker, is anything wrong?"

To this day, I do not know where these words came from (though I have twelve witnesses that say I spoke them). But in a high, squeaky voice I said, "I don't want to talk about it."

The teacher said, "Then I think it's time you learned the motto of the Outward Bound School."

I thought, "Oh, keen! I'm about to die, and she's giving me a motto!"

But then she yelled up to me the words that I will never forget, words that have been genuinely empowering for me ever since. She said, "The motto of the Outward Bound Hurricane Island School is, "IF YOU CAN'T GET OUT OF IT, GET INTO IT!"

Palmer *did* get into it and completed the descent successfully.

Competitive sports provide constant opportunities for developing mental toughness, for getting *into* the challenge when it's not possible to get out of it. Whenever one of your players gets into a tough spot, you can empathize with him but also remind him that this is an opportunity to develop mental toughness. You can help the player learn, or remember, that winning is not the only criterion of success, that it is by trying new and challenging things that one gets mentally tougher; and that it's normal for things not to work out so well the first few times you try something new.

The interesting thing about reminding players of this is that often their performance improves as they readjust their focus from a fear of failing to a willingness to try to develop the positive character trait of mental toughness.

2. **Having fun:** It may seem strange to see the ability to have fun near the top of a list of positive character traits. However, I am convinced that the ability to enjoy challenges and take pleasure in struggle is a character trait that can be developed and will make for happier, more successful people.

Mahatma Gandhi was once told by a Western journalist that he should take a vacation. He responded by saying, "I'm always on vacation." And this in the middle of a ferocious nonviolent resistance campaign with the fate of an entire subcontinent at stake. I believe that much of Gandhi's success was related to his ability to enjoy the challenges he faced.

Parker Palmer's Outward Bound story reminded me of the bleakest and most triumphant moments in my own Hurricane Island Outward Bound experience. My lowest point was being awakened at six o'clock the first morning after we set sail. We crawled out of our sleeping bags, undressed, and put on our swimming suits. Then, one by one, we jumped into 50 degree water in Penobscot Bay off the coast of Maine. As I awaited my turn, I reflected on the absurdity of paying money to "get" to do this. The water was so cold it forced the breath out of my lungs in a violent gasp.

However, I realized that this was the routine. Every morning I would have to jump into the ocean. There really was no honorable way to get out of it, so I decided to enjoy it. The standard approach was to hold onto the side of the boat when you jumped in so that you could immediately come right back out. I began to think about trying something more daring. I started by jumping in without hanging on. Then I tried to lengthen my stay in the water by a few seconds each time. Our last night on the water, a boatmate named Bill and I made a pact. In the morning we would each jump into the water and swim *around* the boat. The next morning we kept our commitment to each other and were so high when we got back on the boat that we *almost* decided to go in again. The challenge of braving the cold, cold water had become exciting, even fun, as I came to appreciate the incredible state of mental alertness I experienced following each bracing dip.

Most people who are truly successful in their lives enjoy what they are doing. They see a challenge as an opportunity rather than a threat. They have confidence that they will survive even if they fail. Because they are having fun, they put more of their energy into trying to figure out how to solve the problem, and less into unproductive worrying. And win or lose, they still are able to enjoy the process.

3. **Winning and losing with class:** I used to talk to my players about good sportsmanship, but I now incorporate sportsmanship into the concept of "class," which seems to have more motivating power. Where "being a good sport" often can seem like a passive behavior (and one more often required of losers), winning and losing with class seems to give young people more to grab onto.

I shudder when I see ballplayers whine whenever a call goes against them. Either coaches are now teaching players that constant whining about bad calls can cause a referee to give them a break on the next call, or players are simply acting immaturely. Either way, it bugs me. Conversely, I take delight in seeing a player respond to a bad call or a tough loss with class.

I ask my players to refrain from clapping when an opponent misses a free throw. I encourage them to help an opponent up after a collision. I insist that they give a rousing cheer for the other team at the end of a game whether or not we win (although naturally the cheer tends to be louder when we win). I try to point out examples of classy behavior to my players whenever I see it, whether it is displayed by one of us or by a member of the opposing team. And I stress that class never involves cheating or sacrificing your principles to win a game.

4. **Courage:** Courage isn't the absence of fear. If you're not afraid, you're not demonstrating courage. Courage is doing what you think is right or necessary in spite of being afraid. Piet Hien captured it perfectly with his little verse:

> To be brave is to behave
> Bravely when your heart is faint.
> So you can be really brave
> Only when you really ain't.

Eleanor Roosevelt said, "You gain strength, courage and confidence by every experience in which you really stop to look fear in the face. You are able to say to yourself, 'I have lived through this, I can take the next thing that comes along.' "

When children are given support and encouraged to see scary situations as opportunities to develop their courage, they can feel more free to try to deal with the challenge. When there is overemphasis on success and it seems that only winners are worthwhile, who in their right mind would want to tackle something scary?

5. **Setting and commitment to goals:** Setting goals is not something that everyone automatically does. Many people are mostly passive about their own development. They go to school where the teachers tell them what they are supposed to learn. They turn on the TV which reinforces and encourages them to not make any decisions. And all too often they join athletic teams where the coach is constantly telling them what they need to do.

Goal-setting is a positive character trait. Help your players determine what *their* goals are for the season. Ask them to think about what they want to get better at, and what they want to accomplish, and to come back to the next practice with a clear idea that they can share with you. One year I started the baseball season by taking players aside at the first practice and asking them what their goals were. Many of them might not have thought about it before then, but they all came up with something.

With my basketball teams, I ask players to choose a "spot" and a "move" that they want to perfect. The former is a place where they will practice again and again so that they can become deadly at that spot. When they get the ball at their spot, they begin to develop confidence that they can score from there. The latter might be a hook shot, a behind-the-back dribble, or any other maneuver that will give them a good chance of getting open when they are closely guarded. It's amazing what self-confidence can come from having a spot that one owns and a move that usually can get one open for a shot.

Then, of course, one must make a commitment to achieving goals. If a player says she wants to learn to be deadly on left-handed lay-ups, help her develop a plan for achieving that goal. If a player wants to be able to play first base, ask him how he can improve his catching ability to the point where he could be successful there. Periodically come back to players to ask them how they're doing on their goals. It's fine for them to change their goals, but too often the goals are simply forgotten and drift off into never-never land. If the original goal was too lofty, help them break it down into a more do-able piece of the overall goal.

Sometimes the goals need to be quite modest for players of modest ability. For example I have encouraged some baseball players to set and attain the goal of reducing the number of called third strikes they take. Many beginning players are so afraid of the pitched ball (and of making a mistake) that it is almost impossible for them to swing the bat. So when they start swinging and missing at the third strike rather than taking it, that is an improvement!

These are just a few of the positive character traits that a coach could focus on. I try to keep them to a manageable number and hit them over and over again, rather than being exhaustively complete. But in any event, you get to pick your own. You can characterize the character trait as you see fit (e.g., "class" vs. "sportsmanship"). But I encourage you to think about, and then write down, the traits you want to emphasize and teach your players. Before talking about how you go about teaching whatever traits you choose, let me emphasize the importance of effort to achieving one's goals.

The Centrality of Effort

I am somewhat sheepish about admitting this, but when I was a young athlete, I didn't realize that I could get better by making efforts to get better. I really didn't believe that if I were willing to work hard at something over a long period of time I could improve significantly. While I never had the potential to be as good a basketball player as Magic Johnson or a baseball player as Jose Canseco, I could have been significantly better than I was. I really didn't know that then.

Now I look back and feel some sadness that I didn't reach my potential as an athlete because I didn't put in as much effort as I might have, because deep down I didn't really believe it would make any difference.

Awhile back I attended a workshop by an organization called the Efficacy Institute that postulated two different models of development. The first and traditional model (what Joyce Gibson, the workshop leader, called the "American Model" of development; also known as the "entity" model) could be summed up as "you either have it (ability) or you don't." People either have athletic ability or they don't. If you don't have it, there isn't much hope for you to become a competent athlete. People who are great athletes obviously "have it" and that's why they are great.

The Efficacy Institute contrasts the traditional model with what they call the "Efficacy Model": "Self-confidence plus effective effort leads to development." Notice that it is not effort alone, but *effective* effort supporting and supported by a sense of self-confidence.

I once attended a basketball clinic at which Golden State Warrior Chris Mullin talked about shooting a basketball. He described the hours and hours of shooting practice, day after day, for many years, that resulted in his great shooting ability. He indicated he sometimes got annoyed when people would refer to him as a "natural" shooter, as if all the time he spent developing his shot had nothing to do with it.

Psychologist William James once noted that the only thing we bring to our life is the amount of effort we put into it. Everything else, our physical talents, our personality, the amount of wealth of the family into which we are born, are given to us. But what is up to us is how hard we are going to try.

If you can communicate to your players that it is the

amount of effort they are willing to put into becoming better at fielding or hitting in baseball (shooting or rebounding in basketball, or kicking with their weak foot in soccer) that will determine how good they can become, you will be giving them an invaluable gift. And by recognizing the gritty efforts by players that don't have as much natural ability, you'll be teaching them a valuable lifelong lesson about the centrality of effort.

DIMITT AND DEFENSE

In every sport there are aspects of it that are determined largely by effort. Defense and rebounding in basketball, for example, are mostly matters of effort. As George Sheehan noted, "There are days when you can't get the ball in the basket, no matter how hard you try, but there is no excuse for not playing good defense."

I like to ask my players to tell me who gets the most rebounds? They will respond by saying such reasonable things as "the person who is in position," or "the player who blocks out the best," or even "the taller players." My response is that the person who gets the rebound is the person who *wants* it the most. Likewise defense is a gutsy thing where effort and hustle can make up for a great lack of ability.

I've begun introducing the concept of DIMITT to illustrate this point. DIMITT is an acronym for "determination is more important than talent." In a single "word" it sums up the message that I want the players to remember, that it is their effort on each play that mostly determines whether they will grab the rebound or keep their man from getting off an easy shot. Often now, when we break from a huddle, instead of "Defense!" or "Rebound!" the cheer will be "DIMITT!"

TRYING TO LOOK LIKE YOU'RE TRYING

I remember a football coach who wanted everyone to growl. He seemed to think that if you were growling while you were blocking that you were trying harder. Maybe he was right, but I do know that I rebelled against what seemed to be trying to look like I was trying. I refused to growl and consequently I didn't suit up for varsity games much when I was a sophomore even though I believed I had more ability than some of the upperclassmen that did. One week during practice I decided that I would growl and see if it made a difference. I growled from the beginning of practice to the end each day that week and was rewarded by seeing my name move to the varsity list. However, I just couldn't keep it up and so the next week I went back to my normal behavior and didn't suit up for the game. By the time I got to be a junior, the team needed me and so I got to play whether I growled or not. But I never forgot what I still believe to be the inanity of growling to show you are working hard.

I worry a bit about coaches stressing effort so much that players begin to work hard at looking like they are working hard. I've had baseball players who really didn't want to swing the bat, who were looking for a walk every time up, who would stride magnificently into the pitch each time with no intention of actually swinging at, let alone hitting, the pitch. I've had basketball players who weren't strong enough to make a free throw the regular way, but who didn't want to shoot it underhand because it didn't look cool. In Chapter 7 I discuss the "way-to-not-be-graceful" way of getting players focused on results rather than how they look. If you are on the lookout for trying-to-look-like-they're-trying players, you can help them focus on getting the job done rather than simply trying to fool people (maybe including themselves).

122

TEACHING POSITIVE CHARACTER TRAITS

There is really no mystique to teaching positive character traits. It can be approached as you would approach teaching any skill. There are four basic steps: (1) introduce and define the character trait; (2) look for opportunities to illustrate the concept as the season progresses; (3) reinforce, model, and intervene when appropriate; and (4) look for stories to share with the players.

The first step is to introduce and define the positive character trait in a clear and involving manner. For example, when introducing mental toughness, I might say something like, "Mental toughness is when you recognize that you are going to make mistakes, sometimes costly mistakes, but you tough it out and do the best you can anyway." Or, "Mental toughness is when you get into a tough situation but you don't give up. Instead you try even harder to get through it."

Then I would try to get the players engaged in the concept so that they begin to make it their own. "Can anyone think of a situation in which they saw someone who demonstrated mental toughness in a difficult situation?" If the players aren't able to come up with much I wouldn't let it bother me. I've got them for the entire season, and I'm only introducing the concept at this point.

As the season progresses I look for opportunities to illustrate the concept. "Hey guys, did you notice when Sara had the ball stolen from her, instead of moping about it she hustled back on defense and helped keep the other team from getting an easy basket? That's mental toughness!" Sometimes the opportunities come from the opposing team. "Boy, I'm impressed with that pitcher. We had the bases loaded with nobody out and he didn't get discouraged even after he walked in a run. That's mental toughness."

The guts of teaching positive character traits, as with any skill, is to reinforce, model, and intervene at key moments. When I see my star player starting to lose her cool because she's getting fouled and the referees aren't calling it, I say, "Kristin, you've got to realize that the other team knows that they have a much better chance of winning if they can get you upset. So they are going to try to bump and push you to see if they can get you thrown out of the game. Because you're such a good player, this is going to happen to you a lot. Can you work on your mental toughness and keep focused on the game rather than getting upset the way they want you to?"

And later, after Kristin has played the entire game while being mauled without losing her composure, I tell her (either in front of the group, or to her privately depending on her personality and the situation) that I was proud of her demonstrating mental toughness in a tough situation. Naturally, as her coach, I will do what I can with the referees and the opposing coach to protect her from getting mugged on the floor, but ultimately only she can determine her response to the situation.

Lastly, as discussed at some length in Chapter 3, stories are a principal way we learn and teach. I look for stories to share with my players. For example, I clipped an article out of the paper several years ago about a high school coach in Georgia who discovered after the season ended that he had inadvertently used an ineligible player for a brief period during an inconsequential basketball game early in the season. His team had gone on to win the state championship. Even though there was virtually no chance of anyone else reporting the violation, the coach reported the violation himself, which meant forfeiting the championship. In my mind, that coach and team had the best of both worlds. They had won the championship and knew they were the best team. At the same time they had the satisfaction of a noble gesture, giving it all up for a principle. To me, that is class and what real coaching and teaching character is all about. So I share that story with my players, their parents, and other coaches.

TEACHING CHARACTER AFTER THE SEASON IS OVER

Finally, at the end of the season during our post-season party, I call attention to all the positive character development that has been going on. I talk about each player and the progress made during the season, both in terms of skill level and contributions to the overall team effort as well as the character development I have observed through the season.

It's interesting to note that often the greatest teachable moments happen after the season is over, when players are listening carefully to hear what the coach is going to say about them and each of their teammates.

One of my first years coaching I had the only girl in the league on my team. She had a difficult season but she hung in there and finished it out. At the end of the year I presented her with a copy of *In the Year of the Boar and Jackie Robinson* by Bette Bao Lord, because like Jackie Robinson and Shirley Temple Wong, the delightful and spunky heroine of the book, she had showed a lot of courage being the only "different" player in the league.

One of the great things about competitive sports is that it offers innumerable opportunities for coaches to help build character in young athletes. Look for those opportunities and you'll be able to help your players become better human beings and citizens, as well as better athletes.

7

Making the Most of Mistakes

The team that makes the most mistakes will probably win . . . The doer makes mistakes, and I wanted doers on my team—players who made things happen."

—John Wooden
They Call Me Coach

Mistakes are the bugaboo of coaches. They can lead to defeat, frustration, and even despair. If I had a dollar for every time a mistake has lost a game for my team . . .

I have seen more coaches lose their cool over a player's mistake at a crucial juncture of a game. As much as I believe what I say in this book, I have to work hard to be positive in the face of a mistake that costs my team a game. But for a coach who is developing human beings and athletes, mistakes offer a silver lining.

THE LIFEBLOOD OF LEARNING

Mistakes are the lifeblood of learning. Without the willingness to make mistakes and learn from them, learning shrivels up.

John W. Gardner has noted the connection between learning and mistakes:

> One of the reasons mature people are apt to learn less than young people is that they are willing to risk less. Learning is a risky business, and they do not like failure. In infancy, when children are learning at a phenomenal rate—a rate they will never again achieve—they are also experiencing a great many failures. Watch them. See the innumerable times they try and fail. See how little the failures discourage them. With each year that passes they will be less blithe about failure. By adolescence the willingness of young people to risk failure has diminished greatly. And all too often parents push them further along that road by instilling fear, by punishing failure or by making success seem too precious. By middle age most of us carry in our heads a tremendous catalogue of things we have no intention of trying again because we tried them once and failed—or tried them once and did less well than our self-esteem demanded.

As we get older we tend to want to avoid mistakes because it destroys any illusions we may have about ourselves. But it is precisely the willingness to experiment and accept the numerous trials and errors that come with it—that drives the learning process.

Years ago my wife took a workshop from Sister Grace Pilon who has many great ideas about teaching young children. Of all those many ideas, one all by itself was worth the price of the workshop. From the first day of school, Sister Grace says over and over and over again to her students, "It's okay to make a mistake."

I have since tried Sister Grace's mantra ("It's okay to make a mistake") with a wide variety of children in classroom and athletic situations. Invariably, the initial reaction is slight—at this point it's just words. However, when the first child makes the first mistake, the magic words hit home. Invariably there is a whoosh of held breath signifying a release of tension when the child realizes that this particular adult, unlike most others, is not going to come down on her for making a mistake.

The message may need to be repeated again and again, so ingrained is the fear and loathing of mistakes in this society. So with my teams on the baseball field or basketball court, there is a constant refrain: "It's okay to make a mistake."

MISTAKES AND CONCENTRATION

A player who is worrying about making a mistake is not concentrating on doing what needs to be done to successfully complete a task. He is like the people in Manly Wade Wellman's *Who Fears the Devil?* who couldn't keep their minds off what they *weren't* supposed to think about:

"I'll turn this potful of pebbles into gold," the fat man told us at midnight, "if you all keep from thinking about the blue monkey."

He poured in wine, olive oil, salt. With each he said a certain word. He put on the lid and walked three times round the pot, singing a certain song. But when he tipped the pot over, just pebbles poured out.

"Which of you was thinking about a blue monkey?"

All allowed they'd thought of naught else. Except me—I'd striven to remember exactly what he'd said and done. And all vowed that goldmaking joke was a laughing thing.

One midnight a year later and far away I put pebbles in a pot at another doings, and told the folks: "I'll turn them into gold if you all keep from thinking about a red fish."

I poured in the wine, the olive oil, the salt, saying

129

the word that went with each. I covered the pot, walked the three times, sang the song. I asked: "Did anybody think about a blue monkey?"

"But John," said the prettiest lady, "you said not to think about a red fish, and that's what I couldn't put out of my head."

"That was to keep you from thinking about a blue monkey," I said and took up the lid.

Inside the pebbles shone yellow. The prettiest lady picked up two-three. They clinked together in her rosy hand.

"Gold!" she squeaked. "Enough to make you rich, John!"

"Divide it up among you," I said. "Gold's not what I want, nor yet richness."

The coach who harps incessantly about *not* making mistakes runs the very real risk of inadvertently filling her players' heads with mischievous blue monkeys.

Once when I was coaching a team of very young children, a boy named Ivan was having a terrible time hitting the ball. Even though the ball was stationary on a tee, Ivan had missed the ball completely twice. It was late in the game and he was smart enough to know that how he did here might determine the outcome of the game.

I called time and whispered something to him, to which he nodded. He went back to the plate and smashed the ball off the tee for a triple driving in the tying and go-ahead run. Ivan's dad yelled at me, "What are you, a magician? We're all yelling at him and it doesn't do any good. What did you say to him?"

I had simply asked Ivan if it was okay for him to make an out. He had nodded his head that he understood (remembered, perhaps) that it was okay to make a mistake even in this clutch situation. He relaxed and went back and powered the ball, as he was capable of whenever he focused on the task rather than on whether he would fail.

A few years later one of my players was fouled with no time left in a basketball game with the score tied. Before he shot his two free throws I asked him if it was okay to miss them both. He acknowledged that it was and then made the first one, winning the game.

I can also recount numerous situations where the same conversation has occurred and the player has not succeeded. It isn't magical as Ivan's father assumed, and it doesn't work all the time. But helping players to remember that it is okay to make a mistake does help them focus on the task at hand and that in turn will increase the likelihood that they will succeed.

MISTAKEN GOALS AND EFFECTIVE EFFORT

We err if we believe that our players want more than anything to win. We are kidding ourselves if we think they are primarily out to improve their skills in a sport. And we are wrong, wrong, wrong if we assume that having fun is what's mostly on their mind. Rarely is any of these top in the mind of a young athlete.

Most players have what Rudolf Dreikurs called "mistaken goals." Dreikurs pioneered the concept of "mistaken goals" to explain why children misbehaved (see Chapter 15). But the concept also explains a lot about why young athletes behave the way they do and why the way a coach deals with mistakes is so critical.

So, what is it that most players spend most of their time worrying about? Most young athletes, like most adults, want more than anything else to avoid looking dumb.

Nobody wants to look bad in public, and there are few situations so public as a sports contest. I believe that the single most prevalent mistaken goal of young athletes is to avoid looking dumb. And some of them try incredibly hard to keep out of situations where they are at risk of looking dumb.

Let's be clear. Kids do try and they try hard when they are out for sports. But as we discussed above, what they are typically trying to do is avoid looking dumb. Missing a flyball because they just couldn't get to it may be preferable to getting to it and missing it anyway. In the first situation, it wasn't their fault, they just weren't close enough. In the second situation, everyone can see that they blew it.

I recently saw a shortstop on an opposing team who missed what should have been an easy bloop fly in short left field because he wasn't trying as hard as he might have. He loped over toward the ball in a movement that looked like it was being performed in front of the mirror. He didn't get to the ball, but he did look graceful. I used the example to tell my players that the purpose was to "not be graceful," that if we are so concerned with how we look when we are trying to make a play, we often won't make it. "I don't care if you look ungraceful out there. Put your energy into trying to make the play and 'don't be graceful.' "

For the rest of that year, the kids hustled like crazy to get flyballs without more than occasionally looking like they were trying for a highlight film. And whenever someone put everything they had into making the play, obviously not watching themselves while they did it to see how cool they looked, teammates and coaches would recognize their effort with something like, "Way to not be graceful!"

A coach who makes it okay for her players to make mistakes will, over time, get more effort toward the goals of trying to win, developing skills, and having fun than a coach who reacts to each mistake like it was the end of the world.

For the coach who wants to win (and which coach can honestly say that he doesn't?), learning to make the most of mistakes makes sense because it leads to kids refocusing and increasing their efforts on making the play.

Fred Miller mentioned an incident when his daughter, Hillary, a competitive swimmer, was 11 years old. When she was disqualified for a race in "her best stroke," Fred suggested that it wasn't so bad if she were disqualified once in awhile. If she was never disqualified, it might just mean that she wasn't trying hard enough (to get off to a great start). She went back to the next race which was in "her worst stroke" and recorded a personal best time.

One of the great things about sports is that it can give children the chance to experiment with making gigantic efforts without horrible consequences when they fail. They can see how it feels to give everything they have to a task, something a surprising number of people don't ever have any experience with.

MISTAKES AND SUBSTITUTIONS

A common occurrence is for a coach to remove a player immediately after an obvious error. After a player goofs, most athletes are embarrassed. They have just looked dumb in front of friends and foes, parents and strangers. By removing a player after an obvious error, a coach is saying that it is *not* okay to make an error. (Or, "It's okay to make an error as long as it's not costly.") He is accentuating the embarrassment of the original error. He is saying gratuitously, "Boy, were you *ever* dumb!"

The coach's response should be just the opposite, no matter how difficult it may be in that moment to be positive. This is the moment when the player needs emotional support. Obvious, dunderhead mistakes in front of the whole world are great opportunities to communicate that you care about the player independent of ability. Don't blow it by pulling the player out of the game and intensifying the embarrassment.

Aside from the psychological reasons for not removing a player in this situation, there are also sound coaching reasons as well. Often foolish mistakes result from nervousness. After making the foolish mistake, the player may settle down and be the *least* likely player to make the next error. It may also be that the substitute may be the person *most* likely to blow the next play. After all, he saw what happened when his teammate messed up. He may have a hard time concentrating on making the play if he's worried about looking dumb himself and getting yanked out of the game.

That is not to say that there aren't times when you need to take someone out of a game. And it may make sense to replace someone—for example, a pitcher who just isn't able to get the ball over the plate today. But it should always be the coach's objective to make substitutions in such a way as to protect the pride and self-esteem of the player.

I try to always have a conversation with a player when he or she is about to be taken out of a game, even to give them warning ahead of time, if possible. Again, life is not perfect and there are plenty of times when I'm not able to do this. But I try to let them know why I'm replacing them, and generally to use the experience as a chance to communicate with them. If during the roar and hum of the game I don't have the chance to explain my action, I try to make sure that I do talk with them later during the game, or at least after it ends and the quiet emerges.

MISTAKES AND CREDIBILITY

Perhaps the most important reason why coaches should make the most of mistakes is because every kid knows that adults can be two-faced. All adults tell kids to "do as I say, not as I do." Every kid has seen adults espouse values in the abstract and then violate them in the specific when it was in their interest to do so.

It's easy to tell a kid you like them, that you accept them no matter how they perform. But the child has learned differently. It's easy for a child to disregard pious statements, but it is a different matter when a coach responds positively after a costly mistake. There is no more dramatic way to communicate that you care about a person, and that you mean it when you say that mistakes are okay, than after that person has made a costly mistake. In reality, coaches who are interested in developing their players as people should welcome costly mistakes for this reason.

MISTAKES AND INTERVENTION

Sooner or later, no matter how relentlessly positive you are as a coach, there will be times when bad things are going on and you simply need to intervene. For example, often older players will pick on or make fun of younger players. Or a player will just lose it and throw a fit when a call goes against her. Or someone will be careless about swinging a bat when another player is too close. I've seen players square off against other players on the basketball floor when they felt they were being manhandled. At times like these it is the coach's responsibility to intervene, and the sooner the better.

One of the wonderful things about drilling into your players that it is okay to make a mistake is that when you need to intervene to stop something harmful, it is easier than it otherwise would be. Once Eric, my best pitcher and a wonderful boy who is usually well-mannered and polite, got frustrated with an umpire's call and threw his glove down in disgust. I was embarrassed and angry. I called him over to the sidelines and told him that if he ever did anything like that again, I would pull him right out of the game.

I am glad I intervened immediately but I wish I hadn't threatened to embarrass him in front of his teammates and parents. What he did was unusual for him and I could have conveyed that it was unacceptable (and unclassy) behavior without coming down on him so hard. Nonetheless, he accepted it and went back to his business of pitching without a complaint. I am confident that he was able to take my uncharacteristically harsh response to him because of the context of it being okay to make a mistake on our team. He had made a mistake and he shrugged it off because people were always making mistakes and on our team it was okay. As it turned out I had also made a mistake (for which I apologized to Eric), which leads me to what happens when the coach makes a mistake.

WHEN THE COACH MAKES A MISTAKE

It is easy to forget that adults are usually just bigger kids. Adults make mistakes. But usually we try to cover up our mistakes, especially to keep them from the awareness of our children.

Last baseball season we lost a crucial game because the umpire called the infield fly rule on a pop-up that bounced foul before any of the fielders could touch it. This was a clear mistake by the umpire, as my assistant coach and I discovered *after* the game. We probably would have won the game had we had the wits to successfully challenge the call. But we didn't, and we lost.

We began our next practice, as we usually do, by going over the good things that each of the players had done in the last game. We also acknowledged that the reason we had lost the game was because of an error on the coaches. By owning up publicly to our own errors, we helped to reinforce that it truly *is* okay to make a mistake on this team, even if you're the coach.

A few years ago a parent of one of my players lost his cool in response to a particularly bad call by the umpire. The call, in my opinion, was flagrant and in favor of the other team, but my player's parent's behavior in charging the umpire and yelling at him in front of the kids also was uncalled for.

He realized it and almost immediately came to me to apologize. All I had to say was "it's okay for adults to make mistakes too." He gave the trademark whooshing sigh of relief and that closed the situation. For the remainder of the season he never again lost his cool. He also didn't have to spend energy justifying his inappropriate behavior by talking about how bad the umpire's behavior was. Since it was okay for adults to make mistakes, neither of us had to dwell on it.

NO BUTS

Once at a dinner with a group of Stanford MBA students, I raised the notion of mistakes being central to development and success. Every person at the table agreed with me but not a single person was able to agree without putting a qualifier on it:

> "Yes, mistakes are good as long as they aren't thoughtless mistakes."
> "Yes, mistakes are okay, but certain kinds of mistakes can't be tolerated."
> "Well, sure, mistakes are acceptable, but not the same mistake twice."

My position is that mistakes are good—period! Saying that certain kinds of mistakes are okay but others are not is really just saying that some mistakes really aren't mistakes at all.

Fear of making a mistake is a paralyzing force that robs athletes of spontaneity, love of the game, and a willingness to try new things. It is the no-buts approach to mistakes that gives the sense of psychological and emotional freedom that can unlock the learning process and occasionally release truly inspired athletic performance.

THE SAME MISTAKE AGAIN (AND AGAIN . . .)

If you stay with coaching even a short time you will run across players who make the same mistake again and again and again. Most coaches will have the tendency to become negative, to say, in effect, it's okay to make a mistake but not the same one over and over.

I have struggled with this issue for a long time. I have had baseball players who continually leave third base too soon when a sacrifice fly is hit and are called out. I've had basketball players who just can't seem to go back up with a rebound without dribbling and then having the ball taken away.

When a coach sees this happen again and again, it becomes very difficult to continue to believe and act as if you believe that mistakes are okay. I think it helps to try to understand exactly what it is that is the mistake and why it is happening. Becoming negative and criticizing the player doesn't help in any case. And, in fact, a recurring mistake can be used as a symptom to try to find out what the problem is and to rectify it.

For example, the player who leaves third base early may be anxious about the play at the plate. He may not want to collide with the catcher or get hit by the throw to the plate. In his anxiety, he may forget to look at the outfielder and see the ball into his mitt. At this point it is worth asking if he has been taught to see the ball into the mitt—if he hasn't, start there rather than giving up on the idea that mistakes are good. If it is the anxiety that is the problem, then you need to help him address that. For example, you can show him ways to protect himself during the slide.

The basketball player who always dribbles even when she doesn't need to, giving the defense time to catch up, is probably simply exercising a habit. Kids like to dribble. In time they get so they don't feel comfortable shooting without dribbling at least once first. Breaking a habit takes time and repetition getting rebounds and going up without dribbling in practice again and again before the new habit of going right back up replaces the old habit. It's hard to come down too much on kids making this mistake when you see major college ballplayers doing the same thing almost every time you watch a game.

WHERE GOOD JUDGMENT COMES FROM

Lynn Frank used to say whenever he or I (or both) screwed up, "You get good judgment by exercising bad judgment." I would go so far as to say that in many cases that is the only way that people develop good judgment. Therefore, as coaches who want to use youth sports to develop young people of character and high self-esteem, we need to learn to make the most of mistakes.

8

Making Practice Time Productive (and Fun!)

Most teams play like they practice.
—Unknown

Nothing drains the life out of a bunch of excited, motivated people in an organization more than meetings that are unorganized, go on forever, and fail to result in any decisions. It's not that different for kids who want to play baseball or any other sport. Unorganized practices, where kids stand around for much of the time, drain the excitement and wonder out of young heads and bodies.

A recent study of youth sports programs in the United States, by Martha Ewing and Vern Seefeldt of Michigan State University's Youth Sports Institute, reported the results of a survey asking boys and girls who had dropped out of sports what would cause them to want to play again. Both groups said the most important change would be if "practices were more fun."

So let's talk some nitty gritty here. Practice is where the rubber meets the road for young athletes and teams. Practice is where the results of a team are developed. Practice, much more than games, is where most athletes spend most of their lives in their sport. How a team practices determines how it plays. Practice sessions are where the players discover whether the coach knows what he is doing and whether he has a commitment to helping the team become as good as it can be. Practice is critical.

Yet for all the books I have read and coaching clinics I have attended, I have found very little information, beyond various sets of drills that can be used by coaches at different levels of different sports, on how to organize a practice session. This is unfortunate because organizing productive practice sessions for a group of young athletes is an underestimated challenge. Organizing practice sessions to be productive and fun isn't easy. It isn't intuitive. It isn't the most exciting of discretionary activities. But it is the key to whether a group of players approaches its potential as a team.

THE HABIT OF OVERLEARNING

Many years ago in college I began to play table tennis somewhat seriously. Whenever I stopped playing for a while I would be confronted upon my return with a backsliding backhand. I might have been working conscientiously on my backhand for some time to the point where I was gaining some degree of power and control. Yet after returning from Christmas vacation, for example, I would find that my backhand had reverted to its pathetic previous state. This was my first introduction to the insight known as "last acquired, first to go."

A few years ago I heard Ted Sizer, Dean of the Education School at Brown University, talk about education. At one point he shared a slogan from the football coach at a prep school for which he had once been the headmaster. The coach used to say, "Show me a quarterback that thinks and I'll show you a losing team."

This phrase really bugged me. It seemed the antithesis of everything I believed about sports. Sport was an opportunity for kids to *learn* to think. What could he mean by such a cynical statement? And why was Ted Sizer, who I respected a great deal, repeating such tripe? So I asked him, and the explanation made sense. Sizer pointed out that in the heat of an athletic contest, what most determined the outcome were the *habitual* responses of the athletes. There usually wasn't enough time to think things through leisurely. You made a decision quickly or the moment for a decision passed. In many cases it didn't even seem like a decision—you just reacted. Outstanding teams and individuals had practiced almost every conceivable situation that might come up in a game and reacted in a habitual way with the appropriate decision.

When I thought back to my table tennis experience, it made sense to me. The only way to truly acquire a skill is to overlearn it. In the heat of a pressure situation when decisions must be made quickly and skills must be executed instantaneously, performance degrades. A player who can make a lay-up with ease in practice finds the backboard seems strangely tilted as she goes for the game-winner with a defender in her face. Another player who knows he should go "back door" when being overplayed will forget in the heat of a tight game and allow the opponent to steal the pass. A shortstop who knows you have to catch the ball before you can throw it will nevertheless look prematurely toward second base and allow the potential double-play grounder to head toward center field.

Repetition is the key to overlearning, which can lead to outstanding athletic performances. If you don't practice a move over and over, it is unlikely that you will ever learn to do it well in the heat of competition. But how do you get kids to repeat skills or plays over and over again until they have made the appropriate response a habit? This is a constant challenge, and one that often confounds me. Nothing works all the time, but this chapter covers some of the things I have learned about making practices productive and fun.

RECOGNIZING THE CHALLENGE

The first step in dealing with any challenge is to recognize and acknowledge it. There is a curious tendency among coaches to act as if organizing a practice were an inconsequential act. As a result, there tends to be little idea sharing among coaches about this critical activity. So my first piece of advice is to recognize that organizing an effective practice is an art and requires a commitment to make it happen.

The second piece of advice is to make the commitment, to yourself and then to your players, that you are going to work hard at doing the best job you can as a coach to help them develop as players and as a team. My friend Leo Redmond once told me about how his high school coach got him hooked: "We were engaged because he cared. We stayed until we got it." Care enough to get them to stay until they get it.

MAKING A COMMITMENT TO LEARN

Once you have decided that you are going to become a good/better/even better coach, there are numerous resources available to you. There are more books than you might believe about virtually any sport that you might want to coach. Check some of them out. Take from them (including this book) what seems useful and ignore the rest.

Attend coaching clinics offered by local college or high school coaches. These clinics are useful not only for the information presented by the official presenters but because if you share ideas with other coaches that you meet at the clinics, you may get lots of valuable ideas from them. At virtually any clinic you can attend, there is more than likely someone sitting in the audience who knows as much about the sport as the official presenters. Often these people are excited that someone is actually interested in their storehouse of ideas and best practices.

Fred Miller has the habit of asking managers he meets at conferences or elsewhere what their three best management ideas are. He notes them and uses the ones he finds helpful. The same can be done with youth sports coaches you know. Ask them for open-ended ideas or for specific suggestions such as how to coach against a zone press in basketball. In particular ask them what tricks they have for making their practices hum. I recently attended a clinic by Guin Boggs, boys basketball coach for Washington High in Fremont, California. He mentioned that he started each practice by having the coaches and players clap to get them in a positive frame of mind. Every coach may not want to use that technique but it's an interesting way to get players' attention and participation right from the beginning.

Another surprising source of information can be your players. Unless your players are in their first year in a sport, they probably learned some things in earlier years. Ask them how their coach last year dealt with a specific problem. Often you will find that at least one of your players will remember. And occasionally you will have a player who has useful ideas that come out of her own head, if you take the time to ask.

A further way of bringing more brainpower to the situation is to see if you can recruit assistant coaches from the parents. It is very likely that at least one of your players will have a parent that played this particular sport as a kid. Ask them if they would be willing to help you coach the team. Then give them plenty of opportunities to share whatever ideas they may have about given situations.

BEING PREPARED (IN WRITING)

There is an old saying that if you don't know where you are going you will end up there. You need a destination and a map. And until you "think it and ink it," neither the destination nor the map take on a life. Thinking and writing are inextricably bound together. It is too easy to be fuzzy in one's thinking if one doesn't write down the thoughts. I have found that I can get by most of the time without a written plan for practice. Consequently more often than I would like to admit, I do just that: I get by. But if I want to truly make the most of the limited time my team and I have together during a season, I need to think out ahead of time what I want to do during each practice and write it down. I also know that I have ideas during the week that are good ideas. But I rarely remember them at practice time unless I write them down as they come to me.

Most of my ideas for practice come from games (see Chapter 9), either the experience of the most recent or the anticipation of the one coming up. In either case it is essential that I write down my thoughts or I will lose most of them by the time the next practice rolls around. If there is an area of our play that the most recent game has indicated we need to work on, we will drill on that in the next set of practices. If our next opponent has a particular strength that we need to neutralize, we will also work on that in practice. The only time that we don't have a tailored practice session is if we played our last game perfectly (unlikely), or I don't know anything about the upcoming opponent (unlikely), or it is simply a case of my not following my own recommendations (more likely than I care to admit) out of either laziness or busyness with other parts of my life.

I recently coached a team of eighth-grade girls in an invitational tournament. The girls were on several different teams and had never practiced together. Many of them didn't know each other. We had only four practice sessions before the weekend tournament. I realized that there was limited time to teach them what they needed to know before the tournament, so I spent a lot of time thinking through what I wanted to do with each minute of the four practices. I also told the girls at the beginning that we had a total of five and a half hours of practice before the tournament and that we needed to make the most of the time available. They heard me, they paid attention, and they learned a huge amount in a short period of time. They learned so much largely because I knew what I was doing and they responded to the cues.

I was coaching another team at the same time for the duration of a season. I was so struck by the contrast of how well the tournament practices went compared to those of my regular team. I finally concluded that because I had the regular team for the entire season, I acted as if we had a lot of time and there was no particular urgency to learn any particular thing. The players picked up on my attitude and were not nearly as serious about practicing as the tournament team. Again the key seemed to be that with my regular team I usually didn't take the time to plan out (and write down) a practice plan that would take advantage of the limited time available.

In this case it was already midseason (a difficult time to establish new norms). I not only wrote down my practice plans for the next few sessions, but I also distributed copies to each of my players. At the beginning of practice I went over with them what I wanted us to cover during the practice to get their commitment to give it their best effort, which they wholeheartedly gave (once they understood that I was committed to having that happen).

Having said all this about the importance of a written practice plan, let me add that a poor practice plan in writing is better than no plan at all. There are days when I simply don't have a clear idea of what I want to cover in practice that night. Nonetheless, if I start to write down at least a few of the points I want to cover, the practice session comes off better than if I totally wing it. If you are a perfectionist like I am, you may have the tendency to procrastinate because you don't have the perfect practice plan in mind. Don't kid yourself that by putting off writing down a practice plan, you will get some great insight later. It is the act of writing itself that usually gives me other ideas that result in a better practice. I will repeat myself and say that a poor practice plan in writing is better than the best practice plan that exists only in the coach's head. So write it down!

BUILDING AROUND A CORE

It's hard to be creative all the time. It's hard to come up with a unique practice plan for every practice. I try to develop a core of activities, usually centered on fundamental skills that need constant reinforcement. For example, I may ask each basketball player, as soon as they arrive for practice, to begin a routine of shooting from close in and moving out as they get warm. Then when we come together as a team we begin with a lay-up drill that starts easy and gets more difficult. We typically end practices in a similar fashion each time as well, for example, running "liners" (see Chapter 13) and shooting free throws.

There are at least three advantages to building around a core practice schedule. First, it helps you remember to continue to focus on fundamentals as the season progresses. It sometimes becomes easy to assume that players have progressed beyond certain activities when they still need drill on them. Second, it cuts down on wasted energy. Each player knows that they always do certain things at certain times during the practice. You don't have to communicate at length to get players to do an activity that they've done many times before. It is simply time to do it, and they are used to doing it so they do. Finally, it allows everyone to focus most of the creative energy on learning the new things that are introduced in any particular practice session. Everyone is less distracted by the routine things that simply get done without a lot of thought.

THE FIRST PRACTICE OF THE SEASON

A fellow teacher from Wyoming once shared his first-day-of-school ritual with me. Before class he would strategically place a wastepaper basket in the aisle. After all of his students had entered the classroom and taken seats, he would make his entrance. He would "stumble" on the basket, "lose" his temper, and kick the basket across the room (making certain not to hit any student, naturally). He would then yell, "Who put that wastepaper basket in my way!?!?" After that performance, he said he rarely had any trouble keeping order in the classroom.

I don't subscribe to that kind of theatrics, nor do I even believe that he actually did it himself. But it's a great story which illustrates that students' expectations are set on the first day of school. And for a team, expectations are set at the first practice. It is possible, but rarely easy, to change expectations in midseason (or even at the second practice). I learned this, to my chagrin, in my first year of teaching. I had the confidence of two years of experience working with emotionally-disturbed children with severe behavior problems. How hard could it be to teach "normal" third-graders?

What I didn't understand was how the Behavioral Learning Center, where I had worked, had very intentionally set expectations in a hundred different ways that made it possible to manage the behavior of some very troubled children. I waltzed into my first day of teaching normal kids and set a tone that the children interpreted as "we can do whatever we want 'cuz Mr. Thompson is such a nice (i.e., 'permissive') guy."

Within a few days things were out of control, and try as I might, I was never able to reestablish the tone and expectations that I wanted during that year. I did not make that mistake again. The next year I established a much more serious set of expectations for the class and they responded. The ironic thing about it is that I was actually able to be more positive with the latter class because the underlying structure established early on made it possible to deviate from the structure without things feeling like they were getting out of control. During the first year I ended up responding negatively to the kids much of the time because their behavior felt so out of control to me much of the time. A little bit further on in this chapter I talk specifically about how to set expectations of behavior that will allow you to give your players some degree of autonomy. In the meantime, let's talk about your opening speech to your players.

At the beginning of the first practice I give a brief but heartfelt speech to the players. My first goal is to endorse them and let them know that I am excited about having them on my team. If it is a situation where I literally picked them, as in a Little League draft, I tell them that: "Do you know why you are on this team? Because I wanted you on it. I got to pick the players I wanted, and you are them." If I didn't choose the players, I still make it clear that I am excited about having them (as individuals) on my team. I want them to know right from the start that they will be "among friends" (see Chapter 5) on this team.

The Big Three and Rule Number One

I then talk about this team's Big Three goals and Rule Number One.

There are three goals I have this year for our team. The first is to have fun. Basketball (or baseball or soccer or . . .) is mostly about having fun. If you aren't having fun playing basketball, why would you want to do it? It's not a job. It's not homework. It's supposed to be fun. So that is our first and most important goal.

The second goal is to try our hardest. I don't particularly care whether we win a lot or not (although, of course, winning is more fun than losing). But I do want each of you to try hard on every play. If you try hard, we will be much more likely to win, and we'll have more fun. Trying hard and having fun are linked to each other. Almost no one I know has fun without putting some effort into the activity. So I want you to try hard *and* to have fun.

The third goal is to be a good sport. It is very important to me that you display good sportsmanship all the time. That means being a gracious winner and a dignified loser. I want you to win with class and lose with class.

Now these three goals together are quite difficult. Any one of them alone can be easy. For example, it's easy to be a good sport if you don't care about the outcome and don't try hard to win. And it's easy to have fun if you win all the time. But I want you to have fun even when we lose. And I want you to try your hardest to win, but to keep your composure when we lose.

So those are the three objectives we have. In addition, Rule Number One on this team is . . . well, does anybody have any idea what it might be? (If they come up with good ideas, I say something like "that's a good idea, but it's not Rule Number One.") Rule Number One is that it's okay to make a mistake. Why would that be Rule Number One? (Often the kids will come up with answers like "because that's how you learn," which is great.) Because you can't learn anything new without making mistakes. If you want to never make a mistake, the only way to do it is to never try to learn anything new. And I want each of you to learn a lot this season. That means that I want you to make mistakes. And I believe that we'll actually play better if we're trying hard to learn new things and making lots of mistakes.

Now it's time to set expectations of behavior.

Control, Autonomy, and the Gentle Hand

One of the nicest compliments I ever received was from a fellow state agency manager when I worked for the Oregon Department of Energy. He had been assigned on a temporary basis to our agency to advise us on establishing a new program in an area where he had expertise. After spending several weeks with us, he commented to me that he liked the way I managed my subordinate managers: "You have a nice, gentle hand on the reins. They know you're the boss, but it doesn't get in the way of their doing their job."

I was flattered and pleased with the compliment, but as I thought about it, I realized that the way I was managing was pretty much intuitive rather than thoughtful. If my hand on the reins was gentle, it was because of a personal style rather than an intentional managerial strategy. However, from that point on, I began to intentionally cultivate a "gentle hand" style of managing, and later coaching.

For kids in sports, I think the analogy is almost perfect. Young athletes are a *lot* like horses. They want to run free and feel the wind in their mane. They want to burn up energy after being in the stable all day. They want to *go* someplace and *do* something. They also don't really want to be totally on their own.

The single biggest failing I've seen in beginning coaches is a tendency to overcontrol kids during practice. One Friday night several years ago while shooting baskets at the local YMCA, I observed a practice session of a team of third- and fourth-graders with a control freak for a coach. He apparently had come directly from work, still dressed in a suit.

He insisted that the players line up in single file. He then passed the ball to the child at the front of the line who got to take one shot. The coach rebounded the ball and then directed the shooter to the end of the line and passed the ball to the next child, who then got to shoot one shot. This approach was used in spite of the fact that there were two baskets available to the team and they had several balls. In a period of five minutes when each child could have taken 20 or 30 shots each and also gotten to run off some steam by rebounding shots by their teammates, each got to shoot the ball exactly five times.

Each child spent 90 percent of the time standing in line, and, as you might imagine, there was a lot of goofing off and horsing around. The coach repeatedly had to yell at the kids to settle down, stop pushing each other, stay in line, etc. It was a sad situation, but not that atypical in my experience. (In fact, at the other end of the gym there was another team of kids with another coach who also was tightly controlling every move they made.)

What in the world could have been going on with this coach? I believe he was afraid that if he let the wild horses run free he would never be able to get them into the corral again. He didn't have confidence that he could get them to stop running, no matter how hard he yanked on the reins, once his horses experienced the wind in their manes. The irony is that by refusing to give his steeds some rope, they never got going at all. By the end of the session he had become as frustrated as his players from trying to make them act like the calm adults they weren't, as if they were waiting in line for tickets to the symphony.

Knowing You Can Stop the Horse

The key to being able to allow your players some autonomy during practice is having the confidence that you can get and hold their attention when you need or want it. Once a coach learns that he can regain control of the reins, he can loosen up and cultivate a gentle hand.

The ideal practice session allows players to work hard, run off energy, try new things, have some choice about what they do, and converse with their teammates—all while operating within a structure that allows the coach to have some significant measure of control *when she wants it*.

There are some simple techniques that I have found give me gentle-hand confidence. The first and most important is to get players' attention when you want it. The second is to reinforce what you want rather than what you don't want.

1. **Getting kids to listen:** When I coach basketball I tell my players at the beginning of the season that I want each of them to bring a basketball to practice every time since we often run drills where each person needs a ball. When I want their attention, I call them together with the phrase "hold the balls." I make it clear to them that when I yell this I want them all to stop what they are doing and hold the ball. It is *not* okay to bounce it just one more time or take just one more shot. They are to form a semicircle around me and *hold the ball*. Lots of coaches use a whistle, but for various reasons I don't.

   Once I have trained them to respond to this request, I feel very comfortable letting them work autonomously through much of the drills and exercises we do in practice. How do I get them to respond? Read on.

2. **Reinforcing what you like (not what you don't):** A school janitor who was also a dog trainer once told me the secret to training dogs was that you had to be smarter than the dogs. He added that most people aren't, and that was why there were so many untrained dogs. Now it isn't literally true that most dogs are smarter than most people. But it is true that most untrained dogs result from owners who don't understand the principles of positive reinforcement.

   When players do what I ask them to do, I thank them. When they don't, I try to remember to ignore it or to respond to them in a way that will not reinforce the undesired behavior. For example, when I yell "hold the balls," and one player keeps dribbling, I try to ignore that player and say to one or two of the other players, "Thank you for doing what I asked you to do." This is quite effective for younger kids, who are used to getting attention from a teacher or coach for *not* doing what they're asked. The typical scene has all the players except Billy holding their basketball. The coach ignores the nondribblers and yells at Billy, "Billy, did you hear me?! I told you to HOLD THE BALL!" Billy, more often than not, will show the sly smile that indicates his satisfaction for once again getting attention for not complying.

A far more effective approach is to say, "Thank you, Phillip, for holding the ball as soon as I asked you. And thank you, Kristi, for coming right over and kneeling down." Then I start talking to the players who have come immediately. If Billy is still dribbling when he gets within reach, I simply take the ball away from him without making a big deal about it. After a while the kids know that if they dribble in this situation, they will temporarily lose the ball. And believe it or not, that works. Holding a basketball is enjoyable. The little dimples on the ball are pleasing to the hand and the black lines provide a nice tactile contrast. Having a ball to hold or sit on while your coach is talking to you means you have something to do with your hands (shorts and jerseys usually don't have pockets). So, kids don't like having their basketball taken away from them. And losing it without getting any attention from the coach is a double whammy.

For a sport like baseball where kids are much more widely dispersed and sometimes only within earshot, I use a different technique. When I want to talk to the kids I ask them to run in from the infield or the outfield or wherever they are and kneel on one knee around me. At the beginning of the season, I actually have them practice running in (and back out). I say some-

155

thing like, "We have limited time to practice so I want you to run (not walk or saunter or dillydally) when I call you in to talk and run when I ask you to get back to the drills. Okay? And let's practice it right now. Run out to your positions and then when I call you in, run back."

We'll do that a couple of times at the beginning until they get used to responding. During the season, some of the players will forget to run, or be pouting about something, or simply be out of it. Or I may get sloppy and stop expecting it. So periodically I will again remind them of the importance of responding quickly and have them practice it again. If, after the reminder and the practice, one or more still don't run, it is a clear signal that something else is going on. In Chapter 15, I discuss how to deal with defiant or passive-aggressive behavior. Most of the time, however, if I make it clear to my players that it is important to me, they will comply with my way of doing things. And if I am confident of this, I can release control until the times I need to talk with them.

Okay, you've made your opening speech, you've had them practice giving you their attention in response to your cues, and you've set the expectations for the behavior you want and will accept from them. Now it's time to get to the actual practicing. And that brings us to pacing.

Pacing: The Pauses That Refresh

A few years ago I asked the father of one of my players if he was interested in helping me coach since he came to all the practices anyway and he had played basketball in high school. He agreed and helped out during the rest of the season. From him I learned a valuable lesson about the need for punctuation in practices.

We had just completed a scrimmage and I was ready to

continue the same feverish pace when he suggested we take a breather. I followed his lead but was surprised when he simply sat down on the floor. The players were surprised too but they followed his lead and sat as well. He then quietly and matter-of-factly mentioned some things he had noticed during the previous activity. We all sat there quietly for a minute or two and then we moved on to the next drill with renewed energy.

In thinking about that pause later, I realized that the players probably learned more from that practice than most of the preceeding practices because of the pauses that he inserted. In a way the pauses served as punctutation marks to emphasize the lessons we were trying to teach.

Since then I have tried to organize practices in a pattern of teach–drill–scrimmage. First I introduce a skill I want them to learn. I describe it, model it, ask them to talk about what the skill consists of in their own words (see Chapter 4), redescribe it if necessary, and then send them off to practice it, either individually or in small groups. I let them practice for some time, giving them privacy to struggle with it without having me breathing down their necks. Then, ideally, we have the chance to practice it in a game-like setting before the practice session ends. If we are sharing the gym with another team, I try to arrange a scrimmage for the last 15 or 20 minutes. (If we are alone, we will scrimmage among ourselves.) Before the scrimmage I remind the players of what we have been working on and ask them to try to remember to implement this skill during the scrimmage. If it is feasible, I stop the scrimmage in midstream several times to remind them if they are not remembering to incorporate the new skills. I find that when I can move from teaching a skill, to having the players practice it, to trying to incorporate the skill into a game-like situation, the improvement is much greater than if the teaching stands alone.

A final note about pacing. Many coaches I have observed (including myself) overtalk. I have found that the amount of information or motivation I can communicate orally is much less than I want to be able to. Consequently I tend to drive a point into the ground, repeating it over and over, and forget that the longer I talk, the less likely the players are to stay tuned in. So my advice to you (and to me!) is to make your talking brief and to the point, and punctuate it with drills, competitions, breaks for the water fountain, and scrimmaging.

In particular, it is a good idea to keep the talking to a minimum when talking to the entire group. Much of what you have to say is specific to one or two individuals anyway. I have found that it works much better to talk individually with players. I can communicate what I want more easily. The athlete can hear me better since he knows that he is the only one I am focusing on. And sometimes, it can even become a special moment between coach and player, rather than a task of trying to get a squirrely group of kids to pay attention.

REQUIRED PRACTICES?

One of the more frustrating things for many coaches is having players miss practice. Roland Ortmayer, football coach at the University of La Verne and profiled in *Sports Illustrated*, has a pretty relaxed attitude about practice. He says, "I think there is something wrong with a player if he practices every day. Some days your car won't run or your girlfriend requires more attention than football. Maybe it's just a nice day to go to the beach. Heck, I've missed practices, like when I wanted to visit my daughter. They practice better without me, anyway."

I am not quite that relaxed about practices, but I do think that many coaches get too hung up about insisting that their players come to every practice. Then when they don't, they have conniptions. I have never been terribly upset when players miss practice, partly because I believe that making them come is the wrong dynamic, and sets a bad tone for the season. I don't want my players to get into a "have to" state of mind rather than the preferred "want to." It is simple courtesy for a player to let you know if he is unable to attend practice, and I will ask my players to do this. But most of the time, I would rather spend my energy trying to make practices productive and fun and let attendance take care of itself. Which gets us to the fun part.

FUN AND DRAMA AT PRACTICE

The people I know who have the most fun in their lives have a certain lightness about them. They are serious about accomplishing serious things, but they don't walk around like they have the weight of the world on their shoulders most of the time. They look for ways to put some fun into what they do and often, because of that, they are able to get more done because they get tired or bored much less quickly. Rich Kelley, former Stanford University and NBA star, conducted a coaching clinic for Cupertino Hoops youth basketball coaches last year. He approached the clinic from the standpoint of a player.

He asked us what we remembered from our playing basketball in seventh or eighth grade. Most of us had to admit that we didn't remember much. He said that mostly what kids remember about a sport is whether they had fun or not. If they have fun, they keep playing the game. If they stop having fun, they eventually quit.

Although it didn't seem like it at first, this is a big idea. We live in a democracy where people (even children) have a wide latitude to do what they want. If basketball practice isn't fun, very few kids are going to improve much over the course of a single season, nor are they going to continue playing the sport year after year. For this reason, and simply because life is too short to not bring fun into as many parts of one's life as possible, making practices fun is a high priority for me as a coach.

And while most of coaching is targeted to games, practices are where kids spend most of their time with the sport. Rich noted that he must have spent three months of his life in lay-up drills either at the beginning of practice or games. Which is fine because in a lay-up line, kids get to dribble (which is fun), they get to shoot (which is really fun), and they get to talk to each other without the coaches hanging over them (which is also fun).

Yet we coaches often forget how much of a motivation fun is. And we don't spend enough time figuring out what would be fun.

My son recently came home from school having decided that he would not go out for a school sport. He told how a friend who had gone out for it had told him that if players missed a single practice without an excuse from a parent, they were off the team. My son's contemptuous retort: "That's like school after school." On the other hand, he can't wait to practice basketball and often will call me at work wondering if we can go over to the local junior high to shoot baskets before dinner.

There are a variety of ways to introduce more fun into practices. Here are four: competition, reducing the level of play, having coaches play, and bringing a sense of drama to the practice.

1. **Competition (with or without handicaps):** One of the ways to inject fun into a practice is to scrimmage. It is the rare athlete who doesn't want to play in a game or game-like situation. But there are other competitions that can be introduced as well. One of the ways I've been able to bring more enjoyment into baseball practices is to play "work-up" with groups of three or four

players constituting a mini-team. With 12 players on a team we have four mini-teams of three players. One team at a time is at bat and continues until it makes three outs, at which time those players rotate out to the field. Thus there is always a full team of nine players in the field trying to get the team at bat out so they can bat.

For achievement-oriented athletes, there is nothing as much fun as a fair (and challenging) competition. I sometimes assign handicaps to my better players, such as making them shoot baskets only with their left hand, or bat left-handed (reversed, of course, for left-handers) to even things out. Or we have three-point shooting contests, with the teams divided in such a way as to even the odds as much as possible. Or sometimes we scrimmage with no dribbling. We've also simply kept track of the number of picks a player sets during a scrimmage, with each team getting a point for each good pick it sets. When you begin to look for ways to introduce little competitions into practice to create more fun, you'll be surprised at how easy it can be.

2. **Reducing the level of play:** Stacy Geiken told me about a track coach who expected his runners to run their event for time and show an improvement every day! But it's impossible to constantly play up to one's highest potential. There are times when a person needs to withdraw and take it easy for a bit to recharge batteries. Reducing the level of play can often add some fun and motivation to a practice.

For example, to make the game of work-up more fun, we often have the players hit off a tee rather than from a pitcher. This excites hitters because they can try to tee off and hit the long ball. It also gives the fielders lots more action because they don't have to wait for those interminable balls and no-swing strikes. In basketball, we sometimes have shooting contests between teams of three or four using very easy shots. Players can shoot from anywhere inside the key, but since they are competing with one or more other teams, there still is pressure to hit what may turn out to not be such an easy shot under these circumstances.

3. **Having coaches play:** One basketball practice when I didn't have enough players for a full scrimmage, my assistant coach and I played. I did this out of necessity rather than grand plan. However, it turned out to be a great opportunity to model unselfish passing behavior and it made the games more fun for the kids. Now I often will have an assistant play, sometimes to push one of the stronger players. I was interested to note when I visited the practice of a college womens' team that they had some men playing against them to give the women a workout against stronger players than they had on the second team. In baseball we often use a coach with good control to pitch to the players. One concern here is that if the coach gets carried away he can do some real damage to the kids, so I carefully choose the people I ask to participate. This is not the time for a coach who never realized his greatness as a player to reach for the stars.

4. **Bring drama into practices:** One hot winter day (this is California after all) when my fifth/sixth-grade basketball team was practicing on an outdoor court, my wife showed up with ice cream bars for all the players. They were ecstatic. They were tired of practicing and I was in a grouchy mood, so they were glad to have me off their backs for awhile. And they greatly appreciated the idea that someone thought they were special enough to bring them ice cream.

Skip Robidart, with whom I have had the good fortune to coach baseball, has what he calls a "slurpee drill" that he uses sporadically at the end of practice. He will have all the players go *deep* into the outfield where he will hit towering fly balls. Each kid who manages to catch one of these truly monstrous hits earns a slurpee courtesy of the coach at the local convenience store right after practice. Somehow each of the kids almost always manages to enjoy a slurpee.

Another technique I have begun using recently for basketball is to bestow jerseys on players who implement a desired behavior in a scrimmage. Recently our small basketball team had been getting beaten because we were being outrebounded and players were allowing opponents to drive to the basket unchallenged if it wasn't their man. So in the teach and drill parts of the practice, we worked on blocking out for rebounds and "helping out" to prevent easy lay-ups. During the scrimmage part of the practice, I announced that anyone who was observed blocking out or helping out during the scrimmage would get to wear a gold jersey for the rest of the scrimmage. One of my players said, "But then everyone will try to block out or help out so they can wear the jersey." Right! And that's exactly what happened.

Sometimes coaches get so goal-oriented that we lose sight of the potential for turning a wonderfully exciting game like basketball into a drudgery. If you begin to look for ways to surprise your players with dramatic touches, you'll come up with lots of things that will cause players to never know what to expect.

These are just a few ideas I've come up with or run across. You undoubtedly will be able to come up with your own ideas—for introducing competition, reducing the level of play, having coaches participate, and bringing drama into your practices—that are tailored to your specific team. And when you do, you will be surprised at how much more enjoyable practices can be, both for your players and for you.

THE LEVELS OF DELEGATION

One of the most prevalent reasons why time is wasted at practices is that a coach can't be in several places at once, and instead of getting other parents and assistant coaches involved, a coach will often try to keep all the kids together. This results in a lot of standing around. And the biggest reason that coaches don't get other adults involved is that they're not comfortable delegating coaching and teaching assignments to other adults.

Delegation is not just a problem for youth sports coaches but one that plagues management in organizations of all kinds. I encourage you to experiment with getting other adults involved in helping you coach. Here are some simple guidelines for delegating part of the responsibility for creating successful practices to your assistant coaches or parent helpers. First, however, decide what level of delegation is appropriate for any given task. At the same time, determine how your assistant(s) feel about how you delegate. Some assistant coaches do not feel comfortable unless they know exactly what you want them to do. Others may feel frustrated if you insist that they do everything by your method.

Delegation can be presented in a much more complicated manner but I think of delegation as having three basic levels.

1. **See and do:** The most basic form of delegation is to have your assistants watch you teach a skill with a group of players and then replicate with another group. For example, I might demonstrate, using a subset of the team, how to block out for a rebound while the rest of the team watches (which often means they are daydreaming or gossiping or thinking about a television show they saw the night before rather than really paying attention). Then I split the group up into smaller groups, with an adult taking each one to teach, demonstrate,

and have them try the same thing. If I have enough adults to cover each of the groups, I will rove and watch how each assistant is doing and offer advice as needed. If I need to take one of the groups and thus am unable to observe the other groups, I will ask the assistant(s) afterwards how it worked out.

2. **Plan and preview:** The next level of delegation gives more authority to the assistants. Ask your assistant ahead of time to think about how she would teach a particular skill and be prepared to explain what she plans on doing before unveiling it at the next practice. This puts the responsibility squarely on the assistant and will bring out the best in high achievement-oriented coaches who will take it as a challenge to come up with an approach that will do the job. It also gives you the chance to review the approach beforehand to ensure that there isn't some fatal flaw with the procedure.

3. **Do and report:** A more complete level of delegation involves asking your assistant(s) to figure out how to teach some skill, do so at the next practice, and then talk with you afterwards about how it went. Naturally this also involves the greatest amount of risk that the skill will be improperly taught.

However, this isn't brain surgery we're talking about. It isn't as if someone's life will be lost if an assistant coach teaches a group of players to shoot a lay-up off the wrong foot. That can be easily corrected (assuming that there is reporting at some point) and the more completely you delegate to most people, the more likely you are to get a high quality response. And besides, in a real game situation, a player had better know how to make a lay-up off either foot since she won't always have the luxury of getting it exactly right as she bears down under full speed with one or more opposing players hanging on her neck.

Before leaving delegation, let me return to an idea introduced in Chapter 4, on engagement. Having kids teach each other is also a form of delegation and can be particularly helpful to make practices as productive as possible when you don't have other adults to help you.

A FINAL WORD ABOUT PRACTICE

When I was a high school trumpet player, my band teacher, Glenn Whaley, took the trumpet section to hear Doc Severinsen play. He told us that he hesitated to do so because it often had one of two outcomes. Responding positively, young trumpet players would become so inspired at what was possible that they would work harder than ever before. However, responding negatively, young musicians would give up, believing they could never play like Doc Severinsen. In our case, neither occurred. Most of us just continued at about the same level of effort, but it was inspiring to hear in person someone like Severinsen using the same instrument that we were struggling with. It might have been even more useful to have gotten a chance to watch him practice. All we saw and heard was the final output without any understanding of how he got to be that good.

So in that spirit, I encourage you to arrange to take your team to observe a local college or high school team practice (depending on the age of your players). Most coaches will be happy to have you observe, and many will even let your players talk with their players afterwards. It is interesting to see the reactions of your kids when they see how hard college or even high school players work during practice. And for kids who want to play in high school or college, it can be inspiring.

9

Coaching During a Game

When it comes to game preparations, I'm basically a worrier; that is, I try to anticipate the worst that can happen and prepare accordingly. I never use the same game plan from game to game because the problems facing our team are different in every game. I want my game plans to represent the very best effort that I am capable of giving on behalf of my team. It's the least I can do, if I expect my players to give their best efforts toward winning.

—William E. Warren
Coaching and Winning

Games are different. How kids perform during games matters more than during practice, and they know it. Therefore, they tend to get nervous, and because they don't know how to deal with nervousness, their performance often degrades. A player who can lay down a perfectly good bunt in practice may have all kinds of difficulty in a game situation. An 80 percent free throw shooter may miss five in a row in the waning minutes of a crucial game.

This is contrary to conventional wisdom that says that competition improves performance. But there is a significant body of research, compellingly summarized in Alfie Kohn's book *No Contest*, that demonstrates that performance degrades in a competitive environment.

When performance degrades, players often get depressed and frustrated. At these moments they need the support

167

and insight of their coach to help them weather what is an unavoidable part of any sport. Baseball, in particular, with so many plays hinging on the judgment call of an umpire, is subject to wide variations in outcomes: a pitch called a ball instead of a strike; a foul ball that just missed being a double that would have turned the game around; an easy flyball that gets taken by the wind and drops in for a hit with the bases loaded.

THE COACH AS CHEERLEADER

The most important role a coach can play in a game situation is to be a cheerleader and advocate for the players, no matter what they do (or aren't able to do) in the game. The reason it is so important for coaches to support their players in game situations is because the athletes are the most vulnerable at that time. They are on public display for everyone to see. If they fail at something that is important to their self-image, the last thing they need is for someone who supposedly cares about them as a person (not just as an athlete) to get down on them.

When a coach lets his players know that he is for them no matter what, they can turn their inner energies toward doing their best in the game.

But the results are often just the opposite, with coaches blaming players for losing. It is sometimes almost unbearably tempting for a coach to complain about or criticize a player after a difficult game when the player didn't do as he was coached. I've been in situations where I've worked for weeks with a kid on blocking out for rebounds and then in a key situation the player forgets to block out and the other team scores.

You can look in the sports pages of almost any paper after a weekend of sports and read quotes of coaches criticizing their players for failing to make the big play. Awhile back, a college football coach was particularly direct in the media when he singled out one of his players for failing to make a last-second goal-line tackle that would have saved a win. I certainly am not a football expert, but I did see the game and it seemed clear to me that the entire team was confused and out of position on the last-second play. The player in question, while out of position to make the tackle easily, was the only player close enough to even make the attempt. Just before the last play, the coach had called a time-out to talk over what was likely to happen. However, rather than take some responsibility himself for the un-prepared state of his team, the coach dumped complete fault for the loss on a 20-year-old college student.

But let's say that I am wrong. Let's say that the coach prepared the team perfectly for the goal-line stand and the player in question simply blew it. I still maintain that the coach crossed a line of disloyalty to his team and players by criticizing this player in the news media for the entire world to read about. A coach who expects loyalty from his players (and who doesn't want that?) needs to demonstrate the same loyalty back, rather than telling the world about their failings. And given the symbolic importance of sports in this society, it is not inconceivable that the criticized player will go to his grave still grieving over his "failure" and the coach's blasting of him in the media.

One could make the case that a 20-year-old college player is really a professional (being the recipient of a scholarship worth thousands of dollars and the opportunity possibly to play professional football) and needs to be tough enough to stand up under the criticism of a big-time college coach. I don't buy that argument, but even if I did, there are all too many examples of youth coaches exhibiting the same behavior. Thankfully the media usually isn't so concerned with the foibles and miscues of Little League athletes and so youth coaches usually aren't interviewed by reporters immediately after a heart-rattling loss. But it does occur.

Several years ago a local Little League baseball team went a long way in the end-of-season tournament that ultimately determines who gets to play in the Little League World Series in Williamsport. I had seen the team in question play and they had a terrific group of 11- and 12-year-old athletes. They had outstanding pitching, great defense, they ran the bases well, and they hit the stuffing out of the ball. Their only problem was that the further they advanced, the more likely they were to run into other teams that pitched, defended, ran, and hit as well or better than they did. And eventually it happened. They were finally eliminated by a team from another part of California. I didn't see the game but I read about it in the local paper. The coach of this particular team was asked by a reporter about the game. Instead of stressing how his star pitcher had performed brilliantly throughout the season, and had, in fact, been a big factor in the team getting as far as it had, he criticized his ace pitcher. He said that he didn't know what had happened to the boy. "He just didn't come to play today." The reporter in his dimness took down what the coach said word for word (assuming he wasn't misquoted), so that all of those who knew the boy and all of us who didn't could read about his failure in the newspaper.

COACHING UP TO THE KIDS

Several years ago I attended an all-school reunion of my high school in West Fargo, North Dakota. I had a great time getting together with some of my old basketball teammates of more than 20 years ago and our coach, DeWitt Batterberry. We didn't have a great team, but I was reminded of how much fun we had playing basketball. At one point Coach Batterberry mentioned a local coach who he particularly admired, partly because he never criticized his players to anyone outside the team. In a crucial football game, one of this coach's players fumbled on a last-minute play and that led to a disappointing defeat. When the coach was given several opportunities to blame the fumble and the fumbler for the loss, he declined. Batterberry said, "He stressed that the opposing player had tackled his player with his helmet right on the ball, causing it [the ball] to squirt out of his grasp. He made it sound like *anyone* would have fumbled in a similar situation." Batterberry ended by saying, "He always coaches up to the kids."

Imagine what this high school kid who fumbled will remember about his football experience and coach compared with the memories of the college player who missed the tackle and the Little League pitcher who lost the big game. Coach Batterberry's phrase says it all: Coaching up to the kids means supporting them in their most vulnerable hour, when they've made a mistake that loses a game.

THE THRILL OF THE CROWD AND TEACHABLE MOMENTS

In spite of the evidence that most often a competitive situation will tend to decrease performance, it is also true that an audience sometimes can enhance performance under the right circumstances. Sport psychologist Dorcas Susan Butt notes that "dominant (well-learned) responses" are "enhanced by an audience while non-dominant (poorly learned) responses" are "lessened by an audience." In layperson's terms this means that when an athlete is performing an action that he knows *how to do very well*, his performance may well improve when performing before a crowd. However, the reverse is also true: When performing a skill or activity that one is *not* totally secure in performing, the performance level is likely to decrease with a crowd present.

The implications of this information are important. It is rare that an athlete finds himself in a teachable moment during a pressure-filled game. And it is a rare athlete who is able to learn something new and successfully implement it without having been able to rehearse and practice it many times before trying it in a game.

This is yet another reason why coaches need to work hard at being supportive in a game situation. Because of the pressure the players are under, there are fewer teachable moments in a game than in practices or scrimmages. Players under pressure are less able to hear and understand what a coach is saying when he introduces something new in a game situation. By being a supportive cheerleader, the coach can maintain a strong, supportive relationship with his players and use the experiences of the game to create teachable moments in practice at a later time.

Therefore the behavior of coaches in games should be different from behavior in practices. Instead of trying to teach kids new things, coaches should focus during the game on recording what needs additional or new teaching and further work by the players. After the game, at the next practice, the coach can set up a practice situation that will teach the needed skill or response. The coach can also debrief the game and talk with her players about what the other team was doing that gave them problems—for example, how they were able to force so many turnovers with their full-court press.

A coach who prepares her players adequately for a challenging game situation, such as a full-court press, can sometimes find that her players can't wait to play the team that pressed against them so successfully the last time. The previous game serves as a benchmark that challenges them to improve. They want to see if they can do better this time. So let's talk about game preparations.

PREPARING YOUR TEAM FOR GAMES

Pressure is part of athletic contests and many of life's challenges. A coach can never guarantee that his team will win or even play to their potential in a given game. But he can go a long way to prepare his players to deal with the predictable pressure situations that recur in game after game. The place to start is with a game plan.

1. **Have a game plan:** When your team is about to compete against a team that you have trouble beating, it helps immeasurably to have a game plan that you can share with your players to give them confidence. Even when the plan may not be a great one, just having a plan and communicating it to your players can go a long way toward relieving their (and your) anxieties about the upcoming contest.

   Last basketball season we played a team that we knew well, one which always gave us a tough game. This team had been very successful thus far in the season while we had struggled a bit. Many of the players on both teams knew each other and had friendly rivalries. Both sides looked forward to the game with a mixture of enthusiasm and anxiety. Because I really wanted to win this game, I spent a good bit of time figuring out what we would need to do to beat them.

   I knew that the other team got innumerable baskets on breakaway lay-ups on the fast break. I told my players that if we could keep them from getting the easy lay-ups we would win because the other team was not a terribly patient team. They were used to getting lots of easy baskets and, if denied the lay-ups, would begin to fire up long shots from the outside. I was willing to risk being beaten by them if they happened to be hot from the outside, but I didn't want to see them run back and forth on the court beating us with two-foot chip shots. I also didn't think they were likely to beat us with outside shooting because the lack of fast breaks would tend to irritate them, which would throw their outside shooting off as well.

   During practice we worked over and over on a get-back drill where players match up and race back on defense as soon as a shot is put up. We also used a drill that matched players one on one, with the offensive player taking the ball to the basket from half-court and the defensive player trying to prevent them from getting close to the basket. If the offensive player was forced to stop dribbling or veer to either side away from the basket before shooting, the defensive player succeeded whether or not the basket was good.

While many of my bright ideas don't work, this time things clicked. The other team got only two or three lay-ups the entire game. They were held to about 60 percent of their typical scoring, and we won by five points. We were helped when one of their best rebounders sprained an ankle early in the second half, but we were ahead even while he was in the game. In one sense it may not have mattered too much if my game plan was the right one, because our players believed in it and made it work. And almost always a poor plan is better than no plan at all. The exception is when a plan becomes so sanctified that a coach and team fail to make adjustments because they weren't in the plan.

2. **Making adjustments:** After spending time earlier emphasizing that there is a limited amount of successful teaching you can accomplish in a game, I must note that there is without a doubt the need to adjust to unexpected conditions. But I believe that having even a flawed plan gives you a reference point that usually makes it *easier* to make sense of what is happening and adjust accordingly. And there are some other ways that you can make it more likely that you will be able to adjust when the need arises.

   a. *The coach's mental preparation:* To be able to make adjustments, you need to prepare yourself to look for and recognize patterns in the game and anticipate that those patterns may require you to adjust. I have found that for me to do my best as a coach in a game situation, I need to take time before the game to get psychologically ready. Recently I agreed to speak to a group on a Saturday at 9:00 AM on a day when I had a basketball game starting at noon. I figured I would be done with the presentation by 10:30 at the latest and still would have plenty of time to prepare for the game. However, right after my speech I was reminded that I had promised to prepare a memo, for all the coaches in our league, to be handed out at the games that day. I had forgotten about the memo but quickly wrote it and got copies made. Although I worked efficiently, I still ended up getting to my game only moments before it started with no chance in the meantime to give it any thought.

This game was against an undefeated team that beat us by a single point earlier in the season. On this day one of their strongest players as well as several other players were missing. We played well and led for much of the first half but fell behind in the second half when their best player began to kill us with a deadly combination of outside (three-point) shooting and driving lay-ups. We ended up losing by a lot.

It was only after the game that I realized that the other four players hadn't hurt us very much. A box-and-one defense with one of our players sticking like glue to their top player while the other four played a zone might have shut him down and given us the chance to win the game. I am convinced that I would have seen this during the game had I been able to prepare by sitting quietly for 15 minutes to think about the game before it started. The box-and-one is not unfamiliar to me since another team had used it on our best player earlier in the season. It didn't work very well against us because we had some other players that were also strong, and they exploited the openings provided by it. But the team we were playing on this particular day might have been particularly susceptible to it with their other star missing from this game. I just didn't think of it until long after the game was over because I hadn't given myself any time in which to prepare to adjust.

A similar situation occurred when I was assistant coach this past baseball season. I came to the game groggy from having been wakened from a not-long-enough nap. The day was hot and I was feeling out of it. As I sat on the bench watching the leadoff hitter for the other team taking signals from his third base coach, I might as well have been in a straight jacket. I saw the batter, the most powerful hitter on the team, react with surprise and call time-out. I saw him walk to the coach and I even heard the coach say to him, "Only if it's a good pitch." Did my brain react? Noooooo . . . my trance continued as the batter laid a bunt down the third base line that went foul while our third baseman belatedly charged the plate. Then, to compound the situation, on the next pitch the batter laid down a perfect bunt—the third baseman once again was playing too deep—and beat it out for a single. All of this I allowed to go right past me because I hadn't prepared myself mentally for the game.

b. *Anticipating the opposition:* When I was an MBA student, I played a computer simulation game called Mark-Strat. In this game, each week, teams of students would plan a strategy for our imaginary company. We would decide how much money to spend in the next "year" on research and development, how many sales representatives to hire, what products to introduce, etc. We would turn in our decisions and return a week later to find out how well we had done. We would get our sales results and then have two hours in which to make decisions for the next year. At the end of the term there was a debriefing with all the teams describing their strategy. We had started out well but then had floundered badly. No matter what we tried, it didn't seem to work.

I was quite surprised then at the debriefing session to discover that one of our competitor teams that was the most successful had taken several sneaky steps to undercut us. They had figured out early that we were likely to be their strongest competition. While we were deciding what we wanted to do without *any* thought to what the competition was up to, they were intentionally planning a strategy that included steps to deflate everything we tried. And, because we were so naive, it worked. We couldn't figure out why our products weren't going anywhere. It turned out that the competition had introduced some products *only* to compete with ours and keep our prices down so that we wouldn't be able to make enough profit to put any money back into new product development or improvement of existing products. Then they focused their main firepower on other products with little competition and those products took off and made them very rich (at least in MarkStrat dollars).

MarkStrat was an interactive competitive game much like basketball or baseball or soccer. Good coaches can be depended upon to try to figure out some way to respond to the strengths and weaknesses of your team. One way to improve your ability to adjust quickly in a game is by trying to put yourself inside their heads. Ask yourself, "What are the strengths and weaknesses of my team? What would I do against my team if I were the coach of the other team?"

You, after all, know your team better than anyone. If you make an inventory of your team's strengths and weaknesses, you will find it relatively easy to anticipate many of the moves that opposing coaches will make against you. You can then incorporate drills and exercises into your practices the week before the game that will act to neutralize the opposition's moves. This way, anticipation and adjustment become part of your game plan.

c. *Adjusting to officiating:* One of the realities of games is that much of what happens is beyond the control of the players and coaches. The officials make calls that can turn a game around. There is no getting around a large degree of subjectivity because referees and umpires rely on their perceptions, which can differ drastically from one official to another.

Many coaches go ballistic over the calls of referees while others seem to deal with them and move on. The savvy coach will incorporate the style of the refereeing into his coaching. For example, if in the beginning of a basketball game the referees call everything very tightly, a coach can either complain about it or adjust. Complaining about it will tend to get the players to also complain rather than focus on the adjustments needed in their own game. The wise coach will use the information gained in the first few minutes of the game and work with his players to adjust accordingly.

When officials make calls tighter or looser than expected, the coach might call a time-out to alert his players to this phenomenon and encourage them to adjust their style of play accordingly:

> Hey, these referees are calling things *tight* so keep your hands to yourself out there. They are calling fouls for reaching in even when you don't even touch the other player. If you reach in, they will call it no matter what. So, don't reach in.

While a complainer-coach will spend energy yelling at the referees and then getting frustrated when her best players foul out, a coach who takes the officiating as part of the competitive landscape will be able to adjust within the first few minutes of a game.

d. *The final adjustment:* But after all of this planning and adjustment, what if the plan you work so hard to come up with still doesn't work? This happens more than I like to think about. Sometimes the talent level of the other team is so high that a perfectly formulated and implemented plan still leaves you behind. Sometimes the plan didn't anticipate some strength of the other team that proves decisive. Sometimes the officials intrude into the play in unanticipated ways. Sometimes we simply aren't able to implement what we have planned and practiced. Sometimes, we just have an off day and nothing goes right. What do you do then? Often there is nothing to be done except lose gracefully, and plan to return to fight another game, knowing that you did what you could to try to win.

3. **Pep talks:** I am skeptical of the emotional Knute Rockne-style pep talk and "Win One for the Gipper." The prototypical locker room pep talk is designed to fire up the players and get them to play with emotion. However, more emotion is not always better. High levels of emotional arousal can work against development of the mental concentration that is necessary to execute in a game the way one has been practicing.

Robert Nideffer addresses this issue in his book *The Inner Athlete:*

> The situations in which you would want to psych up an athlete are definitely very limited. There is too much psyching-up going on. You should treat arousal like a loaded gun. The athlete who is psyched up is bordering on being out of control. He has a limited control over his attentional processes, so he must

rely more on his environment to provide direction. To function effectively, either he must be lucky or the environmental situation must be stable.

And competitive athletic contests are anything but stable. I recently attended the 1992 North Dakota State Class A Boy's Basketball Tournament to watch my high school alma mater, the West Fargo Packers, defend the state title. I was impressed by many aspects of West Fargo's play but one thing in particular stood out. They didn't beat themselves. Each player appeared focused and intent on playing the best basketball he was capable of playing. Observers might even have concluded that they were passionless, but what I saw was rather a concentration on the task at hand that few college or professional teams ever approach.

Twice during West Fargo High's successful drive toward its second consecutive state title, they came up against two very talented teams playing with obvious great emotion. In one of West Fargo's last regular season games, the incredible hype surrounding the game seemed to get to the other team, which not only lost the game but then failed to qualify for the state tournament the next week. That allowed a much weaker team to advance. And in the state tournament final game, against perhaps West Fargo's toughest opponent of the season, the other team's star player seemed so emotionally aroused that he got ejected early in the second half when he refused to accept a traveling call against him. Without him, the Packers won easily in a disappointing, anticlimactic game.

There are some illustrative scenes in *The Breaks of the Game* by David Halberstam in which Bill Walton of the Portland Trail Blazers mentally prepared himself for the upcoming game:

He would sit in his home or his hotel room in

those hours and actually see the game and feel the movement of it. Sometimes he did it with such accuracy that a few hours later when he was on the court and the same players made the same moves, it was easy for him because he had already seen it all, had made that move or blocked that shot. He loved that time, he had it all to himself, he was absorbed in his *feel* for basketball. He was amazed in those moments at how clearly he could see the game, see the spin on the ball and the angles from which different players were coming. Moment by moment in that time he became more confident until when he arrived in the locker room he was absolutely ready . . .

In Walton's case he used visualization to imagine himself quieting the opposing crowd in an away game by shutting down the other team's star player.

His favorite games were the close games with great rivals on the road, the noise of the opposing crowd rising in crescendo as the game progressed and then (in his own words) the silence at the very end. The silence was his own personal reward.

Mental concentration is the key to successful execution in a game, and a pep talk that distracts a player from concentrating on what he needs to do in the game is likely to be counterproductive.

Often I suspect that it is the coach who has not taken the trouble to develop a game plan and who has not prepared her team for the upcoming game who will try to take a shortcut by giving an emotional pep talk at the beginning or at the halftime of a game.

In lieu of an emotional pep talk, I tend to review the game plan with my players before the game. I will remind them, or ask them to remind all of us, what we need to do to win the game. If we have been working hard on blocking out for rebounding against a larger team, we review the steps in rebounding. If we know something about the team we are playing, we talk about who will guard who, paying particular attention to any of our players who are likely to need some help in guarding an overpowering player on the other team.

And finally, especially before a big game, I end by reminding the players that basketball (or baseball or soccer or . . .) is supposed to be fun. I want them to enjoy the game as well as do well in it. And, of course, I believe that people who have fun with what they do perform better than those who don't. So in one sense I guess it fits with a traditional pep talk since in both cases the goal is to encourage the team to rise to the occasion, play its best, and win!

HELPING PLAYERS DEAL WITH PRESSURE

Sometimes the most important lesson a coach can impart to a player is how to deal with pressure.

1. **Alien monsters and nervousness:** I remember reading a science fiction story when I was in high school involving an earthling who ended up on another planet. He was terrified of the monsters that he encountered there. Mysteriously, every time a monster was about to destroy him, the monster was zapped and died. Eventually the earthling discovers that on this alien planet, his fear is a deadly weapon. Anything that causes him to be afraid is suddenly vaporized. As long as he is afraid, he is invincible.

   The next time a monster approaches him it destroys him with little fuss. What happened? He forgot to be afraid because he didn't realize that he still *had* to be afraid. When he wasn't afraid, the deadly ray failed to materialize out of his brain and he became lunch for the monster.

When I taught second- and third-graders, I often had them put on performances for parents or another class, sometimes singing and dancing, sometimes dramatic readings. Many times the children would become so nervous that they would flub their lines and feel silly and embarrassed.

I found myself asking them if they were nervous. When they almost always said "Yes," I told them that was good because if they weren't at least a little bit nervous they wouldn't be on their toes to do their best.

I really believe that some nervousness is good, partly because it is a form of energy and energy is required to give a good performance, whether in sports, music, or dramatics. It takes energy to do your best and nervousness can be transformed into useful energy if channeled properly. During the 1991 NBA Playoffs, Los Angeles Laker star James Worthy was interviewed on television before a key game with the Portland Trail Blazers. He was asked about fear and nervousness, to which he replied, "I like to be a little bit afraid, to be nervous. It usually conjures up some good energy."

We've all seen performances that were just a little bit flat. Often it is the lack of nervous energy that causes the flatness. Just like the earthling who forgot to be afraid, performers who don't get at least a little nervous often don't get up for the performance. So . . . before every big game I ask players if they are nervous and encourage them to welcome the nervous feeling as a way to help them slay the alien monsters that lurk on the playing field.

2. **The elephant and the bamboo shaft:** Sometimes, however, it doesn't help much to be told that a little nervousness is good, because the player isn't feeling just a little bit of nervousness, but a lot—so much nervous-

ness, in fact, he isn't able to function anywhere near his normal capability. Eknath Easwaran in his book *Meditation* tells this story:

> On festival days in India you will often see a huge elephant, caparisoned in gold and gorgeous cloth, carrying an image of the Lord on its back through the village streets. Everyone enjoys the sight: the musicians with their drums and cymbals in front, then the beast slowly lumbering along and the devotees behind, all on their way to the temple.
>
> But there can be one difficulty. Stalls of fruit, vegetables, and sweets line the narrow, crooked streets, and the trunk of the elephant, as you may know, rarely stays still. It sways back and forth, up and down, constantly. So when the procession comes abreast of a fruit stall, the elephant seizes a shelled coconut or two, opens his cavernous mouth, and tosses them in. At another stall the big fellow twists his trunk round a bunch of bananas suspended from the roof. The mouth opens again, the whole bunch goes in with a thud . . . you hear a gulp . . . and that's the end of it.
>
> The humble people who own these stalls cannot afford this kind of loss, and to prevent it the man in charge, the mahout, asks the elephant to grasp a firm bamboo shaft in his trunk. Though not sure why, the elephant, out of love for his mahout, does as he is told. Now the procession can pass safely through the streets. The elephant steps right along with his stick held upright in a steady trunk, not tempted to feast on mangoes or melons because he has something to hang on to.

Young athletes' minds can be like the trunk of an elephant in a market, flittering here and there and coming back again and again to the fear of failure or a nervous imagining of all the things that might go wrong in the upcoming game. Sports psychologist Tom Tutko notes: "You cannot focus your mind fully on two things at once. When you need to pay attention to a certain play you can't be worrying about the last one or the one coming next. But if you are anxious, you are more likely to focus your mind on the anxiety than on the task at hand, since the anxiety—with all the body feelings it stimulates—tends to be more compelling."

A coach can provide the equivalent of the elephant's stick to help young athletes deal with anxiety in a pressure-filled situation by giving them some specific tasks to perform early in a game. Once the game gets rolling, most players can roll with the punches most of the time and get into the flow of things. For example, I always try to start a basketball game with a play for the opening tip-off. Each player knows what they are to do, and they are encouraged to focus on playing their role expertly. In baseball, pitchers can be asked to try to hit various spots as the catcher moves the glove around.

A coach can also provide techniques for his players to deal with the anxiety that comes up in crunch situations in every athletic contest. Perhaps the most anxiety I can remember feeling at one time has been while on one of several ropes courses. Although there is very little *real* danger involved (you are connected by two cables to a thick wire above your head), the *perceived* danger can overwhelm you (you are, after all, 30-60 feet above the ground). While on a ropes course in Northern California run by an organization called Catalyst, I once again experienced the panic that being high above the ground inspires in me. The Catalyst instructors, however, gave us some great advice for how to coach each other through difficult spots. Two of their suggestions can apply to almost any situation: breathing and feet.

When one of us would begin to tremble at what we were about to attempt, we would be coached with the suggestion to remember to breathe. Once I focused on it, it was amazing how fear and anxiety disrupt the body's natural breathing. You can literally forget to breathe and then your body tries to force rapid, shallow breaths to catch up. It is hard to feel grounded with any task when you are not breathing properly. The second piece of advice dealt literally with grounding. We were asked to concentrate on feeling our feet on the log we were perched upon. Being so high above the ground can cause one to feel very up in the air emotionally as well as physically. By focusing on feeling your feet you begin to get a sense of security. The combination of remembering to breathe and to feel my feet beneath me helped me gather my inner resources to do what I needed to do. And these two pieces of advice can be lifted word for word from the ropes experience to the athletic fields and gymnasiums. A softball pitcher who must pitch a strike or walk in the tying run is likely to forget to breathe deeply. And she can get more grounded by experiencing the feel of her feet on the ground. And both of those little mental tasks will tend to leave less mental energy for worrying about the bad things that might happen.

A similar idea came from a friend who told me about some golf lessons she had taken. When she putted, an instructor would hold up math flash cards above the hole. While she was putting she was to yell out the answers to the equations displayed on the flash cards. She was amazed to discover that her putting dramatically improved when her conscious mind was occupied (like the elephant's trunk) with a little problem that would keep it from imagining the million different things she might do wrong to miss the putt.

Last year I watched videotapes of the West Fargo boys team winning the 1991 Class A North Dakota State Championship with an impressive display of free throw shooting at the end of each game. I noticed that many of the players seemed to be talking to themselves before and as they were shooting. In some cases it was quite apparent that they were talking out loud, but it was impossible to determine what they were saying. Try as I might, working with the VCR rewind switch and trying to read their lips, I was unable to make any sense of it. After the final victory, one of the Packer stars was asked by a television announcer about the amazing accuracy at the free throw line. He mentioned that Bob Torgrimson, their coach, had given them a good way to focus themselves when shooting free throws, and they had simply used that technique and the shots had dropped.

Now I was even more curious so I asked my mother in West Fargo to try to find out what the players were saying to themselves. She investigated and came back with the answer: "Bounce, bounce, sight. Bounce, shoot." When you think about it, it almost doesn't matter what you say to yourself when shooting free throws. It's like solving math problems when putting. If you have practiced shooting free throws for a long time, you have developed the muscle memory for how to shoot the free throw properly. Your conscious mind, once again like the elephant's trunk, will only disrupt your normal proper functioning. So you give it a stick to hang on to so that the subconscious muscle memory can do its thing.

OPPORTUNITIES TO TEACH CHARACTER IN A GAME

One of the great opportunities of hotly contested games is that they offer countless chances to teach and reinforce lessons on character. Earlier I mentioned that I recently coached a team of eighth-grade girls in a basketball tournament. It was a team of considerable talent but made up of girls from several different co-ed teams in our league. Thus, the girls hadn't played together as a team before. We had time for only four practice sessions, and with other activities, not all the players were able to come to all four practices.

Nonetheless we won our first game handily. The semi-final game found us behind at halftime, but we ended up getting stronger as we played together more and held the other team scoreless in the last period to win. A couple of our girls were banged around pretty hard in the latter part of the game. They didn't lose their temper but came close in a couple of incidents. Before the championship game, I addressed the rough play directly with them. I asked them why the other team was getting rougher. They came up with several reasons. I told them that I thought they started getting rougher because they were frustrated. They were getting beat, and it made them frustrated, and it showed in their play. I went further and told them that they should take the rough play as a compliment because if the other team felt they could beat us fairly, they wouldn't have to resort to that kind of play. One of my players had fun with this idea: "Thank you for beating on us. It's so nice to know you admire our style of play."

In the championship game, we held a consistent 10-12 point lead throughout most of the second and third quarters. But midway through the third quarter once again the other team began to get physical. They were throwing hips and setting very rough moving picks (that looked a lot like football blocks). In several cases, our players were getting clubbed pretty good with no foul being called. I substituted for two of our best players who, because they were around the ball most of the time, were the targets of much of the physicality. I told them that they were being singled out because they were such good ballplayers but they needed to focus on the game and not retaliate in kind.

Our players began to respond by complaining to the

referees, which I didn't like. At the same time, the other team began to creep back into the game. Eventually one of our players committed a hard intentional foul that kept the opposing player from scoring an easy lay-up, just as the third quarter ended. At the quarter break I called the girls together to say as forcefully as I could that I was not happy. And I made it clear that it was not the narrowing score that bothered me but our loss of composure and discipline. I acknowledged that they were getting roughed up but that the appropriate response to that was to focus even harder on playing the game.

They came back in the fourth period and played the best basketball I could ever have asked them to play, outscoring the opposing team 12-3! They ignored every rough play (and there weren't as many as before because when they were concentrating on their game, the other team had trouble even fouling them). They had faced adversity and risen to the occasion, ignoring the distractions of rough play and putting everything together for an incredible quarter of basketball against a rough and tumble opponent.

After the trophies and awards were handed out, the tournament director made a special point of telling me that he was impressed by how well our girls had played, but also by their sportswomanship and how they had kept their composure.

Games offer innumerable opportunities to teach kids about character that just aren't available when the stakes aren't as high. And sometimes you find positive role models in the strangest places.

Recently, against my better judgment, I watched a championship kick-boxing match on a hotel television screen. Kick-boxing is every bit as brutal as boxing, with the added attraction that kick-boxers are able to punish their opponents with kicks to the head and body. It was the first "real" such match I had seen (Jean-Claude Van Damme movies don't count) so I was prepared for something like professional wrestling, with the kick-boxers taking cheap shots at each other whenever the opportunity presented itself. Imagine my surprise when the combatants displayed not only good sportsmanship but clear respect for each other. There were numerous (passed-up) opportunities for one or the other fighter to throw a sucker punch in the breakup of a clinch. At the beginning of each round they touched gloves in a congenial way before then trying to batter the other into submission. And at the end of the hard-fought contest, they both spontaneously threw their arms around each other and hugged. After the decision was announced—the champion narrowly defended his title—both fighters were gracious, almost effusive, in their praise of the other. It was an inspiring example of two athletes of great character who put everything they had into trying to win but refused, time and again, to cross the line that would have diminished themselves and their sport.

Sport psychologist Dorcas Susan Butt might have been talking about these two kick boxers when she wrote:

> . . . If athletes understand that the sport in which they participate is greater than themselves and will continue longer than they will, and if they have a clear picture of its organization and rules, and understand that it places the highest value upon the development of competence, then the athlete will be able to concentrate fully upon developing his or her own competence and appreciating the competence of others.

THE MISSING ELEMENT IN MOST GAMES

Enjoyment is often the first thing that goes out the window in a game. Almost everyone has trouble remembering to enjoy a hotly contested game in which something is at stake. We've discussed various ways that a coach can support her players, but perhaps the most important support a coach can give her players in tense, pressure-filled competitive games is to continually remind them to relax and simply have fun. They will grow up soon enough and strange though it may seem in the moment of truth in a hard-fought game, it really won't matter all that much who won a particular game many years later. But what does and will continue to matter are the values that those athletes take away with them from those contests. The lessons that young athletes learn, often from their coaches, in the crucible of a "big game" can have a lasting impact on how they live the rest of their lives. And one of the most important lessons you can help them take away is how much fun it can be to give your best effort in a competitive sport.

10

Handling Parents

The toughest thing kids have to face is the unfulfilled lives of their parents.

—John W. Gardner

The game was close. We were behind but battling back, and now trailed by a single run. Our batter hit a ball into left-center field. For a moment it looked like the center fielder had a chance to make the catch but he couldn't get to it. He did, however, dive vaguely in the direction of the ball. But then, instead of getting up and chasing after it, he rolled on the ground in agony. It wasn't clear whether it was physical pain or the emotional pain of seeing the ball get away from him that was the source of the disturbance.

Meanwhile our baserunners were chugging around the bases with the runs that would clinch our victory. But wait! The umpire, who happened to be the parent of a player on the other team (might he be the dad of the center fielder?), calls the play dead and sends the batter, who had already reached third, back to first base. The other two runners are also ordered to return to second and third so that no runners score on what looked to be at minimum a triple and more likely a home run.

One of my parents cannot contain himself at this injustice. He charges up to the umpire and complains strenuously about the unfairness of it all. "Even if the center fielder is hurt, you can't stop the play until it's over. You can't send the runners back. That's not fair. The center fielder is not in any danger from the play." The umpire, who was enlisted after much coaxing by the other team's manager when the "regular" umpire didn't show up, is not taking this outburst kindly. It may well be his first ever (and probably his last) experience as an umpire. "Well, then, *you* ump if you can do it so much better!" he grumps as he stomps away.

This brings forward a parent from the other team who is not merely defensive. He (a college professor) is ready to duke it out with my parent (an engineer) before the other manager and I get between them and calm things down.

What's wrong with this picture? The most amazing thing to me is that this is a tee-ball game between first- and second-grade children! That parents could become so out-of-control angry about a small-fry game still boggles my mind after seven years.

THE SOURCES OF LITTLE LEAGUE PARENT-ITIS

More than almost any other factor, it is parents that give would-be coaches pause. I have only occasionally glimpsed the "Little League parent," but even one time is too many. It is an ugly picture. As kids get older, parents tend to become more belligerent, as if they acknowledge that it was okay to just have fun when the kids were young, but now that they are in seventh grade (or sixth, or fifth, or . . .) it's time to win.

In this chapter I discuss the sources of Little League parent-itis, how a coach can prevent it from getting out of hand, what parents need from a coach, and how a coach can meet parental needs to ensure that the kids have a good experience free from the worst influence of overinvolved parents.

The sources of parental misbehavior are many. Part of it comes from a normal phenomenon of distorted perceptions. Some of it can be traced to a desire to relive lost (or never-were) days of glory through one's child, and some of it comes from a subconscious concern that other people judge one by how one's child behaves on the athletic field. To be fair, I should also add that there is almost always an element of true concern for the child, and it is this noble strand that is the coach's best ally in learning how to handle parents.

1. **Distorted perceptions:** It goes without saying that parents tend to think that the umpire, referee, linesman, etc. will make calls against their kids' team. It is clear that partisans at a sporting event tend to interpret referee calls in a biased manner. As a coach, you can defuse a lot of negative energy by calling into question the distorted perceptions of your players' parents.

During a soccer game that my son was in, many of the parents on our team became outraged by a call made by one of the referees. I volunteered that it looked to me like it was a good call. There was an almost audible release of tension as parents seemed to be reviewing the play in their heads, since someone who was "on their side" (me) called into question their perception.

Distortion of perceptions is not a disease that affects only other, "bad" people. I certainly am not immune. Any time that I badly want our team to win, I become susceptible to distorted perceptions. Recently my basketball team was being soundly trounced by a team that I really wanted to beat. One of the best players on the team passed up an easy lay-up to give the ball to another, weaker player. I became enraged at what I took to be an obvious insult to our team's ability. I said as much to

195

Jim Nakasuji, my assistant coach, who challenged my perception. He pointed out to me that the other team, like ours, had some weaker players and the other coach had directed his better players to ease off (since they were way ahead) and give the weaker players chances to score. Jim pointed out that we did exactly the same thing when it was clear we were going to win.

In retrospect I see that my perceptions were wildly off base. But the heat of competition distorted my thinking. The lesson here is that this is *normal*. In a competitive sport when you're trying hard to win, it is absolutely normal and commonplace to experience distorted perceptions. It is normal, but it is also unhealthy and harmful to players to allow those distorted perceptions to go unchallenged. It is a sad and ugly thing to see parents and coaches act on distorted perceptions. Even worse is when players themselves begin to see the world through distorted perceptions. They tend to stop trying as hard, whine after every call that goes against them, and generally lose the degree of mental toughness they will need to succeed in sports and in life.

The person in the best position to deal effectively with distorted perceptions is you, the coach. How? Begin the season by telling parents some horror stories of Little League parents and coaches you've seen in the past. Make it clear to them that you don't want that to happen with your team and that you are confident it won't. Acknowledge to your parents that distorted perceptions are normal but you don't want them to get out of hand. You might even tell parents and your assistant coaches that you sometimes fall prey to distorted perceptions, and you'd like them to help you see when that is starting to happen.

Simply calling the phenomenon to their attention at the beginning of the season will go a long way toward keeping it from happening or at least from getting out of control.

2. **Reliving past glories:** Sports are one of the few ways left in this society that people have a chance to be a hero. Few of us get the chance at work to do something heroic. It is rare that we get a chance to use CPR even if we have learned it. But competitive sports are *set up* to offer heroic opportunities to people.

Some of us get the opportunity to be a sports hero, and occasionally we come through. I once hit three home runs in a Babe Ruth League game in Colfax, North Dakota, more than 30 years ago. I doubt that anyone else remembers it, but I still can see where each home run went (two down the right-field line and one over the left fielder's head). For a brief moment I was a hero—at the local swimming pool that next week, girls who had never talked to me before hovered around me.

My moments of sports glory have been quite few and modest. Many people haven't had any. In either case, there is the doomed hope that one can live again or for the first time that glorious glory through one's child. Of course if we verbalized it out loud to a friend or spouse, we would realize how out-of-touch with reality it is. But few people do verbalize it to themselves let alone anyone else. Sometimes we verbalize just a part of it. The stated part is: "Why can't Billy hit that slow moving pitch?" or "Why can't Janet make a simple lay-up?" The unstated part is: "*I* could do it."

What's missing here is the realization that Billy and Janet are children who are just learning the game while the "I" speaking is a grown adult who now probably does have the ability to hit a slow-moving pitch from a child or make a simple lay-up. It's not surprising that a 30-some-year-old adult could hit a pitch from a fifth-grader.

But we fail to put ourselves completely in the shoes of our children. When they are our age, most of them also will be able to hit a fifth-grader's pitching. The better comparison for us might be, "Could I hit Nolan

Ryan's pitching?" After all, Nolan Ryan is older than most Little League parents.

And, in fact, arranging situations where parents have to perform (and not just give directions to their children) can have a positive impact by giving parents a whole different way of looking at their child's performance.

I recently had a humbling experience that drilled home to me the usefulness of having parents go through the same experiences that their child athletes do. On the last day of our first Cupertino Hoops basketball season, we had a coaches game. As coaches, we had been yelling at our players all season to play the game correctly, and now we were giving the players the chance to yell at us.

After just a few minutes of running up and down the court I was dragging. It was then that a great insight hit me. I was running down the court after the other team had scored, with my back to my teammate who was bringing the ball up the floor. Now I have yelled innumerable times at my players to not turn their back on the ball when they run, but here I was doing it. The insight came in a flash: I wasn't looking for the ball because I was afraid someone would throw it to me. I was so tired that I didn't want to have to make the effort to catch the ball and then do something productive with it.

The lesson is clear: If possible, get parents into game-like situations where they cannot continue to fantasize unrealistically. Beyond that, I don't have any magic potient to keep parents from trying to relive past glories through their children. However, simply airing the subject with parents and getting it out of the closet will help defuse it. Regularly remind parents that the players are still learning the game. Share with them that it is sometimes difficult for you as a coach to remember that what seems easy for an adult is nonetheless difficult for a child. By getting the ghost of sports-glories-past out in the open, you will have gone a long way toward exorcising it.

3. **Believing "I am my child"**: One of the difficulties of coaching your own child is the concern that others will judge you based on your child's actions, both in athletic performance and social behavior. Part of what drives parents to get overinvolved in trying to control their child's behavior around a sport is the belief that they are judged by others, as a parent and as a human being, according to how their child behaves.

One particularly unhappy situation occurred a few years ago with a baseball player whose father was on him *all* the time. The boy was a good ballplayer, but his father tried to direct his every move. He regularly yelled out instructions on where to position himself before each hitter. He gave him batting feedback without ever apparently stopping for breath. The results were not good. The player, who had the ability to be a terrific hitter, hit almost nothing. He typically tried to get a walk, and because he was short, he often did. But whenever he came up against a pitcher with good control, he was a sure out because he rarely swung.

In talking with his dad, it became clear that he took every move his son made as a personal threat to his own self-esteem. He expected perfection from his son. What he got was reduced performance from a young athlete with a lot of potential who was too busy resisting his father's control to be able to concentrate enough to hit the ball.

This isn't intended to be a happy talk book. I am not going to say that other people won't sometimes judge a parent by the behavior of their child on the athletic field. Sometimes people do think, when they see an athlete misbehave, whine, or throw a tantrum on the playing field, "Where did her parents go wrong?"

But there is lots of evidence that most parents are

too self-consumed worrying about what other people are thinking about them and *their* child to spend much time examining the behavior of other people's kids.

As a coach you can help take the pressure off parents who confuse the identity of their child with their own by making it clear that *you* don't judge them on that basis. You can say to them early and often that the player's behavior in practice and games is the joint responsibility of the player and you, the coach. If there are problems which you don't anticipate, you may call on the parent for help, but you don't expect their kids to be perfect. And they don't need to apologize for, or feel bad about, how their kids perform.

Acknowledging that you know they might tend to feel responsible for their child's behavior but that you won't blame them should go a long way toward defusing this problem.

WHAT PARENTS WANT FROM A COACH

Parents want to be reassured that they have done right by their child. They want to be able to believe that they are doing a good job as a parent. They, like their children, want to feel a part of a successful team. As a coach you probably don't want to get involved with parents at the level of a psychotherapist. But there are some simple things that you can do to help your players' parents become constructive forces for the team. Here's my short list of what parents want from a coach.

1. **To be in the information loop:** Tell parents when practices are going to be. Tell them when practices are going to end. Try to end practices when you say they will end. In the part of the world where I live, people's lives are already complex and overscheduled. Make it easier

for them by giving them a realistic notion of when practices will end and then end them on time.

Tell them about the season. Give them as much advance information about games as possible. Tell them when the season ends, whether there will be playoffs, and whether there is an all-star game. As a first-time baseball coach I was surprised at all the hoopla at the end of the season, with the tournament of champions and the all-star tournament. After I had coached for a few years, I began to assume that parents and players knew all about them. In one case, one of my best players was unable to play in the all-star tournament because his family had planned a trip to Japan at that time. They had planned the trip for the end of the baseball season and I hadn't bothered to tell them that their son was a likely all-star and how long the all-star tournament was likely to go.

2. **To hear good things about their kids:** Tell parents good things about their children. Don't make up false things, but find some area where a player is making improvement or effort and share that with his parents. I try to speak to each parent at least once before, during, or after every practice and talk about what Julio or Kristi is working on and how it's going. Parents want to know that their children aren't going to grow up to be criminals or bums. You can reassure them that at least in this one area, sports, their kids are upright citizens who are trying hard and making progress.

3. **To see their kids play:** Play each child as much as you can. Parents want to see their kids play. Many sports programs for younger kids have a minimum playing time rule. However, many coaches treat such a rule as a ceiling on playing time for weaker players rather than a minimum that can be exceeded. Even in games that are won in the first inning, coaches will play the weaker players only the required minimum number of innings. As the kids get older and the importance of winning in-

creases, the playing time rules tend to drop away. And the weaker players play even less. I am amazed at how conservative coaches are about playing weaker players.

I have seen many, many situations where a coach has passed up an opportunity for a weaker player to participate in a game that is already won or lost. If you look for the chance to play your weaker players more often, you will find situations where you can do it without hurting the chances of your team.

4. **To be included—to also be "among friends":** Chapter 5 describes ways that you can build self-esteem by helping your players to feel they are "among friends." Most of the ways that you build self-esteem among players will work just as well for parents. Adults appreciate it when the coach learns their names, jokes with them, expresses appreciation to them, etc. And they, in turn, will want you to succeed and be willing to help you.

HOW PARENTS CAN HELP YOU

Parents, when properly dealt with and appreciated, can become a potent force to reinforce the messages you are trying to send to your players. And in some cases, positive parental involvement can even help your team win more games.

When my son was playing soccer several years ago, I had a bad attitude about it. I didn't realize it at the time but I was tired of sports. The baseball season had ended after seeming to go on forever. Soccer practices were beginning two months before the season started. The soccer coaches wanted to go to a tournament every weekend, including one that was an overnight trip several hundred miles away. The soccer season was going to extend well into January or February, which was basketball season, my favorite sport. I was burned out on long sports seasons (and soccer, in particular), and I didn't try to hide it from anyone, including my son.

I don't believe that it was a coincidence that he began to play poorly. Unlike before, he rarely kicked the soccer ball around, outside of practice. He became unenthusiastic about practices and even games. And his play suffered.

It wasn't until sometime later that I concluded that my constant complaining and lack of enthusiasm about soccer was contributing to his halfhearted efforts. The next soccer season I made a point to be upbeat about soccer, and he rebounded with his usual enthusiastic play. My being a sourpuss about soccer made it harder for him to feel good about the amount of effort it takes to play a sport.

The lesson here for a coach who wants his players to be enthusiastic and positive about the team and the sport is to recognize the impact parents can have on a player's attitude and effort level. I recommend discussing this impact with parents at the beginning of the season and encouraging them to be visibly upbeat about the season with their child.

Then try to get them to agree to help you create a terrific experience for the players on the team by following these guidelines for a coach–parent partnership.

GUIDELINES FOR A COACH–PARENT PARTNERSHIP

While you will not always be able to get parents to be active forces to help you get your messages across to the players, if you can give them some concrete guidelines about how they can help, you are more likely to forge a potent coach–parent partnership that will benefit everyone. Here are my guidelines.

1. **Don't put the player in the middle:** It is common for parents to disagree with the coaches of their youngsters. Even when a disagreement doesn't surface to the coach, it can result in parents complaining to their child about the coach's strategies or policies. Talk with par-

203

ents at the beginning of the season and ask them to talk directly with you if they have a problem about the way you are running the team. If they think, for example, that their child is not playing enough or is playing the wrong position, or whatever, they should come to you and discuss it. If parents are openly and repeatedly invited to talk with you about problems they have, they are less likely to complain in front of their child.

2. **Give you feedback:** This may seem like a repeat of the first point, but it is important enough to single out as a separate item. If you tell parents that you want them to talk to you about what's bothering them and/or their child, they will do so. Not only will they come to you, they will be less likely to complain to their child, or to gossip behind your back with other parents about all the horrible coaching moves you are making. They may even be astonished, since in my experience, the norm is certainly not for coaches to encourage parents to tell them when there's a problem.

Also encourage them to tell you when something is bothering their child, such as a physical ailment like a cold or the flu, a death in the family, or problems in school that might affect their behavior in practice or a game.

One year I had a player on my baseball team who was very hard of hearing. It wasn't until late in the year that another parent who knew the kid in question asked me about how I was handling Jake's hearing loss. I felt like a total dunderhead when, before I could stop my mouth from letting it out, I said, "What hearing loss?" It was all clear to me then, all of the times I had gotten so frustrated with Jake because he seemed to be purposely disregarding my instructions. Many's the time I had to restrain myself from yelling, "Are you deaf?!"

You can only benefit from encouraging your parents to engage in full disclosure about your players.

3. **Don't give instructions during a game:** When I coach I

often have individual players working on specific things that may not be apparent to observers, even parents. It drives me up the wall to have parents yelling instructions to their kids during a game. One basketball game we were playing a one-player team. The entire offense revolved around one very quick point guard who had failed to demonstrate that she had an effective outside shot. The other team's single play seemed to be to set multiple picks for their point guard and let her drive to the basket. I asked my point guard to drop way off and dare her to shoot from the outside. By dropping off, my player could also more easily avoid the picks and keep her from getting the lay-up. Our plan was working splendidly when one of our parents began yelling to our point guard to "get out on her." Fortunately, our player ignored the directions, I explained our strategy to the parent, and all was well. But too often, players are put in the no-win situation of trying to please both the coach and the parent. It is difficult for the player to resolve this situation and that means the coach needs to deal with it.

I ask parents to tell me if they have a suggestion to improve their (or another) child's play, so that I can tell the player, if appropriate. That way, the player won't be confused by conflicting instructions. Even if the parent's suggestion is a useful one, it may not be helpful to the player to have the parent yelling it out in the middle of a game.

4. **Provide positive support for their player:** Perhaps the most important thing a parent can do is to be there for the athlete. Competitive sports are stressful to players and the last thing they need is a critic at home. Be clear with your parents that you want them to be a cheerleader for their kids. You want them to focus on the positive things their child is doing and leave the correcting of mistakes to you.

5. **Be part of the "home court advantage" for the team:** In

205

Chapter 14 I discuss how to create a home court advantage for your team. Parents can be an important part of this atmosphere. Ask them explicitly to help create a home court advantage. Tell them why the home court advantage works and that you want their help in making it work for your team. Once they understand the concept, they will likely become enthusiastic and relentlessly positive forces from the sidelines.

6. **Don't disparage the other team:** I want to win but I don't want to win at the expense of diminishing the players and coaches on opposing teams. I once observed a baseball coach who pretended to shout encouragement to his players while really trying to discourage the opposing players. He would yell to his pitcher things like, "Just throw strikes. This guy hasn't gotten a hit all season."

   I want my team to win by playing their best and beating the best that the other team has to offer. Winning by demoralizing the other team's players is not for me. I ask my parents (and players) to be careful to avoid inadvertently saying things that have a demoralizing effect.

PARENTS AND CHARACTER DEVELOPMENT

Another area where positive parental involvement can be effective is in keeping kids involved when the going gets tough. In particular I have seen situations around all-star teams where parents could have made a huge difference.

All-star teams bring out the absolute worst in parents. Players who have been the stars of their individual teams now have to jockey with other stars and only one or two of them can play shortstop. To go from playing shortstop to right field, or even worse, to sitting on the bench most of the time, is difficult enough for the players. And since the minimum playing time rule often no longer applies during an all-star tournament, many players who played all game every game all season long now find themselves watching most of the game from the bench. When the parents also express a lot of resentment, it is a rare child who can make the best of the situation.

In several all-star situations, parents have pulled their kids off the all-star team because they felt they weren't getting enough playing time, or that their "natural first baseman" (i.e., he is left-handed) wasn't getting to play first base. One tragic situation I observed up close occurred during the middle of a hard-fought all-star tournament game. Our team had already lost one game in a double elimination tournament, and we were narrowly hanging on to a lead largely because of a great effort by our best pitcher.

The parent of a child—one who had played first base all year but who now was mostly sitting on the bench—challenged the manager in the middle of the game when the boy playing first base made an error. He got into a shouting match with the manager, which upset the manager and coaches and probably some of the players as well, since the parent was not taking pains to keep his voice down. The parent eventually stomped off back to the bleachers, the game resumed, and we eked out a narrow victory to keep our hopes alive in the loser's bracket of the tournament.

The irony here is that although the manager was irate at the parent, he was influenced by his criticism. The next game happened to be against a much weaker team, and he told me he planned on starting the irate parent's son at first base for that game. Alas, it never came to be because the parent yanked his son off the team. The next game was an easy victory, with all the players getting to play a significant amount of the game. Some of the players who hadn't played before in the tournament went on to make great fielding plays and get hits.

I still feel badly about the dilemma the yanked player

was put in. It would have been hard for him to come out ahead. If he got to start after his father's tantrum, he might well think that was the only reason. He could well imagine his father expecting him to do especially well since this was his big chance to show the manager that his father was right. With that kind of pressure, it wouldn't have been surprising if he would have had a bad outing. And it is a rare event when you come up against a weaker team the further you go in an all-star tournament, as we did in this case. As you keep playing, you face better and better teams, so even your superstar players begin to falter. The cards were stacked against the child by the father's action, and it didn't have to be that way.

The parent might have used the situation to help the player become mentally tougher. He might have said something like, "It must be frustrating for you to have to sit on the bench, especially if you believe you can do a better job than the kid playing first base. But you're going to face many situations like this in life, and I encourage you to continue to work hard in practice and show the coach that you're ready to go in and make a difference when you get the chance. If you really work hard in practice, you may get that opportunity. So hang in there." He might have gone the whole nine yards and added, "In the meantime, you can help your team from the bench by volunteering to coach the bases, warm up the outfielders, and cheer for your teammates."

The father also might have gone to the manager privately and talked diplomatically about the situation. For example, he might have said something like, "Hector is a little frustrated by not getting to play and it seemed to me that he might be able to help your lineup defensively at first base. You know he played first base all year with his regular team. Is there something he can do to get a chance to play more?" It is a rare manager who won't listen to a parent who approaches in the right manner. And in this case, I think the manager would have responded by giving him more playing time in a way that would not have increased the pressure on the boy.

By the way, it wasn't at all clear to me that *Hector* was itching for more playing time. He may well have been content to not play that much given the high quality of the competition. Nonetheless, either of these approaches would have supported the player and made it easier for him to deal with the situation rather than put him into a no-win bind.

WHEN ALL ELSE FAILS— INTERVENING WITH A PARENT

Most of the time the suggestions in this chapter have worked for me. When people in organizations get clear signals about the kind of behavior that is expected of them, they usually try to comply if they have the ability. When parents get clear signals of what your program of parental involvement is and isn't, when they are clued into the sources of Little League parent-itis, when they hear lots of good stuff about their children from the coach, when their kids get to play a lot and are progressing and having fun, they tend to go along with the program.

But sometimes, your best efforts aren't enough. Then the parent who apparently hasn't read or heard your repeated statement of parental guidelines comes along. Or worse, the parent has read them but ignores them. He yells out instructions during games. She focuses on her child's mistakes and won't let them go. He dresses down the player in front of others. She just generally gets in the way of the player having fun and learning the sport.

In this situation there's no alternative to intervention because that's part of the responsibility of a coach who is serious about developing his players as athletes and people. So, go ahead and do it. Take the parent aside, away from everyone else, and, in as matter-of-fact a way as possible, tell him what you observe him doing and what the negative consequences for the player and the team are. Ask him to refrain from doing it.

A key to handling this successfully is to not make it seem like a big thing. This may be difficult if it has started to annoy you and you've let it go on longer than you feel you should have. But if you can handle it in a straightforward way, your chances of the parent going along will be greatly enhanced.

The other essential element is to focus on the behavior that you observe and why it's a problem. For example, you might say, "I've noticed that you often yell out instructions to Paul during a game. We both know that Paul sometimes forgets to back up throws to the bases and to think about where to play each hitter, but I am trying to get Paul to concentrate on thinking for himself and remembering to do those things. When you yell instructions to him, it makes it harder for him to learn to think through these decisions on his own. I'd appreciate it if you wouldn't yell instructions any more. Okay?"

I've said elsewhere in this book (see Chapter 2) that it is easier to confront someone with the need to change their behavior when you have created an atmosphere of positivity in which they feel accepted and able to make mistakes without censure. If you have done this, the likelihood of even needing to intervene with parents will be dramatically reduced. And if you do need to intervene, the parent will be much more likely to respond positively to you when you do.

THE NOBLE STRAND

I mentioned at the beginning of this chapter that in addition to distorted perceptions, a desire to relive past glories, and a belief that the parent is the child, there was a noble strand of concern that every parent has for their child. Most parents want their kids to do well because they love them. If this noble strand is not readily apparent—and with some parents it may not be—it still is down there somewhere ready to be drawn out into the open by how you interact with the parents.

It's not necessarily easy, but I am convinced that by following these suggestions for dealing with parents you will be able to tap into the noble strand with each parent you run across. And it's worth the effort.

11

What About Winning?

Usually coaches win if they can;
if they can't, they build character.
—Austin Henderson, a character in
Thomas J. Dygard's *Quarterback Walk-on*

After years of talking about the importance of building character and self-esteem and having fun with sports, I still get depressed when a team I'm coaching loses. A few years ago, as my son was recovering from the flu, our fifth- and sixth-grade basketball team played a game that we could probably have won if my son had played. He bugged me to let him play until I wanted to scream. I really wanted to beat this particular team since they had beaten us narrowly the year before, and I believed that we had improved more than they had. He wasn't really *that* sick any more. Nonetheless, I didn't let him play.

After we lost the game, I couldn't stop asking my wife over and over, "Do you think I should have let him play?" (Sandra: "No way.")

Now, from the distance of several years later, I have no doubt that I did the right thing. This was a noncompetitive league that didn't keep standings. There was no honor at stake. My other players performed very well, each getting more playing time than they would have if the entire team

213

was there. And they nearly won the game anyway. My son continued his recovery and came roaring back the next week. I'm sure that no one other than me even remembers the incident. Nonetheless, losing that game still bothers me.

In this society, winning seems to be everything. Major political leaders with decades of honorable public service are derided as "losers" when they come in second with millions of votes in a presidential campaign. We hear daily through the media of major college coaches who brutalize their players, display an atrocious lack of sportsmanship and, in general, act like three-year-olds throwing tantrums. Yet this behavior is tolerated *as long as they win*. This society exacts a heavy cost from those who make the "wrong" choice when forced to choose between winning and building character.

IS WINNING THE *ONLY* THING?

What exactly did former Green Bay Packers coach Vince Lombardi mean when he said, "Winning isn't everything, it's the only thing"? Did he mean that it was okay to cheat to win? Did he mean that he was willing to risk the health of a player to win? Did he mean that he would overlook the violation of a team rule or substance abuse by a star player so that player could continue to be part of the team? Apparently in later years, Vince Lombardi tried to clarify the record saying he had been misquoted, that what he really said was "*Trying* to win is the only thing." I feel better about this statement because it emphasizes effort (something a person can control) over outcome (something a person rarely can control). Nonetheless, youth sports is not war, and even trying to win needs to be balanced against other goals of participation in sports, such as having fun and learning good sportsmanship.

But regardless of what Lombardi may have meant, it's

more important how *you* feel about winning. How important is winning to you?

I've found that it's important to be clear with myself about this, because in the heat of decision-making during a game or season, the lines blur between what's acceptable and what's not. Early in a baseball season it's easier to say you would never pitch a kid with a sore arm. In the playoffs, with something at stake, it's not quite so clear. You begin to think about the pitcher's responsibility to the rest of the team. Upon reflection, you realize that this player will never make it to the major leagues anyway. You wonder if maybe this isn't the peak of his baseball career as a 12-year-old. You wonder if it's really fair to *him* to keep him from pitching in this game. You worry that he may regret not getting to play in it for the rest of his life.

Unless you are a remarkably well-adjusted person, you can't rely on your judgment in the heat of a competitive game situation. You need to support yourself with a written declaration of principle.

Write It Down

I encourage you to explicitly address the question of how much winning means to you. Write down what you are willing to sacrifice to create a winning team. For example, are you willing to risk a player's health to win a game? What if it is a championship game? And what if the player himself wants to go ahead? And what if even his parents encourage you to let him play?

Are you willing to play only the better players on your team to win? Are you willing to risk embarrassing a player by removing her right after she makes a costly mistake in a key game? Are you willing to encourage your players to play rough to intimidate players on the other team?

On the positive side of the ledger, are you willing to leave work early or devote your leisure time to scout other teams? Are you willing to stay up late at night devising strategies to improve your team's chances to win? Are you willing to devote additional instruction time to teaching players on an individual basis? Are you willing to work with your weaker players outside of regular practice times? Are you willing to study games on television with an eye to finding things you can use in your coaching, rather than simply treating the games as entertainment? Are you willing to read everything you can find about coaching your sport so you can be the best coach you are capable of being?

It's important to write down our commitments about winning because it's too easy to be fuzzy in our thinking until we "think it and ink it." We have a tendency to gloss over the complexities of a situation if we do all of our thinking in our heads without making it tangible by putting it down on paper. If you have a written statement of what you are willing to do (and *not* do) to win, and carry it with you to games, it helps keep those lines clear and present.

It's also useful to write down important goals that may, in fact, make it harder for you to win. I may go to a baseball game against a stronger team with the idea that I am going to finally give Zachary the chance to pitch that he has been bugging me about all season. But then we suddenly find ourselves ahead in the fourth inning when he is due to pitch. If I have written down my goal to give Zachary a chance to pitch, it will be easier for me to stick to it. If I haven't written it down, it may be all too easy to succumb to the sweet seduction of the chance to win and play only my stronger players.

So take out that pencil and paper right now and start writing:

> To help every player on my team have a terrific season, I will . . .
>
> Even if it means losing a game I really want to win, I will not . . .
>
> To become the best coach I can be, I will . . .

THE POWER OF OPO

Part of why coaches can get so messed up about the relative importance of winning during the heat of competition is because of the underestimated power of OPO (other people's opinions), both real and imagined. I have been a parent on the sidelines, as well as a coach, and I know what thoughts can go on in the heads of other parents. As a coach I try to manage the expectations of my parents by telling them ahead of time about my values and, in effect, giving them the chance to move their child to another team if they don't like my approach.

Nonetheless I am constantly distracted by what my wild imagination fantasizes may be going on in the minds of other people who watch me coach. Particularly after making a coaching mistake, I am sure that parents and other observers are making comments about what a stupid decision it was.

I believe it's normal, or at least not fatal, to worry about what others think of you. And, once again, having a written statement of my values and how they relate to winning can help rein in the power of OPO.

THE DANGER WITH "TOO-HIGH" STANDARDS

Everywhere I turn I seem to find another article by someone saying that the problem with America is we don't set high enough standards. Recently there have been a spate of opinion pieces about how we need a national standardized test for high school students to make them work harder. Everybody seems to ascribe to the idea that setting high standards leads to improved performance. But there is a problem and that is knowing where high standards end and "too-high" standards begin.

I have seen too many children whose parents have set standards for them that are impossibly high. When they are not able to meet those too-high expectations, they

217

cope by trying other strategies, most of which are not useful, either to the individual or to our society.

I once observed a soccer game in which the coach's son was being driven by his father to play perfectly. The boy was a very good soccer player, but his father ignored all of the good plays he made. He yelled and criticized all of the times the boy didn't come through as his father expected. The boy played well but occasionally an opponent with superior speed or skill would get past him. As the game progressed and it became clear that despite his best efforts, his team was not going to win, and his father was not going to be pleased, he tried a different strategy. He began to get rough. Whereas before he would put all of his effort into trying to make the play, he now began to swing an elbow here or there, to try to knock down the opposing player rather than take the ball away from him legitimately. In the end, his team lost anyway and the other team was angry at the dirty tactics. A good soccer player, who might have earned the respect of the opposition during a hard-fought match, instead walked off the field with a reputation as a dirty player.

I fully endorse setting high standards, for myself and for others. However, I am not naive enough to believe there are no down sides to high standards. When standards are set too high—by that I mean so high that one cannot realistically, solely by one's own effort, ever hope to achieve them—several other things can happen.

1. **Whining:** Often the first response to too-high standards is that players become complainers and whiners. If they are expected to meet too-high standards, they may well turn to blaming their failure on someone else. And since the standard they are being held to is nothing less than defeating the other team, it doesn't help to simply admit the truth (that the other team is better). Instead, the other team cheated. Or the referees were biased. In

any event, the blame is not in one's ability and/or effort. I can't stand being around whiners, although I don't mind whining a bit myself. Somehow it's more palatable when it originates with me.

A side effect of whining is that whiners can miss the beauty in the performance of an "opponent." One reason sports have such power over the minds and imaginations of so many is that they contain moments of incredible beauty. Sometimes the beauty is performed by "our" team, and sometimes by the opposition. Whiners rarely are able to appreciate, let alone acknowledge, a great performance by someone who defeats them.

2. **Cheating:** When winning becomes all important, players will tend to do what it takes to win. And cheating can go undetected and help you win, especially in youth sports where the officiating often may not be top-notch. There are many reasons why cheating is not good. But one reason that is often overlooked is that cheating is rarely accompanied by increased efforts. (Why work harder when you can get what you want so much easier by cheating?) And it is increased effort in response to losing that can make a person an ultimate winner

3. **Dropping out:** Often the child who has too-high standards set for her feels unable to quit the sport that is so important to her parents, coach, or peers. However, if an athlete believes she has the option to quit, too-high standards can often lead to a premature exit from sports. And years, even a lifetime, of enjoyment of sports, and friendship in and around sports, can be lost.

If the child is not able to drop out physically, she *always* has the option of dropping out mentally. In many ways it is a much sadder outcome for a player to go through the motions, rather than making a clean break and finding something in which to passionately invest her energy. Either kind of dropping out is not pretty and is most often where too-high standards lead.

I know of no clear and easy way to determine if standards are too high, but the symptoms mentioned above are some warning signs to look for. Whining, cheating, and dropping out may be symptomatic of too-high standards. If young athletes are discouraged, then a likely cause is too-high standards. And it is appropriate to ask who is setting the standards. Standards that an athlete holds oneself to may be motivating even though apparently stratospheric to others. On the other hand, standards that are set by a coach or parent without buy-in by the player can seem high even though, objectively, they may be well within the reach of the athlete. The bottom line with standards is that they should encourage greater and longer efforts rather than discourage. Standards that discourage are too high!

HOLDING YOURSELF TO COMPARABLE STANDARDS

John Gardner notes in *No Easy Victories:* "One of the problems you encounter in talking about dedication is that everyone wants the other fellow to be more dedicated." Coaching is rife with hypocrisy and double standards. Read almost any book about major college or professional teams and coaches, and you will run across examples of both. You'll find athletes expected to attend class while the coach can skip practice if he feels like it. You'll see players expected to be in tip-top form while the coach is 30 or more pounds overweight. Players are expected to control their tempers while the coach throws a tantrum at the slightest deviation from his game plan.

There is a lovely story about Gandhi recorded by Eknath Easwaran in *Gandhi the Man* that illustrates this point.

During the thirties a woman came to Sevagram asking Gandhi to get her little boy to stop eating sugar; it was doing him harm. Gandhi gave a cryptic reply: "Please come back next week."

The woman left puzzled but returned a week later, dutifully following the Mahatma's instructions. "Please don't eat sugar," Gandhi told the young fellow when he saw him. "It is not good for you." Then he joked with the boy for a while, gave him a hug, and sent him on his way. But the mother, unable to contain her curiosity, lingered behind to ask, "Bapu, why didn't you say this last week when we came? Why did you make us come back again?"

Gandhi smiled. "Last week," he said to her, "I too was eating sugar."

Earlier in this chapter I suggested that one of the things a coach needs to think about is what he or she is willing to sacrifice to win. Are you willing to spend the time that's needed to prepare your team to win? Are you willing to take vacation time, or give up your lunch hours, or take time away from your hobby (assuming you have any hobbies besides coaching) to do what you need to do to help your team win? Are you willing to make a commitment to the team to help each member become all he can be?

I mentioned earlier the soccer coach whose favorite phrase was "Never let up." He would yell it over and over again during games. Now the reality was that all of the players would at some point or another let up. If they hadn't, if they had gone 100 percent every moment of every game, they would have run themselves into the ground. And the further reality is that the coach let up at times. I didn't follow him to work every day, but I am confident that he took coffee breaks, relaxed at times, and went home early from work when he was coming down with a cold. I bet there were even times when he came to soccer practice less prepared than he might have been.

I'm not critical of him for being human and pacing himself at times. But I do see this particular double standard all too often with coaches and their players. By trying to hold yourself to the same standard that you expect your players to meet, you may in fact find yourself with more reasonable (and encouraging) standards for you and your players.

THE PARADOXICAL IMPACT OF POSITIVE COACHING

Sometimes the quickest way to a goal is indirectly. There are times when, in trying to see a particular constellation or star, you have to look away slightly to see it. And I would guess that we all have experienced the frustration of trying so hard to remember something to no avail, only to remember it when we turn our mind away from it.

Winning can be like this. Sometimes when we coach to win we do more poorly than if we come at winning indirectly. I like to start each season with a new group of players by stressing the big three goals: having fun, trying hard, and being good sports. When, as they sometimes do, players ask about winning, it gives me the chance to say that the surest way to win is by trying hard and having fun.

When the overriding goal of coaching is to build character and self-esteem, you will sometimes find that you win *more* than you expect to. Kids with a higher sense of self-efficacy (see Chapter 13) try harder. They stick to a task longer before they give up. And kids who are having fun with a sport practice longer and more often. And those are the elements of a winning effort.

12

Learning from Losing

It's common for us to play over our heads against superior opposition, because this foreknowledge that winning is not an essential part of the experience is what brings out our best performances . . . If you are not intimidated by the idea of losing . . . or "looking bad," you can simply concentrate on playing and sometimes go beyond yourself.
—Thomas Tutko and Umberto Tosi
Sports Psyching

*T*homas Edison was reputed to have tried more than a thousand times to invent the light bulb before he was successful. If he were in a competitive young inventor's league, he would have been branded a failure and probably would have become discouraged long before the light bulb came to be.

Ours is a society that usually doesn't recogize the good try, that pillories individuals and teams of high excellence that don't quite reach the very top. But losing is a part of sports and of life. And an important part.

I recently watched a junior high girls basketball team trounce every single opponent they played by outrageously large scores. Part of the reason they did so was because several of the girls had just finished a season in which they played in Cupertino Hoops, our co-ed league, against and with boys. They had improved dramatically by playing against tougher competition and now they were reaping the reward.

But what kind of a reward? Each game was effectively over before the midpoint of the first quarter. If the Los Angeles Lakers played a local high school team, would we think that made sense? Would we think that either the Lakers or the high school players were gaining from the experience? Just because the players were of the same general age and grade in school didn't mean that it made sense for them to be playing against each other. With virtually no chance of an upset, neither team benefitted from the debacle.

One tragedy of an overemphasis on winning is that we can easily overlook some important lessons to be learned from losing. For example, it is difficult to see how one could develop the positive character trait of persistence in the face of adversity without the adversity. It's hard to develop the ability to keep getting up if you're never knocked down. It's hard to come back the next day and work harder after a loss if you never lose. If we want to use sports to help children learn lessons that will help them cope with life, we need to develop an approach to losing. We need to value losing for the lessons it can bring us and our players.

LIVING WITH THE DISAPPOINTMENT OF LOSING

Losing hurts. As a fellow coach once eloquently put it, "Losing sucks. Winning is more fun than losing."

Last year my baseball team sustained a heartbreaking, come-from-behind loss in the bottom of the last inning. I found myself trying to gloss over the disappointment of losing in such a manner. I actually said things like, "You shouldn't feel bad about this game. Focus on how much you are improving."

Later I realized that I was doing my players a disservice by encouraging them to deny their feelings. In fact I had trouble sleeping for several nights after, replaying the game over and over, thinking if only I had or hadn't made this or that coaching move. I couldn't paper over my feelings but I was encouraging them to do so. Not good.

Now I have come to believe that it is not only difficult to stifle upset feelings about losing, it isn't even a useful thing to do. As I write this, I am suffering the disappointment of having had my basketball team beaten by 20 points. We had won our first three games of the season quite easily and I was unprepared to be beaten so soundly by a team with which I thought we'd be competitive. I came home after the game and took a nap and awoke less tired but still depressed. I felt like I was a failure as a coach. I was embarrassed about how badly we had been beaten. I finally acknowledged to myself, and then shared with my wife, the fact that I was sad and depressed about losing the game, and about losing so badly. Then I could (mostly) let it go and enjoy the rest of the weekend.

I was also finally able, after I acknowledged to myself that I was hurt and depressed about the loss, to analyze what had gone wrong and, most importantly, why. We had missed many lay-ups and offensive rebound put-backs, shots that we normally make. We also were not matched up well on defense. For most of the game, we had the wrong players on the floor to match up with theirs. Our league requires that all players play at least half the game. Normally I am prepared to meet that requirement while making sure that we are well matched up at any given time. This isn't too difficult since the other coach has to meet the same standard.

Further, we missed an opportunity when one of their strongest players got three quick fouls on him (in our league four fouls is the limit). Instead of taking the ball to him and either fouling him out or getting easy baskets while he was being "careful," we let him get away with playing the entire rest of the game. Finally, the other team overplayed us to prevent initial passes from getting to the wings. Normally we would exploit this by going back door

225

to the basket and making them pay for overplaying. This game we didn't, and they ended up getting a bunch of steals and easy lay-ups at the other end of the floor.

Now I had my plan for the next practice. We worked on lay-ups from all directions with pressure from a charging defender. We used a one-on-one-on-one drill with all three players trying for a rebound and then putting it back up. Then hit or miss, all three would again try for the rebound and put it up, and so on for 20 times. We also reviewed what to do on offense when being overplayed.

The other two problems were totally mine. That game day was picture day, and I was helping get each team to the photo room on time. Two of the teams were playing at a Golden State Warriors halftime in three days, and they hadn't been briefed on where to go and what to do. The person who was in charge of the referees had stepped down from that position, and I was trying to deal with the referees while finding another person to take on that responsibility. I had too many administrative duties in addition to my coaching, and I simply didn't have my head in the game. I didn't focus on match-ups until it was too late, and I simply missed the opportunity with their top player's foul trouble. I began our next practice by telling the kids what I thought had gone wrong at the last game and apologizing to them for not having been better prepared to do my best as a coach.

The point of this is that until I faced my shame and hurt at the loss, I wasn't able to learn from the experience. Once I did so, I was able to see what had happened and take steps to keep it from recurring. And then I couldn't wait until we played that team again.

A KID'S PERSPECTIVE ON LOSING
(AND WINNING)

While I was in a serious funk, my players seemed to have a lot less problem with the loss, which in my experience is pretty typical. They were chattering after the game about what they were going to do the rest of the weekend, about next week's game, about great and blunderous plays that had been made in the game. Most of them seemed to have little, if any, of the kind of depression I had about the loss. They seemed to feel fine, which reminded me of a game a year earlier, against a team that I really wanted to beat. The players on that team were mostly eighth-graders, compared to my mostly seventh-graders, so it was a challenge. And the players on both teams knew and liked each other well. This friendly rivalry made it even more enjoyable.

After the big victory I gathered my players outside the gymnasium to dwell upon the thrill of the victory for awhile. I was amazed to hear them talking to each other about the television show they wanted to watch that night, or the latest record they wondered if the others had heard yet, or . . . "WAIT A MINUTE!" I wanted to yell. "Don't you guys realize that we just beat a team that no one ever thought we'd be able to beat? How can you talk about TV or records after playing a game like that?"

I'm sure they enjoyed the victory, but they weren't obsessed with it the way I was. They had winning in perspective—I was the one with the problem. Tom Tutko tells a delightful story about his interaction with his son who had just played a tough soccer game which his team lost. As they were driving home after the game, Tom decided he needed to say something profound to his son. After all, he is a sports psychologist, so he's supposed to have wisdom to dispense. He first offered, "You know that 50 percent of the teams that play soccer always lose?" No response from his son. He then tried another angle. Still no reaction. Finally he reached back over the years: "I remember when I was young, I played in a game that I really wanted to win, and it really hurt when we lost." At this his son slid over in the seat and put his arm around his father saying, "It's okay, Dad." At that point Tom says he knew that one of them was severely disturbed.

227

WHEN THINGS GO WRONG

As perverse as this may sound, coaches who want to make a positive difference in their players' lives should welcome adversity. It is when things go wrong that coaches can have the most impact. When you have a great bunch of athletes who always win, what is there for you to add?

But when you play a team that you fully expected to beat, but find yourself down by 10 runs before you know it, it is easy for players to become discouraged. And that is when you can help them learn to deal with it.

In a recent basketball game, two players, including one from my team, almost came to blows. The week before there had been a similar situation not involving my team, and I was appalled. This wasn't supposed to happen in Cupertino Hoops, which was formed precisely because the other league in town didn't meet our standard. We had gone our entire first season without a single ugly incident, but now we had expanded upward to include ninth- and tenth-graders, and they were more volatile. They moved faster, they were bigger and stronger, and when they collided, they often got angry about it. I was upset about the situation and talked with other board members about it. We came up with a new set of guidelines governing player and coach behavior, and discussed them with each of the referees and coaches before the next games. I thought the issue was closed and, in any event, I was sure nothing similar would happen with anyone on *my* team.

Surprise, surprise. The very next game one of my players was fouled hard as he went to the basket. He expressed some frustration with that, the player that fouled him talked back, and the temperature heated up quickly, with the referee having to separate them. Both players received technicals, and the other player was tossed out of the game. I was devastated. Not only did it seem like the entire program was getting out of control but I took it as a personal reflection on my coaching that one of my players had gotten involved in the kind of incident I take some satisfaction in criticizing when seen on TV.

My initial reaction of horror notwithstanding, there was a silver lining here. This turned into a tremendous opportunity to work with two young men who had a great deal of athletic (and plain old human) potential but who were a little hot-headed. Both boys got a lot of sage advice and support from several different adults. Both also were told in no uncertain terms that this behavior was not acceptable. They shook hands and apologized to each other after the game, and life went on with no further incidents the rest of the season. Time will tell if the incident will have any lasting impact on either of them, but I am convinced that these are exactly the kinds of kids and situations for which positive coaching can make a difference. And the opportunity is greatest to make a difference when things go wrong.

GETTING BACK UP

There is a scene in the movie *Gandhi* that can serve as a metaphor for mental toughness. Gandhi has called for a demonstration protesting conditions for Indians in South Africa. The protest calls for Indians to burn their identification cards. As Gandhi sets fire to his card, a policeman knocks him down with a club. Gandhi gets up and returns his card to the flame. Again the policeman knocks him down, this time harder. Again Gandhi gets up. Each time as Gandhi rises, more Indians, initially fearful of joining the protest, approach the flames with their cards.

My college roommate, Tom Copeland, a distant relative of Robert Bruce, King of Scotland in the fourteenth century, first told me the story of Robert Bruce's spider dream. It seems that after being defeated six times by the English, Bruce had retreated to a cave to recover. While sleeping there, he had a dream in which a spider tried to spin a web up in a precarious, high corner of the cave. The spider spun and failed six times. The seventh time, it succeeded. Bruce took this dream to mean that he too would succeed the seventh time he tried to defeat the English, which he did.

Too often our standard of success is to win at the beginning, but as Harvard Business School's Rosabeth Moss Kanter has noted, "Everything looks like a failure in the middle." Looked at it one way, life is mostly about failures. George Bernard Shaw once said that he noticed that only about 10 percent of what he did was successful so he decided to try 10 times harder. The real test of character is not whether we occasionally get knocked down, but how many times we can get up. And you simply can't know if you are the kind of person who will get back up again if you've never been knocked down. One great thing about youth sports is that they can give young people the chance to get knocked down without getting knocked out. With a supportive coach and team, a knockdown can be a big advantage that can help kids learn to become the kind of person who gets back up, which is as good a definition of a winner as I can imagine.

HELPING PLAYERS ASSESS THE COMPETITION

Young people are not necessarily skilled at assessing the competition. If they were playing the Los Angeles Lakers they would realize that they were not supposed to be able to win. But in playing a team from across the city that has been together for several years with players of great ability, they might get really depressed about losing.

A major responsiblity for a coach is to help players assess their chances against the competition. A few years ago, my team of all sixth-graders was dominant in its fifth-sixth-grade league. They had played together for several years and had suffered through being a team of fifth-graders being beaten by teams of sixth-graders. Now they were the dominant team but it wasn't satisfying (at least to me). The games were so one-sided that I felt embarrassed because there was no way I could make them more competitive given the talent level of my players compared with those on the other teams. I tried things such as making them pass the ball three times before shooting, but that only provided us with even easier shots.

I discussed with them my perception that they were not going to be challenged in the fifth and sixth league, and that the victories there didn't have as much meaning as they would against stronger competition. I asked them if they wanted to move up and play against seventh- and eighth-graders. Every kid except one immediately said yes, and after thinking about it, he also decided he wanted to.

They realized several things: first, that they were not being pushed to improve as much as they might be; second, that it wasn't really much fun or much of an accomplishment to batter teams that weren't of the same caliber; and third, that there is virtually no pressure when you play against someone you aren't expected to beat. We moved up and won only one of our remaining five games. Yet the players were excited and motivated for each game. They understood the level of competition had changed and thus could interpret their losses in a positive way. The great effort they were making was not lost even though they were beaten most of the time. The players were excited and motivated for each game, and their skills improved as they were pushed to rise to a new level of play.

THE LOOSE FREEDOM OF THE UNDERDOG

Most athletes at one time or another experience competing as an underdog. When I was a high school quarterback for the West Fargo Packers, we played against an exceptionally strong Fargo Shanley team ranked number one in the state. The *Fargo Forum* ran an article about our game with the lines: "Can the Packers beat Shanley? Will the sun rise in the west?"

231

Try as we might, we couldn't make the sun reverse direction (although after more than 20 years I still use that line to remind myself in which direction the sun comes up). But we did play a terrific game. I remember throwing three touchdown passes as we came closer (though not very close) to beating Shanley than any team did that year. I have no doubt that the fact that everyone expected us to be soundly trounced by Shanley loosened us up to the point that we were able to play our best game of football of the season.

A FINAL REASON FOR APPRECIATING LOSING

There is a great scene near the end of the *The Hobbit* by J.R.R. Tolkien in which Gandalf (the voice of John Huston in the movie) responds to Bilbo Baggins (the voice of Orson Bean), who is confused about the adventure he has just participated in. " 'You don't really suppose, do you, that all your adventures and escapes were managed by mere luck, just for your sole benefit? You are a very fine person, Mr. Baggins, and I am very fond of you; but you are only quite a little fellow in a wide world after all!' 'Thank goodness!' said Bilbo laughing . . .''

Winning can do strange things to our heads and our sense of balance. We may have the best talent in the league on our team, but we attribute our team's success to our great coaching. I have had moments of delusions of grandeur about what I might accomplish as a coach if I were to make it a career rather than a passionate voluntary activity. Losing restores us to balance. Losing helps us realize that there is more to life than what goes on between the first base line and the third base line. We coaches, whether of children or of college athletes or of professionals, are really just quite little fellows (and fellowettes) in a wide world after all. Losing helps us remember that.

13

Nurturing Outstanding Individual Competitors

> "Jonah Brooks will catch in the place of Piney Woods," said Dutch. "Piney been summonsed elsewheres than here this fine and pleasant afternoon . . . His mind is in the hemisphere . . . I have spoke to him both in private and ate him out in public, and I wrote both his father and his mother . . . I must figure out another means of throwing fear in his heart. I do not know. Any observations?" . . .
>
> "Some boys do not answer to fear," said Red.
>
> —Mark Harris
> *A Ticket for a Seamstitch*

The first rule of medicine, international development, and coaching kids is "Do no harm."

David Hilfiker's wrenching book, *Healing the Wounds*, illustrates how even a competent and dedicated doctor can end up harming a patient in the attempt to cure him. The film *Black Robe* describes how seventeenth century missionaries to the Hurons inadvertently laid the groundwork for the devastation of the tribe. There are hundreds of examples from more recent history of well-meaning foreigners intent on improving the lot of tribal peoples in developing countries who instead disrupt the native culture with tragic consequences. These dangers are well understood by most practitioners in medicine and international development.

This danger is less well understood by practitioners of youth sports. I have seen many instances in which coaches try to motivate talented athletes to become great competitors but end up doing more harm than good, largely because of misperceptions about motivation.

In this chapter I look at what it means to be a great competitor. We may all think we know one when we see one, but what exactly is it about the great competitor that is different? And what separates the outstanding performer from the merely good performer with the same level of talent? I first discuss what I believe are the characteristics of a great competitor. Then I describe the crucial concept of self-efficacy and how it relates to outstanding performance. Finally I suggest some ways for coaches to *help* (because you can't make it happen if they don't want it more than you do) their players acquire some of the characteristics of great competitors.

THE CHARACTERISTICS OF THE OUTSTANDING COMPETITOR

Watching an outstanding athlete perform is like viewing a work of art. There are some people who are so talented that even other athletes come to watch them practice. Rick Telander, in his poignant book about inner city basketball, *Heaven is a Playground,* describes how people would come from miles around to watch 14-year-old Albert King dominate playground games against major college basketball players. Few youth coaches are going to be coaching an Albert King or a Pete Maravich. But some will if they stay with coaching long enough. For those remaining, there are useful lessons to be gained from understanding what, aside from sheer physical ability, makes an outstanding competitor—lessons that can benefit *all* athletes.

I have identified five characteristics of outstanding competitors. A top competitor tends to be someone who (1) is internally rather than externally motivated; (2) seeks and is energized by challenges; (3) sees his development as a process under his control rather than a fixed capability; (4) is independent and willing to risk violating conventional wisdom; and (5) can accept both success and failure as part of the game.

1. **Internal motivation:** Since B. F. Skinner and the behavioralists, it has been clear that positive reinforcement works better and with fewer unpleasant side effects than negative reinforcement. However, it is not well understood that there is a difference between the performance of individuals motivated by internal factors and those motivated by external factors.

   There is evidence that great athletes are motivated more by their own internal goals than by external rewards such as fame, money, and status. It is internal passion for the sport that unleashes super performance. Michael Jordan, the athlete who has perhaps made more money from his rare talents than any other, had this to say about his motivation: "I love the game for the game, not just for the money. If I wasn't getting paid, I'd still be playing the game of basketball somewhere. A lot of people don't understand that." And a lot of coaches don't seem to understand that fear and greed aren't as powerful motivators as joy and love of a game.

   To develop the kind of skills even remotely approaching those of a Michael Jordan, an athlete has to *like* to play the game. You simply don't get to the highest level of skill without an incredible amount of practice. And most people aren't willing to put in the significant amount of practice time needed to develop high-level skills unless they enjoy the activity itself, over and above whatever external rewards they can gain from being a star athlete.

   I recently read a passage in a book by a nationally famous parenting expert that made me irate. The expert was asked for advice by a parent who wanted his reluctant child to play a sport. The "expert" responded that it was the parent's responsibility to select the sport that he believed would be best for the child and do whatever it took, including, if necessary, forcing the child to participate. If there is a prescription for mediocrity and joyless participation in sports, this is it.

Read almost any biography of a great sports figure and love for the sport comes shining through. Many athletes have made great sums of money from their talent but it was the love of the game that came first. They didn't start playing the game because they expected to make a bundle of money from it. They are primarily internally motivated. They enjoy their sport so much that you could imagine them saying, "What! They pay me to do this?" And you could believe it. Olympic speed skating champion Eric Heiden is a case in point. After winning multiple gold medals, he passed up the opportunity for lucrative endorsements to go to Sweden to study and take up bicycle racing.

John Gardner, in *Self-Renewal*, put it as well as anyone could: "Everyone has noted the abundant resources of energy that seem available to those who enjoy what they are doing or find meaning in what they are doing . . . How many times have we seen people leave work that they care deeply about to do something that does not interest them because it will bring more money or higher status or greater power? . . . Such people would be refreshed and renewed if they could wipe the slate clean and do *one little thing* that they really cared about deeply, one little thing that they could do with burning conviction."

Too often coaches try to increase a player's motivation by giving them external rewards. There is no question that most people, even the kind of top competitors we are talking about here, will respond in the short term to the chance to gain a reward or avoid a punishment. But it is a mistake to believe that you can motivate someone to achieve great things by holding a carrot in front of their nose or threatening to whack them with a stick. And sometimes the addition of external reinforcement, even positive, can actually decrease motivation and performance, as I discovered with my son and the piano.

When my son was in the first grade, he began taking piano lessons. He seemed to enjoy it and, in the (completely objective) view of his father, to have some talent for it. However, as he progressed in piano, the tasks he was asked to perform got more and more difficult. He began to be less interested in practicing and more interested in getting maximum time outdoors playing with his friends. He began talking about wanting to quit taking lessons. His mother and I ignored him for awhile but soon it got to be difficult. He was quite unhappy about having to practice the piano and take lessons.

This was hard for me to take because of the déjà vu factor. I had started piano when I was six but had complained so much about not being able to be outside playing baseball that I finally drove my mother to relent and set me free from the piano. Now these many years later, I was seeing the past repeat with my son, and I wasn't willing to give up without a fight (or a deal).

I told Gabby that if he would continue playing the piano for six months, I would take him to Disneyland. He agreed and dived back into his piano lessons. He practiced, attended his lessons, and continued to develop as a pianist. I was feeling pretty proud of my strategy and the results. As they say, pride goes before a fall and in the fall after our summer trip to Disneyland, Gabby began again to say he wanted to quit.

This time I tried to bribe him with a trip somewhere else, and he initially agreed but within a few days said he really wanted to quit. When I told him one too many times about my experience as a young pianist who now wished he had stuck it out, he replied with irrefutable logic, "But I'm not *you*, Dad!"

He quit, and we let him because in our family we try to keep to a minimum the things that you have to do whether you want to or not. And playing the piano wasn't one of them. I also didn't want him to come to hate the piano, and I could think of no way more likely to have that result than to force him to play it against his will.

Later, as I learned more about internal and external motivation, I discovered that I had done exactly what would be likely to cause him to *stop* playing the piano rather than continue. People tend to "attribute" their actions according to the motivations that are apparent to them. I increased the external motivation for him to play the piano and ended up simply substituting external motivation for internal. When Gabby first started playing the piano, he did it of his own free will. If he had an internal dialogue with himself about why he played the piano at that point, he could only have concluded that he did so because he wanted to, perhaps even because he enjoyed it. After the Disneyland bribe, he would be more likely to attribute his decision to play the piano to the fact that he was earning a trip to Disneyland.

Often a player who has been primarily motivated by internal mechanisms, such as love of the game, becomes the focus of external rewards for his performance. He begins to attribute his motivation to the external rewards. I have heard of wealthy athletes who "long for the hungry days" when there was no confusion about why they played the game. There were few or no external rewards. Like Jerome and Bix who play their games alone "beneath the spin light" in Bruce Brooks' wonderful book, *The Moves Make the Man*, they were doing it for their own internal reasons.

The phenomenon of external rewards undermining, even displacing, internal motivation is beautifully captured in the following story, appropriately entitled "Applied Psychology" from *A Treasury of Jewish Folklore* by Nathan Ausubel.

In a little Southern town where the Klan was riding again, a Jewish tailor had the temerity to open his little shop on the main street. To drive him out of the town the Kleagle of the Klan sent a gang of little ragamuffins to annoy him. Day after day they stood at the entrance of his shop. "Jew! Jew!" they hooted at him. The situation looked serious for the tailor. He took the matter so much to heart that he began to brood and spend sleepless nights over it. Finally out of desperation he evolved a plan.

The following day when the little hoodlums came to jeer at him, he came to the door and said to them, "From today on any boy who calls me a 'Jew' will get a dime from me." Then he put his hand in his pocket and gave each boy a dime.

Delighted with their booty, the boys came back the following day and began to shrill, "Jew! Jew!" The tailor came out smiling. He put his hand in his pocket and gave each of the boys a nickel, saying, "A dime is too much—I can only afford a nickel today." The boys went away satisfied because, after all, a nickel was money too.

However, when they returned the next day to hoot at him, the tailor gave them only a penny each.

"Why do we get only a penny today?" they yelled.

"That's all I can afford."

"But two days ago you gave us a dime, and yesterday we got a nickel. It's not fair, mister."

"Take it or leave it. That's all you're going to get!"

"Do you think we're going to call you 'Jew' for one lousy penny?"

"So don't."
And they didn't.

As coaches we tend to act as if we can increase a player's motivation by adding external motivation to his or her internal motivation. But the evidence is clear that external rewards decrease internal motivation in many situations. Use of external rewards can boomerang and coaches would be wise to try to help athletes develop their own motivation rather than relying on external rewards.

My friend Paul Solomon summed it up one morning while we were running together: "It's hard to be driven when you're being driven." Outstanding competitors are driven by their own internal motivation. If they have a coach who insists on driving them, either with rewards or punishment, the end result may not be increased motivation but simply a substitution of external motivation for internal motivation, and less chance that the individual will achieve greatness as a competitor.

2. **Energized by challenges:** We have all seen outstanding players who seem to disappear in the waning moments of a close game. Most people have bad days when they'd just like to be able to stay in bed with the covers pulled up over their heads. But, day in and day out, outstanding competitors usually want to be the ones on the spot at the end of the game. Make them or miss them, they would rather shoot the free throws with no time left on the clock than have a teammate do it. If they are in the on-deck circle with two outs and the tying run on second base, they want the batter to somehow get on so they can get their crack at driving that run in. If there is a sudden death shoot-out to determine who will win a tied soccer game, they want to have a chance to drive the ball past the goalie.

Outstanding competitors seem to relish challenges. During the 1991 NBA championship series, the excitement was obvious in Magic Johnson's voice when he talked about the Lakers getting to play the Chicago Bulls and Michael Jordan in the finals.

Psychologist David C. McClelland first presented the idea that different people have different needs, some for affiliation with other people, some for power, some for achievement. He found that people with high needs for achievement would work with their surroundings to create acceptable challenges for themselves. For example, when asked to play a game in which the object was to toss rings over a peg from any distance they chose, they would place the peg just far enough away to be challenging. Other people with less need for achievement would place the peg either so close that they were assured of making most of the tosses, or so far away that there was little chance of hitting it.

Need for achievement can be contrasted with "failure avoidance." Let's look at two different young athletes of the same age with the same physical ability, one an achievement-oriented person and the other failure-avoiding. The failure-avoidance person may well choose to play in a league of athletes of the same age, even though he has much more ability than his peers. Because failure is so unsavory, he chooses to play with his age group rather than experimenting with playing against older kids who might push him to develop. The achievement-oriented athlete, on the other hand, will tend to discount any success he might have playing with athletes who are clearly below his ability level. He will want to play with people who will challenge him. This is the equivalent of pushing the hat back to make the card toss more challenging.

It is important to realize that all of us have multiple needs. Rarely is someone totally oriented around any one need, such as achievement. You may find an achievement-oriented athlete who chooses to play with his age group because he also has a high need for affiliation. He simply wants to be and play with his friends. In this situation, the need for affiliation is modifying the need for achievement. However, in general, outstanding competitors want to compete at a level that will push them to be their best, not at a level where they can succeed without risk. They respond to a challenge with greater effort and seem to be energized by it.

I began to notice a difference in the play of my son this past season when he played in two different basketball leagues. On Saturdays he played for me on a Cupertino Hoops team. During the week he played for his junior high team. He exhibited an increased level of intensity in his play during the junior high games. It wasn't much of a mystery. The previous year his seventh-grade team had failed to make the end-of-the-season playoffs by one game. He and his teammates were determined to make the playoffs in the eighth grade.

It wasn't that he didn't play hard on Saturdays, but there was something extra present during the weekday games. He worked hard outside of practices to perfect his shooting and ball handling ability. Perhaps because his school team was much shorter than every team they played, he researched (and then faithfully did) exercises that could increase his vertical leap to improve his rebounding. He was responding to a challenge which clearly motivated him to higher levels of effort and performance. And I am happy to report that he and his overachieving teammates did make the playoffs and advanced to the semifinal round before losing.

3. **Seeing development as a process under their control:** In Chapter 5 I talked about the Efficacy Institute and the efficacy model of development: "Self-confidence plus effective effort equals development." Too many young athletes believe that great athletic ability is fixed—you either have it or you don't. Either way, there is not much they can do to increase or decrease their ability to play the game.

Great competitors see the development of their skills as a process which they control. If they are weak dribbling behind the back with their left hand, they understand that they can improve and that they are responsible for making the efforts required to develop that skill. And if that is a skill that is critical to their becoming the best that they can be, they will work at it until they get it right. If they cannot perform the skill in question, they attribute it to their lack of effort. They could learn it if they worked harder and longer at it.

And so they work on their game and seem to continually improve. During the 1991 NBA championship series, Dean Smith, Michael Jordan's college coach at North Carolina, mentioned that Jordan was so much more devastating on offense now than in college because he didn't have a good outside shot then. This surprised me. I had assumed that he had always had all the tools. But Michael Jordan was not able to dunk at birth. He has worked hard to improve and refine his skills even after making it to the NBA.

Part of seeing development as a process concerns how athletes attribute their success or failure. When people fail at something that is important to them, they try to understand their failure and tend to attribute it to a specific cause. Outstanding competitors tend to see the reason for their failure as lack of effort rather than bad luck or lack of talent. Basketball coach Tara VanDerveer was recently asked about her career as a ballplayer by a reporter. She indicated that she hadn't tried hard enough to be really good. Notice she didn't say that she didn't have the natural ability. She could have been great if she had put more effort into it. As sport psychologist Dorcas Susan Butt phrases it, ". . . some people see themselves as acted upon while others see themselves as acting in order to influence outcome." Great competitors attribute their success or failure to their own efforts, rather than the hand that life or genetics has dealt them.

Great competitors also tend to set their own goals. And because they set and own their goals, they tend to be highly motivated to achieve them.

One recent summer I tried a variety of ways to get my son to study algebra over summer vacation so that he might qualify for an advanced math course in the fall. Having failed to fully absorb the external motivation lesson from the Disneyland–piano lessons fiasco, I bribed him to get him to study algebra during the summer. However, predictably, when he got to the end of the external rewards (in this case, the skateboarding equipment he wanted), he stopped studying. I bemoaned his lack of motivation for something that was very important (to *me*). And in the end, he didn't qualify for the advanced math class. He came late to school on the day of the math exam and missed part of the instructions. Perhaps he really wasn't ready for the advanced class, but for sure his heart was never into the whole project.

Shortly thereafter, as I watched him skateboarding on a "quarter pipe," (a skateboard ramp in the shape of one-quarter of a giant pipe useful for doing skateboarding tricks), I was struck by what he had accomplished at a task for which *he* was motivated. The saga of the quarter pipe began one Saturday when my wife and I returned home from shopping to find Gabby feverishly clipping protruding branches in our backyard. It turns out that he intended to clear the brush in our backyard so we could install a *half* pipe (i.e., two quarter pipes connected to make a ramp) for skateboarding.

After some heated conversations about liability insurance, the fact that we rent and would need the landlord's permission, and several other nontrivial objections, he abandoned the backyard scenario and I took a nap. When I awoke, he was energetically cleaning out the garage (which had been a mess for several months). It turned out that his new plan was to put a half pipe in our garage. Well, for some of the same reasons, including a low ceiling, that didn't work out either (although it was nice to get the branches trimmed and the garage cleaned out).

Still he didn't give up. His next approach was to talk with his friend Josh, whose father (much more proficient at carpentry than I) helped them build a portable quarter pipe which Gabby and Josh used for months to perfect their skateboarding technique.

I know of few people as tenacious as my son when he is going after something that is important to *him*. When he is required to follow my (or some other adult's) program, that tenacity is typically lacking. So it is with athletes. As coaches and parents, we often have no alternative to setting limits and requiring certain behaviors. But limits and rules will not create a truly outstanding athlete. The athlete has got to want it. And he has got to want it more than you want it for him. The most you can do is to provide encouragement.

4. **Decision-makers rather than order-takers:** Much effort is expended by good coaches to improve the decision-making abilities of their athletes. When a basketball player gets a rebound, should she dribble up the floor herself? Should she pass to the guard? Should she throw a long pass to a teammate streaking up the floor? Or should she slow it down?

Based on what the defensive back in football sees in the offensive formation of the opposition, should he bump the receiver? Should he drop back a step to guard against the long pass? Should he get ready to come up to help make a tackle? A coach can help players learn to become better decision-makers but not if he is breeding dependent order-takers.

My son recently attended several summer basketball camps. Among the written material he was given in one camp was a set of "principles." One of the principles was that "the coach is always right."

I attend a lot of coaching clinics. During a recent one

which included presentations by some very successful major college coaches, I noticed how one coach in particular seemed to be trying to create dependency in his players. He wanted his players to do well academically, which is admirable. But he stressed again and again how he got them to do exactly what he told them at every moment on (and often off) the court. For a moment I wondered if I were attending a dog obedience class rather than a coaching clinic for developers of young men and women.

I am struck by how often coaches try to reinforce dependency in their players, and how mindlessly the media panders to coaches by repeating and endorsing the idea that the coach is always right. It is so rare that a player or group of players are able to stand up to dictatorial coaches that I smile whenever I see an act of independence on the part of an athlete, even if in some ways it may seem misplaced.

Outstanding competitors tend to be independent and willing to challenge conventional wisdom. They are the *unreasonable* people according to George Bernard Shaw's phrase:

> The reasonable man adapts himself to the world: the unreasonable one persists in trying to adapt the world to himself. Therefore all progress depends on the unreasonable man.

I'm sure there was a coach somewhere who told the young Bob Cousy to get rid of that silly behind-the-back dribble and those outrageous behind-the-back passes. Or perhaps there wasn't such a coach and that's why Cousy perfected his dribbling and passing skills in ways that defied the conventional wisdom of the time. Now you can see grade school kids dribbling behind the back and between the legs, and it is the rare high school point guard who doesn't routinely dribble behind her back. What was sacrilege becomes commonplace in a few generations. Ernesto Cortes, Jr., a community organizer with the Industrial Areas Foundation and winner of a MacArthur Foundation "genius award," put it this way when he spoke at the Stanford Business School last year: "There is a difference between 'tradition,' which is the living ideas of the dead, and 'traditionalism,' which is the dead ideas of the living." There are hundreds of dead ideas afflicting sport, and too many coaches who inflict them mindlessly upon their players.

Each sport evolves, and it is often the heretic like Bob Cousy who pushes it to evolve to the next step. Before George Mikan, who dominated professional basketball in the 1950s for the Minneapolis Lakers, a big man who could run and jump was an oxymoron. Big guys were *supposed* to be clumsy and slow. You parked them under the basket and they got rebounds. It was crazy to expect them to be able to dribble well in a crowd. Imagine the shock to yesterday's conventional wisdom dispensers if they could see the six foot nine inch Magic Johnson playing point guard.

Jim March, in his wonderful essay *The Technology of Foolishness*, points out that we need to legitimize experimentation. "Playfulness is the deliberate, temporary relaxation of rules in order to explore the possibilities of alternative rules." A coach who restricts a player from trying fancy-dancy moves in practice may be keeping him from stumbling onto a move that, with persistent practice, can become an important part of his repertoire. How many potential Pete Maravich's never got the chance to dazzle on the court or field because of a coach who had a system and forced all of his players into it?

5. Accepts success and failure: I believe this is the foundation characteristic. Outstanding competitors are emotionally and psychologically prepared to deal with either success or failure in any given undertaking. It may seem funny to talk about athletes fearing success but it happens all too often. The problem with being successful is that people come to expect success of you. And on any given day you may not want to deal with other people's expectations for you. It may be easier to accept being an ordinary athlete than being a great one, if everyone expects you to be great all the time. Who needs that kind of hassle? Outstanding competitors tend to be able to deal with success and not let fear of it keep them from reaching their potential.

On the other hand, fear of failure also does not paralyze an outstanding competitor. They are able to focus on the task at hand and ignore distractions. When I observed my old high school team, West Fargo, North Dakota, defend its state championship in March 1992, I was struck by the concentration that point guard and eventual tournament MVP Randy Torgrimson exhibited. In one game he was pushed hard after the whistle by a frustrated opposing player. Torgrimson showed no response to the shove. He was so focused on what he and his teammates had come to the tournament to do—win a second championship in a row—that a mere shove didn't even merit a pained expression.

We've all seen teams ahead in the middle of a big game who can't seem to maintain the lead. What often seems to happen is that teams will stop playing to win and begin playing to not lose. Their fear of losing takes them out of their normal play. Usually this means they stop doing what got them the lead in the first place, which allows the underdog team to stage a comeback. And often the comeback fails because once the score has closed again, the superior team reverts back to trying to win rather than simply not losing.

SELF-EFFICACY:
THE CRUCIAL VARIABLE IN PERFORMANCE

Warning: Don't get scared away from reading this section because "self-efficacy" is an unfamiliar term. Most people *don't* know what it means. But if you stay with it, I am convinced that you will find that it is an idea with far-reaching implications for coaching effectiveness, and one of the most important ideas you will encounter as a coach.

Psychology professor Albert Bandura has done pioneering work on the concept of self-efficacy, a person's belief about one's "capabilities to exercise control over events that affect their lives." As Bandura uses the term, self-efficacy is a situation-specific form of self-confidence. For example, a basketball player with high self-efficacy about his free throw shooting will *believe* that he is capable of doing what he needs to, to be able to make two free throws with the game on the line. And his belief about his ability is the most important determinant of whether he will in fact make them. This same person may have overall low self-confidence and low self-efficacy about his ability to learn higher level mathematics, for example.

While the research is mixed about the impact of higher self-esteem on performance, there is a great deal of evidence that indicates that increasing a person's sense of self-efficacy about an activity does lead to higher performance in that activity. In fact the evidence shows that increasing a person's sense of self-efficacy leads to the person:

- trying harder and increasing effort when confronted with obstacles
- abandoning strategies that aren't working and trying new strategies more quickly
- sticking to the task longer before giving up
- setting higher goals for oneself
- having more commitment to achieving goals

- visualizing succeeding and expecting oneself to succeed
- setting more challenging goals for oneself after the initial goals are met

You don't need to be a rocket scientist to realize that increased effort by a person over a longer period of time in pursuit of higher goals will make it more likely that he will succeed.

Much of what determines whether an individual will be successful in performing a task is how that person believes he will perform. But simply telling yourself (or having a coach tell you) that you can do something doesn't mean that you are going to *believe* that you can do it. Bandura's work suggests four ways to increase self-efficacy.

1. **Mastery experiences:** We gain in self-efficacy when we try something and have success with it. We then tend to want to try something a little bit more difficult. In direct contrast with the sink-or-swim method, taking many small successful steps over time will more often produce the outstanding swimmer. Studies of children trying to learn math indicate that having small interim goals resulted in more learning than children with no goals or with only long-term goals.

   Bandura believes effective use of mastery experiences is one reason for former San Francisco 49ers football coach Bill Walsh's success in developing outstanding quarterbacks. "He is very skilled in building quarterbacks' sense of efficacy by inserting them gradually into situations where they are very likely to succeed. In this way, he not only builds the quarterback's self-confidence but also builds the teammates' confidence that the quarterback can produce good results." Bandura notes that developing "carefully structured performance tasks that are likely to bring success" requires real skill on the part of a coach or teacher

2. **Vicarious experience:** People can gain self-efficacy watch-

ing others trying to accomplish a task they also want to be able to do. When I participated in my first ropes course I was scared and not at all confident that I could successfully negotiate those high trees. When the most competent athlete in our group did it, it had little impact on me because I knew I was not comparable in ability. But when others in my group with whom I identified gave it a try, I was emboldened. The extent to which people see other people like themselves (or less talented than themselves) modeling successful behavior, they will get a boost in self-efficacy. I once read that Jimmy Carter was inspired to run for the presidency by his interactions with other candidates. He was surprised to find that they weren't any smarter than he and so decided that if they could do it, so could he. This "if they can, so can I" attitude can be a great motivator.

It even can be motivating for people to watch others fail at a task when it is clear that they are using poor strategies. They can then conclude that they have a chance at doing better if they have a superior strategy. For example, a superior basketball team may lose because the coach played only the starters who became exhausted by the end of the game. Your players might conclude that by having a stronger bench or being in better condition, they could win.

I experienced this aspect of self-efficacy myself many years ago. I was scheduled to testify before a committee of the Oregon Legislature about the Governor's energy program. I was representing the Governor's Office for the first time before the Legislature, and I was nervous. I was scheduled to be the first speaker but the committee chairman noticed that a high ranking state commissioner was in the audience and assumed that he was there to speak for the Governor on this legislation. I expected that the commissioner would defer to me but he didn't. He sat down at the witness table and made a horrible mess. He didn't have any prepared testimony, he didn't understand the legislation, and he was unable to respond intelligently to any of the legislator's questions. As I watched and listened with horror, my nervousness left me and I felt a great and growing self-confidence. I had helped write the legislation and I knew the answers to the questions being asked. I also was angry at the damage being done by the unprepared commissioner who didn't have the sense to admit that he wasn't the right person to be testifying. By the time I got to the witness table, I was utterly confident and was successful in explaining the importance of the legislation and of undoing the initial damage.

It wasn't until many years later when I started learning about self-efficacy and writing this book that I finally understood where my surge of self-confidence had come from. I was observing a poor performance by someone I believed had some skill or ability that I lacked. I attributed his failure to poor preparation and because I was better prepared, my confidence in my ability to do well grew.

A second form of vicarious experience involves visualizing oneself overcoming obstacles to successfully complete a challenging task. Nancy Ditz, Los Angeles Marathon winner, has used visualization in this way. A newspaper article described the results. "Before a recent race, running in the heat scared her most. She imagined searing temperatures and a series of mishaps, including not having her water bottle available at expected intervals along the race course. In her mind's eye, she saw herself remaining calm and not wasting vital energy worrying about things she couldn't control. As it turned out, her water bottle wasn't available at one point during the race. And Ditz remained as calm as she had visualized she would."

3. **Verbal persuasion:** There is benefit to positive self—talk ("I think I can. I know I can.") but it needs to be part of a program and is not some stand-alone mystical quick

fix. Simply saying "I'm getting better every day" unaccompanied by effective effort to improve is not going to make one a great athlete. However, positive self-talk can short circuit negative imagination which impairs performance. For example, if I begin to get nervous about a speech I am about to make, I can remind myself that I am a good presenter. I can tell myself that I have something of interest to tell the audience. I can also get my focus off myself and onto my audience by saying that I am eager to hear what questions they might have to ask me.

If I don't know my subject, and I haven't prepared and rehearsed my speech, and I have annoying speaking habits that I've never bothered to correct, all the positive self-talk in the world is not going to cause me to give a great speech. However, if I have done the necessary groundwork, positive self-talk can displace negative thoughts in my head and help me focus on what I need to do to deliver a great speech.

4. **Interpreting arousal:** When we are in stressful situations, funny things happen to us. Our knees can shake. We may sweat. Our heart may beat rapidly. Most often we interpret these signs of arousal in ways that undermine our self-efficacy (e.g., "I'm really nervous about this game"). However, indications of bodily arousal are not necessarily harmful to self-efficacy. In Chapter 9 I discussed how to try to turn natural stage fright into a positive condition for children by telling them that there is energy associated with nervousness. Without some nervous energy, your performance is likely to be flat. If athletes have strategies to cope with the stress of bodily arousal, they will not be put off their game.

WHAT COACHES CAN DO

Every coach undoubtedly wants his players to work harder on becoming better athletes. The research on self-

efficacy gives some clear direction on how coaches can encourage their players. Here are some guidelines:

1. **Educate them about internal motivation:** Tell your kids
   about the research on the power of internal motivation.
   At the beginning of the season, tell your players that to
   be the best players they can be, they need to be internally motivated. Let them know that they are more
   likely to become great athletes if they love the sport
   and have fun with it. If they work hard only because
   you are yelling at them, they are likely to stop working
   hard when you are no longer there to yell at them.

   Ask them to spend some time thinking about how
   good they want to be by the end of the season. Tell
   them you will do your best to provide them with good
   instruction during practices but that to become really
   good they will need to motivate themselves outside of
   practice. This might be a time when you can introduce
   Bill Bradley's 10-for-13 shooting drill (described in Chapter 3), or an equivalent drill for other sports, and encourage them to complete this drill every day at all of
   the spots where they want to become deadly.

   You might also talk about conditioning in this context. You might begin and/or end your basketball practices with "liners," or, as they called them when I was in
   high school, "crushers" (in which players run from the
   base line to the first free throw line and touch it, then
   return to the base line and touch it; run to the half-
   court line and touch it, return; run to the far free throw
   line and touch it, return; run to the far base line and
   touch it, run all the way back to where they started).
   Then ask who would like to run an additional set. Don't
   badger them to do it. You want to give them the space
   to do it *at their own initiative*. Most kids most of the time
   will run an additional set (or sets), and because they are
   choosing to do so, they will be strengthening their internal motivation rather than simply responding to the

(external) coach requiring them to do it. In many cases, you will find that kids will do several more sets than you would think of inflicting upon them.

In particular, avoid what psychologists call "contingent rewards," which almost always undermine an athlete's internal motivation. A contingent reward is a situation in which the athlete knows beforehand that she will receive a reward if she accomplishes a task. Because of this prior knowledge, she will tend to believe that the reason she worked so hard (assuming she did) is because she wanted the reward. A reward that is given afterwards with no prior knowledge doesn't undermine internal motivation because the athlete clearly didn't know about it.

2. **Encourage them to see skills as acquirable:** People will try harder to learn a skill that they believe is mostly acquirable rather than mostly inherited. Studies have looked at how well people do in trying to improve a skill. In one case they are led to believe that the skill in question is primarily an inherited one; in a second case they are told that it is an acquirable skill. Not surprisingly, people in the second category do much better. This may seem obvious, but I guarantee you that many, many kids don't believe that skill in sports is acquirable.

By emphasizing how players you have known have acquired skills through practice, you can encourage your team members to make efforts to also acquire those skills. Earlier in this book I mentioned how Chris Mullin became a great "natural" shooter through years of practice. Rick Telander, as described in *Heaven is a Playground*, asked Ernie DiGregorio how he became an outstanding college basketball player and NBA rookie of the year in spite of his physical limitations: " 'Six feet tall, chunky, slow, with short arms, chubby fingers, and no jumping ability . . .

" 'You know,' Ernie said . . . 'nobody gets up at six in the morning to play ball. But I did. At twelve years old my mind was made up that I was going to play pro ball. TV did it to me, I think—watching fans go crazy. I started practicing nine, ten hours a day. By myself. With gloves. And I loved it. They could've cut my right hand off and I'd have played one-handed'."

A variety of role model athletes can be useful here. When Guin Boggs gave his shoot-the-lights-out basketball clinic for Cupertino Hoops players last year, he began by shooting 18-foot baskets while he talked. He said some interesting things about his dedication to learning to become a great shooter. He had not been an outstanding high school player and was not recruited by colleges. But he spent an amazing amount of time shooting during the summer after he graduated and then became a walk-on at San Jose State University. Because his shooting had improved so much, he soon became a starter.

Now this is an inspiring story all by itself. But imagine the impact of him shooting all the while he talked and making 95 percent or more of his shots. At one point I counted 63 in a row, followed by 47, followed by 82. He had the kids' attention. And given his lack of major college height, he was a very credible role model for the importance of practice in acquiring skills such as shooting the lights out.

3. **Provide mastery experiences for key skills:** There is an old story about the farm boy who was able to lift a cow. He was asked how he had gotten to be so strong. He replied that he started when the cow was a newborn calf. He lifted it every day without fail and since the cow's growth was gradual, he had always been able to lift it the next day with just a little bit more effort. This story, while of dubious accuracy, has a lesson for coaches. If you break up the process of learning a critical but advanced skill into little steps, most athletes will be able to move from one step to the next without getting discouraged.

Determine what the essential skills for success for your players are, and then devise ways to help your players master them. Let's look at the example of making lay-ups in basketball. Almost any basketball player who has played for several years can consistently make lay-ups in practice. But making a lay-up under pressure in a game situation is something else, attested to by the many missed lay-ups in virtually any hotly contested high school or college game. Sophisticated observers of basketball quickly distinguish those players that are "closers" (i.e., they *make* the lay-ups) and those who often end what starts out as a great defensive play, stealing the ball, by missing the lay-up.

Let's say that you are coaching a group of fifth-graders. To help each player master the long-term goal of becoming a strong closer, you might follow this sequence.

a. Teach the fundamentals of dribbling and shooting a lay-up and work on this in every practice until players can consistently make 90 percent or more of their lay-ups starting their dribble from just beyond the free throw line. Start from the shooter's natural hand side, then from the reverse side, and then straight on.

b. Introduce lay-ups shot after getting a pass while cutting to the basket.

c. Have players shoot lay-ups with the coach standing near the basket and waving his hands to distract the shooter.

d. Introduce the "good hands" drill in which a coach (later it can be done with a teammate) will make a bad pass to players who must adjust to be able to catch the ball and then turn their concentration to putting the ball in the basket.

e. Have the lay-up shot with the player dribbling from just inside the half-court line with a defender just behind the line. The shooter must go full speed to the basket and make it with the defender bearing down on him.

f. Repeat the previous step, starting after getting a rebound and dribbling the length of the court with a defender chasing him.

There are nearly infinite variations that can be introduced into this sequence. If combined with interim goal-setting and charting (see guideline 4), you will find yourself with with a team of closers by the end of the season. This approach of developing a progression of mastery exercises can be applied to almost any skill in any sport, although it will take some time and thought to develop each interim step.

4. **Encourage personal goal-setting and charting:** In Chapter 2, I presented the idea that people tend to do what gets measured. Research has clearly demonstrated that challenging goals are motivating to children (and adults for that matter). And goals are that much more motivating when they are set by the person himself.

Ideally goals will be established either by the athlete herself or by the coach and the athlete together. Start out by asking players to write down the goals they want to achieve during the season. Writing is critical because it sends the signal that this is serious enough to take some care with it. A written record also helps both you and your players keep a focus. It is something that you can look up if you forget. Once the player has formed her goals, keep a copy with your clipboard at each practice for easy reference.

You can help provide feedback on how well your players are doing in reaching their goals, being careful not to take ownership away from them. Positive charting, described in Chapter 2, can be tailored to include goals that the athlete herself selects as well as ones that you ask her to work on.

Charting of goals that are measurable and clear is a critical part of providing athletes with a program of mastery experiences. For example, after teaching the proper way to shoot a reverse lay-up, you can chart each player's reverse lay-ups once a week at practice. You can give each player 10 or 15 chances and keep track of how many are made from one week to the next. Carry the charts with you to each practice so players can assess their progress from one practice to the next. And, of course, the ideal is when the athlete is charting his own progress on his work outside of practice.

Encourage players to set both long-term and interim goals. Children who set both kinds of goals do better at meeting their long-term goals than those who set only long-term goals. It is also wise to minimize the number of goals that are beyond the control of the athletes. For example, having the goal of hitting .300 for the season is partly dependent upon how good the pitching is, something over which your player has no control. That is not to say that you should overrule this kind of a goal. Rather, help the player fill out the long-term goal with interim ones that will help make the larger goal come true. For example, the batter may have trouble hitting low pitches. An interim goal might be to take a certain number of swings per practice, at low pitches, either with a pitching machine or an adult pitching. His interim goal might be to keep on swinging until he connects solidly on a low pitch 20 times each day. It may be difficult to meet this interim goal (given limited availability of fields or pitching machines), but there is little doubt that if he is able to do so, his longer-term goal is more likely to be achieved.

A final point about goals is to try to make them comparisons with oneself rather than other players. The most important thing is continued development. A player who focuses only on his relative standing with another athlete could end up cheating himself in either direction. He might be the best athlete without having to improve much. If he gauges his development only against others, he may well sell himself short. On the other hand, if he matches up poorly against others at the beginning of the season, he may make major improvements but not recognize them because the opposition has also improved.

Once you get your players setting interim and long-term goals that are used to compare themselves with where they started, and charting their progress toward meeting those goals, you will wonder how you ever coached so long without them.

5. **Focus on the do-able parts of any challenge:** You can't make a basketball player grow when she is playing against a taller opponent. But you can emphasize areas of competition that she is able to control. For example, by relentlessly blocking out on rebounds, a smaller person can often neutralize a bigger person. Stress the importance of what your smaller athlete *can* do and avoid focusing on factors beyond her control, such as height.

In describing the factors in her team's second national title in three years, Tara VanDerveer attributed some of it to the superior conditioning of her big players. Many outstanding teams have guards, like Stanford's, who are in great shape. But Stanford's big players also could run the floor all game long, eventually leaving their opposite numbers, who weren't in guard-like condition, gasping by the fourth quarter. No matter what talent level a ballplayer has, he can be in great shape. And sometimes at the end of a game, it is not the one with the most talent who prevails but rather the one with enough energy left to make that last effort.

6. **Encourage generous estimation of relative ability:** In ninth grade I played football for my West Fargo Junior High team. At the end of the year we had an intersquad game with players from our high school B-squad. Each time I was tackled by one or several players from the opposing team, I refused to fall. I kept digging and got several additional yards before I finally was dragged down. My determination to not be easily tackled was in

distinct contrast to how I had run during the regular season games against teams from other junior high schools. It wasn't that I hadn't tried when I played against other teams. But I hadn't tried *as hard* as I was trying in that intersquad game. I knew the kids I was playing against, I was convinced that I was a better athlete than most of them, and I wasn't about to let them tackle me so easily. Against teams from Fargo and Moorhead, I was not so sure about my relative ability, and so I hadn't reached down to find the extra effort as I had in the intersquad game. The irony is that the ability of the high school B-squad members probably wasn't all that much different than that of the other junior high players. Had I tried as hard then I might have been . . . oh well.

Stark realism about one's own abilities is *not* an advantage, and can even be a handicap. Shelley Taylor, in her book *Positive Illusions*, notes, "Increasingly, we must view the psychologically healthy person not as someone who sees things as they are but as someone who sees things as he or she would like them to be."

Imagine an athlete, who believes she is a better basketball player than she really is, driving the lane against a larger, more talented player. Several things can happen here, many of them good. She may make the basket. She may get fouled. Or she may not get fouled but the referee may think she did and call a foul. And then she may make the free throws while causing the fouling player to get into foul trouble. She may have had no business trying to drive the lane against a player who is so much bigger and better. But because of her slightly unrealistic evaluation of her own ability, she did it anyway and it paid off. If her perception of her own abilities was merely realistic, she probably wouldn't even have tried it and none of those good things could have happened.

Jim Pruitt, in *Play Better Basketball*, suggests ways a

player can improve his quickness that border on self-deception. "You are quick if you think you are . . . (this) is true because self-confidence and its product, aggressiveness, are integral parts of overall quickness. The opposite of this fact is the old adage, 'He who hesitates is lost.' *Making an unhesitating move* will help you be quick."

For years, radio host Garrison Keillor ended each of his "Prairie Home Companion" radio show monologues with the phrase, "So that's the news from Lake Wobegon, where the women are strong, the men are good-looking, and all the children are above average" (sometimes adding "every single one of them"). People gain energy through favorable comparisons with others. If you can help your players see that they have the potential to be "above average" (every single one of them) in their sport, they are likely to work harder to achieve that potential.

7. **Desensitize them to pressure:** There is an old saying that the greater part of courage is having done something before. The second time we have to face a challenge, it almost always seems less scary. The process of desensitizing people to a fear has become quite sophisticated in some cases, but the heart of it is exposure under controlled circumstances to that which is feared. And for most athletes, the greatest fear is that one will "choke" under pressure.

There is convincing research evidence that pressure degrades performance of almost any task. A coach can assist a player by desensitizing him to pressure. Sports psychologist Tom Tutko suggests the simple idea of getting players used to handling pressure by introducing pressure situations into practice sessions. For example, I regularly have team shooting contests in which players are divided into roughly equal teams. The team that first makes 13 (or 17 or . . .) baskets from a given spot wins. We talk about how pressure degrades performance and why they missed so many easy shots.

Then we do the exercise again. We repeat this quite often during the season from different distances as the players get better at shooting from longer distances. I've found that you can start with reasonably close distances for shooting because the introduction of pressure degrades performance to make what is normally easy more difficult.

Another exercise is to shoot free throws late in a practice session when everyone is tired. The players shoot a one-and-one. If they make the first one they get to shoot another. If they miss the first one they run a lap, which simulates a game situation where making or missing the first free throw has a consequence. A player who has experienced this artificial pressure consistently in practice will be more used to it when it occurs in a game situation.

Another important component to helping your players learn to deal with pressure depends upon your attitude and behavior. You are a role model to your players. If you have fun with your sport, they will be more likely to do so. If you downplay the importance of winning relative to doing one's best, they will also. And as I have asserted several times in this book, the irony is that when an athlete focuses on doing her best, she experiences less pressure and is more likely to win than if she rigidly focuses on winning as the only thing of value.

8. **Be influence-able:** There is much evidence that it is a person's feeling of having little or no control over his environment, not stress itself, that permits stress to overwhelm him. People who have ways of coping and believe that a situation is manageable do not become stressed out.

A coach is an important part of an athlete's environment. If your players believe they have influence with you, their sense of self-efficacy is likely to be increased. Give them a break. Listen to them, even solicit their opinions about how the team can deal with certain problems or generally improve. Take their advice and opinions to heart and implement them as much as possible.

Sam Saddler, who worked with me in the Oregon Department of Energy, was a master at getting people to agree with his written policy recommendations. Once I asked him how he did it. He said that when it didn't make any difference one way or the other, he did it the other person's way. So much of what we argue with others about just doesn't really matter. We get wrapped up in our authority, when the reality is that many times a player's suggestion about how to run a drill (or whatever) would work as well as our way. Family therapist Virginia Satir put it well: "Beware the tyranny of the one 'right' way."

By being influence-able, coaches can contribute to their players' sense of self-efficacy.

WHAT COACHES CAN'T DO

I have seen a few coaches and parents who are bound and determined to make their kids into superstars. Tragically, they more often have the reverse effect. This chapter began with the first rule of coaching kids, which was "Do no damage." I will end it with a related rule, the last rule of developing great competitors: "You can't do it." As in "*You* can't do it." You can *nurture* it but you can't *do* it without an athlete who wants it *more* than you want it for her or him.

Think about that. It's when people *really* want something that they become truly creative. They tap into a passion that gets them thinking and working to make it happen. A coach can help stimulate that but it ultimately has to be centered in the individual. As much as you may want a particular young person to achieve her potential for sports greatness, *she* has to want it even more. If you want greatness for an athlete more than he wants it for himself, he's not going to make it, and you're not going to make it happen for him.

So relax. Enjoy coaching. Build self-efficacy and nurture the characteristics of great competitors in *all* your players. Ultimately it's up to them. That's the way it works.

14

Helping Individuals Become a Team

People on a meshed team will help each other personally . . . A group of self-dedicated soloists, on the other hand, never ceases its internal competition.

—Bill Bradley
Life on the Run

Sidney Lumet's captivating 1957 movie, *Twelve Angry Men*, examines the inner workings of a jury. Henry Fonda plays an architect who labors to convince his fellow jurors that they should look more closely at the evidence against a young man accused of murder. At the beginning of the film, 11 of the 12 are prepared to find him guilty and get out of there quickly. The architect believes there is something wrong with the case against the boy. He is clever enough to begin to convince other jurors that they should take a second look. The most memorable scene for me is when some of the *other* jurors begin to really tackle the problem of what happened. Once the architect unlocks the minds of the jurors, they *become* intelligent for the first time in the movie. They closely examine the evidence against the boy, and they too begin to uncover inconsistencies.

What begins as a stereotypical case of an all-knowing

leader telling his followers what to do veers off in an unexpected direction as the jurors begin to play off each other's observations and ideas. They become so insightful that they uncover flaws in the evidence that even the architect didn't notice.

All too often the idealized profile of a coach is that of a genius who directs his players like puppets. I believe that the Fonda character in *Twelve Angry Men* is a more suitable ideal of a coach: someone who unlocks the capabilities of groups of people.

BETTER THAN THEY SHOULD HAVE TO BE

Taylor Branch, author of *Parting the Waters*, a prize-winning book about Martin Luther King and the civil rights movement, spoke at Stanford recently. One of the points he made was that leadership often requires followers to be "better than they should have to be." When African Americans are being beaten, they shouldn't have to be nonviolent. When Indians in South Africa were being abused by the ruling government, they shouldn't have had to be nonviolent. When a Nordstrom's clerk is yelled at by a customer, she shouldn't have to be polite back to the irate customer.

When a basketball team has played a more talented team to a standstill for four quarters, they shouldn't have to play an overtime session at an even higher level of performance. They may not believe they have it in themselves to play five more minutes hard, but coaching leadership can and should ask them to try.

Leadership often demands commitments from followers not only greater than they should have to make but sometimes even greater than the followers believe they are capable of making.

Asking your players to achieve excellence, to become more than they believe they are capable of, is a crucial step in developing a high performance team. The story of Roger

Bannister and the four-minute mile is instructive. For years, the four-minute barrier was unattainable. Then right after Bannister broke four minutes, the floodgates opened with many runners achieving times below four minutes. He pushed a whole generation of runners into a new level of performance.

When I was in high school in North Dakota in the 1960s, the state champion mile was typically run in just under five minutes. Recently I attended a junior high track meet here in California at which the winning miler, an eighth-grader, ran the mile in 4:36.

I have to admit that I write this section with some trepidation that it might be taken out of the context of the rest of this book and used to browbeat kids into performing for the sake of coaches or parents. I discussed in Chapter 13 my belief that outstanding individual performances rarely come from people who are motivated primarily by external factors (such as a coach who "drives" them). And in Chapter 11, I covered the impact of "too-high standards."

Here I am talking about inspiring your players as a group to reach for the stars; *asking* them (rather than ordering them) to make a commitment to achieve a level of achievement that most groups rarely experience. In short, to become a team. But before you can expect a group of players to learn to work together as a team, you need to recognize the factors that tend to keep them from doing that.

SELF-PROTECTION STRATEGIES*

Groups are dangerous. Groups can make people do things they don't want to do. Groups can embarrass people and

*As a student at the Stanford Graduate School of Business, I had the privilege of taking a course developed by Jerry Porras and David Bradford, called "Interpersonal Dynamics" (or "Touchy-Feely" as it was known). Touchy-Feely is one of the most popular courses in the school, and for good reason. Many of the insights about groups contained in this section and in the following section entitled "The Requirements of a Successful Team" were first encountered in this course. Naturally, any faulty interpretations are my responsibility.

lower their self-esteem. Groups can take advantage of people and not acknowledge their contribution to the group.

Everyone, children included, realizes the power that a group can have. Whenever we enter a new group, we try to protect ourselves. We worry about protecting ourselves until we become convinced that the group will not hurt us. We engage in self-protection behaviors that minimize the possibility that a group will harm us.

There are four types of self-protection strategies that individuals use when they enter a new group: fight, flight, alliance-building, and scapegoating.

1. **Fight:** Some people respond to the anxiety that comes with uncertainty by trying to organize things to remove the uncertainty. They take charge and face the threat by becoming more aggressive. Fight-response athletes may become bossy to other players and give directions at least partly to convince themselves that there is some sense to the world and to this group of players.

   They may even give directions for things they themselves don't know how to do correctly. The anxiety of dealing with the ambiguity of the situation, and not knowing what is going to happen next, drives them to take charge regardless of their competency to do so.

   It may be that having some take-charge players on your team will be useful, just as organizers are useful in most groups in business as well as sports. The key issue is the goal of the organizer. Is her goal to contribute to a successful team or is it to reduce her own anxiety? Organizing energy when it is directed for the benefit of the team can be wonderful. When the principle motivation is self-protection, more often than not, it will be counterproductive.

2. **Flight:** On the other hand, many of us tend to lie low, to try to get the lay of the land before committing to anything that might expose us to vulnerability. I tend to take my time in a new group, trying to sense where

people are coming from, seeing how I might fit in, testing the waters to see how people would respond if I disagreed with them. And, until I have checked things out, I am reluctant to commit myself to it. Once I become convinced that I am safe in the group, I tend to be a vocal, enthusiastic member. Occasionally people that know me from one setting where I am comfortable will be surprised at my low profile behavior in a setting where I don't feel comfortable.

As with fight behaviors, it is probably useful in most situations for groups to have members who look before they leap. But if the goal of the person is self-protection rather than advancement of the group toward its goals, the person may not speak out when that is exactly what the group needs to hear.

3. **Alliance-building:** Another strategy closely related to the lie-low approach is to look for other individuals within the group that one can ally with. For example, in a group setting I might compliment another member on a comment she made. "I think Muriel has got the right idea with her suggestion that . . ." Now it may be that I really do think a lot of Muriel's idea. But it may also be that what I am really saying beneath the surface is, "Muriel, look how I am supporting you in this group. If you support me, I will continue to support you. Then if the group picks on one of us, at least we'll have an alliance that can protect us." As in the above cases, letting others know that you support them and like their ideas can be a very useful action in a group. But the issue is whether the primary objective of the person sending the message is to move the group forward or to protect himself.

4. **Scapegoating:** Perhaps the most insidious of the self-protection strategies is to seek a scapegoat. If we can blame everything on someone else, no one will think to blame us. Or if they do, we may be able to shift the blame onto the scapegoat.

Some coaches try to focus the attention on a common enemy outside the team. There are lots of examples of coaches who put quotes from the opposing coach or an opposing player on the locker room bulletin board to motivate his team to focus on beating an external enemy. There are few things as satisfying to a team as beating a team that has denigrated its abilities. But resorting to using external enemies can often backfire. While your players' level of effort may increase, it is not clear that concentration or overall performance increases with increased negative emotion focused on an external enemy. A violent, collision-oriented sport like football is one thing. But performance in a sport relying more on finesse and timing like basketball or baseball may actually be harmed.

And if you don't win, the bitter feelings tend to be expressed closer to home, which gets the players (and sometimes the parents) back to looking for an internal scapegoat, possibly including the coach.

While I am ambivalent about the use of external enemies, the use of a scapegoat within the team is always a destructive tactic. I believe it is the coach's responsibility (and that of the leader in any organization) to prevent the group from focusing on a scapegoat internally. Most often when a scapegoat is chosen, it is someone who is a little bit different from the rest. It often, but not always, is the weakest player. It can be a player from "the other side of the tracks." It could be a kid who looks different, perhaps someone who's overweight. It may be someone whose family doesn't have as much money as the norm for that community, which may be reflected in his wearing "weird" clothes.

One reason that scapegoats are so prevalent is that the scapegoated individual often "nominates" himself to be the scapegoat. The child may have habits that bug the coaches and the other players. They may seem not to be trying (and in fact may not be) as hard as the other kids to win. If the team is winning, these habits are easier to overlook. But when you lose, it is easier to look for a scapegoat than to confront the fact that you got beat by a better team, or a team that tried harder, or one that was luckier, or even one that was better coached. Scapegoats are intrinsically different from the first three self-protection strategies in that the use of scapegoats is *never* a positive influence on a team.

You can be confident that your players will continue to engage in self-protection strategies *until* they become convinced that the team poses no danger to them. When most of the coaches and players have reached this level of confidence, you have the potential to become a team in more than name only.

THE REQUIREMENTS OF A SUCCESSFUL TEAM

Professional sports teams have been known to use up a player while he is useful to the team and then spit him out when his usefulness is ended. I was disheartened as a boy when *my* team, the New York Yankees, traded my hero, North Dakota native Roger Maris, to the St. Louis Cardinals only a few years after he had broken Babe Ruth's home run record. How could they do that?! I never loved the Yankees again as I had before that. I learned that sports was a business and one that could treat players as expendable commodities, sometimes even at lower levels of competition. When an organization treats its members primarily as commodities that can be easily exchanged for other commodities, it is unlikely to see a team emerge.

Whenever a new group assembles, there is a sorting out process that it must go through before it can become a team that works together toward a common goal. There are four general requirements that must be satisfied in the minds of your players (and coaches for that matter) before

273

they can begin to work together as a team to accomplish the group goals of playing as well as they can and winning. They are *acceptance* by the group, feeling that one has adequate *influence* within the group, having an *identity* in the group, and believing that the individual will win if the group wins (*goal matching*).

1. **Acceptance:** Each player must feel that she is accepted by her coaches and teammates before she can devote anything close to 100 percent of her energies to improving as an athlete and helping the team win. For example, are the other players going to accept me if I strike out with the winning run on third base? What if I miss the first of a one-and-one free throw that loses a crucial basketball game? On the other hand, if I am successful, will my teammates and coaches be happy for me or just that the team won?

   You can often tell by watching players at a practice which ones feel they really aren't on an equal footing with the others. Until each player is certain he is accepted, he will be conflicted, with wasted energy distracting him from the real job. Many of the ideas put forth in Chapter 5 on building self-esteem address this concern directly. By communicating clearly that your players are important to you regardless of how well they perform, you help them get past this first requirement.

2. **Influence:** Will the coach put me in a situation where I will look foolish, or worse? All groups demand something from their members. Is this team going to make me do something I don't want to do . . . something I believe I am unable to do . . . something that will hurt me . . . or something that is against my values? If so, I will never stop looking over my shoulder. Once I have a sense that I can exert an adequate amount of influence over what happens to me on the team, *then* I can throw myself wholeheartedly into helping the team win. The

suggestions in Chapter 5 on influence-ability and listening are especially useful for helping players believe that they don't have to be afraid in this particular group.

3. **Identity:** Am I an important member of this team, or is it simply that every team has to have 12 players and they had to pick me? Do I have a role that will help the team achieve its goals? If the team wins but I have had no hand in it, I am less likely to rejoice in the victory. In many cases, a player may be secretly (because it can be dangerous to reveal it) happier in a defeat where he played well than in a victory where he contributed nothing.

Last year I had the chance to observe Stan Morrison, men's basketball coach at San Jose State University, conduct a practice. Several times Morrison went to great lengths to praise the group of athletes that were playing the part of the opposing team. He recognized the important role that the "shadow" team played in getting the starters prepared to play at its peak against a given opponent. From the spirited play of the shadow team, it was obvious to me that the shadow players saw themselves as an important part of the team even though most of them rarely saw action in a game.

On the other hand, I recently watched a high school basketball game between two of the top girls teams in the state. At one point one of the star players for Team A grabbed a rebound and turned to pass it to a teammate breaking for an outlet pass. When she recognized who she was about to pass to, she abruptly diverted the pass into a dribble, until she saw Team A's other star player and then passed to her. There were two interesting things about this action. The first is that what might have been a fast break leading to an easy basket turned into something much slower. But the more interesting issue is what the refusal to pass signaled to the nonrecipient. It was an unmistakable vote of no confidence that could hardly have helped her feel she had an important role to play. Every team had to put five players on the floor at every moment, but she was treated, at least in this one instance, as a place-holder rather than a real member of a real team.

Tom Tutko recommends a simple procedure to reinforce each player's identity on a team: ask players to pick a nickname for themselves, something that they've always wanted to be called. Letting players pick the number they want to wear might also be more meaningful than adults would ever imagine. The coach that looks for ways to help each player feel like an important part of the team will find them, and that will help the player meet this need and thus be able to focus on helping the team succeed.

4. **Goal matching:** Each player needs to feel that he wins if the team wins. Every good salesperson knows—and great coaches are usually great salespersons—that the person making the decision to buy a product needs to benefit personally from the decision, irrespective of what the benefits to the organization might be. Robert Miller and Stephen Heiman, in their book *Strategic Selling*, point out the distinction between a "result" and a "win."

A *result* is something that is good in the abstract for the organization. For example, purchasing a new computer system might help the organization improve efficiency, cut costs, and thereby increase profits. But in each sale there is a key buyer who makes the go/no-go decision. A *win* is something that personally and concretely benefits the decision-maker. It is not difficult to envision a scenario in which the organization may benefit from the purchase of the new computer system (a positive result) while the decision-maker will actually lose status and influence (definitely *not* a win). For example, the new system may reduce the need for employees under the decision-maker's supervision. If, as is the case in many organizations, managers gain status and influence by the number of employees they supervise, the decision-maker is not likely to buy a system that will reduce the number of employees under his supervision. The savvy computer salesperson realizes that she needs to be concerned about providing a win for the decision-maker. If she focuses only on the results to the organization, she well may lose the sale in spite of the benefits to the organization as a whole.

The parallel for coaches is clear. All too often coaches will focus on results for the entire team without asking what would constitute a win for the individual players. Like the business scenario described above, it's not hard to imagine a situation in which a basketball team would benefit from the point guard passing more and shooting less. But if the point guard gets his internal goodies from shooting and scoring, the coach would do well to figure out how to convince him that he will benefit even more if the team wins.

One way to directly address this issue is simply to ask each of your players what their goals are. Awhile back I started sitting down individually with each player at the beginning of the season to ask them a series of questions about their goals for the season. My focus was on each player as an individual so I was pleasantly surprised when one of my players said his goal was for the team "to win a lot of games." I was thinking almost totally in terms of individual goals so his team-oriented response impressed me. I have since revised my list of goal questions to include both individual and team goals, and to ask about the interrelation of the team and the individual both winning.

LIKING VERSUS CARING

As coaches, it is a treat to work with kids that we like. And it is even better when the kids on a team all like each other. But it is rare in any situation in life where all the people working together will like and enjoy spending time with each other. It is much more typical to have a mixed bag. You will find it easy to like some of your players and not so easy with some others. Some players will be best buddies with each other, and some just won't click. In some cases players may actually dislike each other, particularly if playing time is a limited resource (as it usually is), and they are competing for it.

As a coach I do not expect all of my players to like each other, but I do want them to learn to care about each other. In one sense, liking someone is involuntary (at least initially; see "The Hard-to-Like Kid" in Chapter 15). You either do or you don't. Perhaps you get to like someone as you get to know them better but in general, liking is instinctive.

Caring, on the other hand, is an act of will. You can *decide* that you are going to care for someone and you can learn to do it. You can decide that you are going to act in ways that benefit another person even if you don't particularly like them. And this is the standard that I aspire to with my teams and players: acting in ways that show we care about each other.

THE PORTABLE HOME COURT ADVANTAGE

Much of the material in this chapter is somewhat theoretical. I firmly believe that there is nothing so practical as a good theory, but the key to making that happen is to be able to figure out how to put a theory into practice in a way that makes sense in the specific situation. The most vivid way I have found of making the ideas in this chapter come to life is the specific application of a well-known phrase, the home court advantage.

I start early in a season by asking my teams why the home team in basketball so often wins. This often sparks interesting thought processes on the part of the players.

Usually they come up with answers such as having the home crowd rooting for them causes players to try harder, play with more confidence, and thus do better.

My friend Mike Saxenian told me about his high school fencing team, which took the sport very seriously. Because they usually got little competition from other high schools, they competed against college fencing teams. What's more, they usually won. He mentioned that he and his teammates were "so obnoxious" about rooting for each other that the other teams tended to become dispirited. In effect, his team took their home court advantage with them.

I tell my players that we can do the same thing for ourselves, that we can take our home court advantage with us by supporting each other in visible, audible ways. I tell them that what typically happens with most teams is that whenever a player makes a mistake, the other players start to criticize him. By supporting each other, by saying things like "it's okay to make a mistake," or "nice try, now focus on the next play," we can create an atmosphere in which we will do better because we become our own home court advantage.

One way of making the home court advantage visible in basketball is by asking players to clap for each other during warm-ups. I recently asked my team of eighth-grade girls to clap twice every time a player made a lay-up in warm-ups, and to clap once every time someone missed one. The idea is that they are supporting each other on every play, but there is an extra incentive to actually make the basket and hear the double clap ring out. From then on, in every game we played, the warm-ups became an opportunity for the players to let each other know they were there with a home court advantage.

In Chapter 5, I described the power of using athletes' names. California Lutheran University men's basketball coach Mike Dunlap has some interesting methods for team building using players' names. He begins practice with a three-person weave with the goal of making 20 baskets in

a row without having the ball touch the floor (you'd naturally reduce the goal for younger players). But he adds a
kicker. Each player must yell out the name of the player he
is passing to as he does so. If any player fails to name his
teammate, it counts as a miss and the process begins again.
Dunlap also runs drills in his summer camp that reinforce
players for making an assist—the ultimate team play in
basketball. The offensive team gets to stay on offense as
long as it scores *and* the player who scores yells out a
thank-you and the name of his teammate who passed him
the ball.

I recently was running at a local track where a karate
club was exercising. They seemed to have great group
spirit so I began to observe their routines. At one point
they ran laps in groups of five with the last person in line
sprinting to the front of the line. As soon as that person
reached the front, the new last person sprinted to the
front and so on.

I was intrigued so I have begun to experiment with this
conditioning technique with my team. I divide them into
groups of four or five and have them run laps around the
field in this fashion. You can run the drill first without any
other instructions. Then as they are huffing and puffing
after getting a drink, you can talk about two different
ways that this exercise can be used by them. They can
think of themselves as individuals who compete with each
other. Or they can use this conditioning drill as a way to
become a team.

I ask them to think of themselves as a team that can
help each other get into better condition. We talk about
how members of a team can help each other get better.
For example, they can yell encouragement to each other.
They can cheer when a slower person makes a huge effort
and sprints to the head of the line. Then we do the drill
again, and we repeat it at least once during every practice.
In my mind the payoff in developing team spirit is even
greater than the payoff in improved conditioning.

AWARDS THAT UNDERMINE TEAM SPIRIT

Sometimes team spirit can be fractured by the selection of most valuable players or other methods for determining who gets how much credit for the team's success. There is an old saying, "It's amazing how much you can get done if it doesn't matter who gets the credit." The reverse is all too true as well. It is depressing how little gets accomplished when people focus on who gets the credit. I tend to avoid MVP type awards, which often backfire with 11 kids coming away feeling like the least-valuable player and resentful of the one. Instead I try to give each child an award that says something about the unique contribution each made to the team (see Chapter 17). However, in many situations you will not have control over the kinds of awards given out. But you can take precautions to help prevent awards from undermining the team spirit you have worked so hard to instill.

Fred Miller tells of how he helped his older daughter, Hillary, feel terrific about the success of her younger sister, Laura. Laura was progressing rapidly as a swimmer, to the point that Fred was informed by the coach that she was about to be chosen as the swim team's outstanding swimmer for the year. Fred recognized a couple of things here. First he realized that a good part of Laura's success was due to the fact that she had an older sister who helped her learn and provided a role model. Second, he realized that it might be hard for the older girl to gracefully accept the fact that younger sister was receiving the top award from the club that both swam for.

Before the swim team's award banquet, Fred told Hillary that if Laura were selected as the team's best swimmer, he would take *Hillary* out for dinner since she had helped Laura become a better swimmer. When Laura was announced as the outstanding swimmer, Hillary was unambiguously delighted for her sister, and for herself. Fred is a master at designing incentives for groups to become teams,

281

but you don't have to be a genius to find ways of linking a group's success with that of each individual on the team.

THE ULTIMATE COACHING HIGH: BEATING BETTER TALENT

There are few things in life more exciting than watching a highly functioning team in action. The old New York Knicks with Willis Reed, Walt Frazier, Dave DeBusschere, Jerry Lucas, Earl Monroe, Bill Bradley, Dick Barnett, and Phil Jackson were a delight to watch. They hit the open man. Players moved well without the ball. Unselfishness reigned.

But one experience that is even more enjoyable than seeing a great team in action is being part of it yourself. If watching a team like this in operation is great, imagine the thrill when you are part of such a team. Occasionally in my years of coaching, things have clicked and the individual players have become a unit, functioning as if with a common brain.

My favorite situation as a coach is to have a team that is a little bit weaker than the better teams in the league. I often wonder at coaches who work so hard to get the most talented players on their team, and then win every game by wide margins. To me this doesn't necessarily say anything about the quality of coaching. And since a more talented group of individuals often can beat weaker opposition even if they don't particularly play well together, it doesn't even say much about whether the group jelled together as a team.

On the other hand, I relish facing a team that has better talent on a player-by-player basis. When you have a group of players who aren't quite as good as the most talented teams, you have the chance to rise to a challenge—as a coach, as individual players, and, most importantly, as a team. In this situation, even losing can be a triumph when you play over your head and come much closer to winning than anyone (except you and your players) would ever have thought you could. And when you win, it provides a feeling of deep satisfaction for each contributing member of the team. It means that you have realized the ultimate— you've created a team, an organism greater than the sum of the individual parts.

And no one has better defined what a team is all about than one of my players this past season: "Just caring about each other and wanting each other to do well." If you can help your players achieve that state of mind, you will have helped them become something rare and wonderful—a true team.

15

Coaching the *Special* Kids

> *It is only as a child's total uniqueness is respected that he can permit his individuality to unfold.*
>
> —Dorothy Corkille Briggs
> *Your Child's Self-Esteem*

O_{ne} of the greatest challenges a coach faces is dealing with special kids with special needs. It's hard enough to coach a team of players who are all pretty similar in age, ability, interest in the sport, and background. When one or more of the kids are special in some important way, it gets more complicated.

This chapter examines several of the most common special situations you may find yourself in, and offers some suggestions for how to deal with them. One qualification: *most* kids are special and within these categories, you'll find an infinite variation. For example, every coach's kid is not the same. Some are good athletes, some are not. Some play for themselves, some play to meet the expectations of their parents. But with that caveat in mind, let's plunge ahead.

I consider coaching the *superstar* (including a special case, the *big kid*) as well as the *weak athlete*. I look at how to deal with kids with *behavior problems*. I show how you can learn to like the *hard-to-like kid*. I also examine the needs of *solo* children such as a girl on an otherwise all-boy's team or a youth of color on an otherwise all-white team, and of *handicapped* athletes. I discuss the *sibling in the shadow* of an older athlete in the family, the child who becomes a *scapegoat*, and the *uncoachable child*. Then I look at a situation that many coaches face, that of coaching *your own child*. Finally I address the *unspecial* kids who often get overlooked because they don't fit into any of the other special categories.

THE SUPERSTAR

Most coaches love to have a superstar on their team. Each year around Little League baseball tryouts, you can almost see the saliva on the chins of the coaches when players of great talent are available to be drafted. It's fun to win, and it's fun to have the confidence that if things get tough near the end of a game, you have a player that can pull something out of a hat. Sometimes this can backfire, however, and result in something I call the *place-holder effect*, a phenomenon that often plagues a team with a superstar.

1. **The place-holder effect:** Last year I watched our junior high team play in a tournament. They were not expected to do well given that there were two very strong teams, each with a monster superstar. Both superstar eighth-graders were taller than six feet and muscular, and could handle the ball well and shoot from the outside. Our local team had some talent but didn't have any single player that could take on either of the superstars. Nonetheless our local team defeated one of the two favored teams on a last-second shot before losing a hard-fought final to the other team.

   The key to the underdog's success in the first game was that the other team overrelied on its superstar. Our team got behind early when every player on the other team was contributing. It looked like a blowout.

But as the game continued and it became clear that our guys weren't going to fold, the other team began to go more and more to their star to make something happen. What was initially a mismatch became even as it turned into a team of five against one superstar player, supported by a cast of place-holders. In the final minutes the ball became a hot potato with no one except the star willing to handle it. Time and again the star ended up receiving the ball at the top of the key rather than underneath, where he had been virtually unstoppable. He tried to force something, which was about his only alternative since his teammates weren't trying to get open. Usually it didn't work, and our team came from behind and won it.

In the final game, it was a different story against a *team* led by a superstar. The other players participated in the offense and made things happen. They set picks and drove to the basket. They brought the ball up the floor and got it to the star down low where he scored again and again. He was clearly the dominant talent on the floor, but the rest of the team played with and off him and they were unbeatable.

When you have a superstar, it's natural for a coach to relax and simply go to him or her whenever it's crunch time. But the place-holder effect is destructive to the development of a team, it often doesn't result in winning (as noted above), and it also isn't fair to the star. It puts incredible pressure on the superstar to perform miracles. But, being a superstar, the athlete often does perform miracles, which can lead to yet another problem: special treatment.

2. **Special treatment and reaching one's potential:** When a superstar is treated by different rules, it can result in a sub-optimal experience for both him and the rest of the kids. By treating the superstar more leniently, you implicitly tell the other players that a person's value is determined by their ability to play this game. This is

not good for their self-esteem. But most nonsuperstar kids adjust to the fact that the world *does* value people more if they can produce (in this case entertainment for the fans or victories for the coach), for at least as long as they continue to produce. Ironically it is often the budding superstar herself who is harmed most by special treatment. We all have seen players who, at an early age, seemed destined for athletic stardom but for some reason didn't achieve what seemed to be within their reach. Often this is because they fail to develop all of their skills fully, because they haven't needed them until they reached a higher level of competition.

What's most harmful to the superstar is not that he will get a big head, although that is certainly not desirable. It is rather that he will not learn the important lessons he needs to learn to really excel at the highest levels. Sydney Harris has noted that at the early levels of competition, it is almost always physical skills that determine the outcome. As athletes get older it usually is mental attitude (together with more than a bit of luck) that determines the outcome. This may be partly because the differences in ability between the players get smaller and smaller as the weaker players drop out and an athlete moves up, notch by notch, to stronger competition. But there is an unfortunate tendency for athletes that mature early to pick up sloppy habits. These bad habits don't seem to be a problem at first but can all too often prevent the athlete from reaching the highest levels of performance as he ages.

A beginning player who may perform like a can't-miss superstar may only seem like a superstar in comparison with the low level of competition. He may be motivated in sports by the ease with which he can excel as a young athlete. As he gets older, he may get easily discouraged as it is no longer so easy to dominate. His dedication to the sport may diminish. He may say to himself that he is just not as interested in that sport as he once was. That may be true, but it also may be that he isn't used to having to work so hard to be above average when, up to now, he has been outstanding with little effort.

I recently attended a basketball game between two highly ranked college teams. The talent level was quite exceptional, as you would expect, but I was amazed to see some of the top players in the country unable to go to their left. Whenever an opening appeared to their right, they capitalized on it and usually scored. But if the defense overplayed them in that direction, forcing them to go left, they had to give up the ball. Undoubtedly each of these players were superstars in their high school. They probably were able to excel without ever having to learn to go to their left. But now they had moved to a higher level where the competition was such that one couldn't rely only on the right hand.

If a coach wants to do right by his superstar player, he will push him to develop skills way beyond what he needs to excel at the level he is now on. In some cases it may be the best thing to move the superstar up a level or two. If that's not possible, the coach should work with the player to be thinking about what he needs to be able to do to succeed at the next level.

Special treatment is also setting the superstar up for a big fall when she rises to the level where she is just another ballplayer. And everyone in every sport (except for the very few Michael Jordans) ultimately reaches the level of their mediocrity. The superstar who has been treated like royalty will have an unusually difficult time putting out continued great efforts to excel when the royalty treatment ends.

And even Michael Jordan will one day grow old and lose the sharpness of his skills as new superstars rise up to push him aside. As a friend once mentioned to me, the opposite of "disabled" isn't "normal," it's "temporarily abled." There is a common occurrence in the business world when chief executive officers (CEO's) of companies retire or lose their jobs. There is a tendency to believe that people treat you with respect and affection because of what a wonderful person you are. When the power and status of being the ruler of a company is gone, the CEO who is used to ruling is often faced with a rough transition back to the world of the normal. So, for a variety of reasons, a coach who gives a superstar special treatment is not doing her a favor.

3. **Bringing out the best in teammates:** One potential frustration for a superstar is playing with teammates who can't approach his level of play. On the one hand, it can be exhilarating to be so much better than anyone else on the floor or field. However, it can be maddening to make a terrific pass that is dropped by a teammate who lacks the coordination and court sense to anticipate and handle it.

   I try to articulate to a superstar player what made Magic Johnson such an outstanding basketball player and a consistent winner: he made his teammates better players. Magic had skills beyond those of most of his teammates for years before he came into the NBA. Rather than showing up his teammates, which he surely often could have done, he made them look good. So, for example, if the superstar's teammates have trouble handling his no-look passes, you might pose a challenge to him to soften up the passes so that they can handle them. At the same time you can work with and encourage his teammates to rise to the challenge of always looking for the ball since it may magically appear. You can also encourage him to round out his game by stressing team-oriented activities such as assists and passing, or setting picks for teammates. For a basketball player who can drive to the basket and score with ease, you might have him work on learning to dish off to teammates.

4. **Self-handicapping:** An incident from my Outward Bound

experience also provides some insight for coaches with superstars. When we were on the ropes course high above the ground in the trees on Hurricane Island in Maine, some of us were terrified of the easiest segments. Others were nonplussed at the hairiest way-above-the-ground challenges. I particularly remember the inclined log which began 10 or so feet above the ground. From there it slanted upward to about 30 feet with little slits carved into the log every few feet. Trying to make my way up that log without grabbing onto the cable above my head was one of the most terrifying experiences of my life. For Tye and Lynne, however, it just seemed like fun on a big jungle gym. They made it more challenging for themselves by walking the log with their eyes closed, then backwards, then backwards with their eyes closed. They provided their own handicaps so they could push themselves to a higher level of performance when the situation didn't adequately challenge them.

A coach can work with a superstar in the same way to encourage her to give herself handicaps that will make the game more challenging and spur her development so that she can progress to the highest levels of performance. A star soccer player can be encouraged to play an entire practice using only her left foot to kick the ball. A baseball pitcher can give himself only three balls before walking a batter. A big basketball player who is a natural center can play point guard and work on shooting from longer range. When one begins to look for ways to push a superstar's development through the use of self-handicapping, there are limitless possibilities.

THE BIG KID

Often a basketball coach will find himself with a gigantic kid on his hands. In this situation, it is the rare coach who is able to look into the future and understand that this kid may not always be a giant. The normal tendency is to teach the big kid to stand under the basket and snarf up easy rebounds and convert garbage baskets. If he stays big enough long enough, he may never learn to handle the ball or shoot well enough to play any position except "giant." This is fine except that eventually the rest of the world starts to catch up. Even gigantic athletes eventually encounter other giants if they keep progressing to higher levels of play. And at the highest level, you can be sure that some of the giants will have skills beyond planting themselves near the basket and reaching.

I realized this recently when I coached two tall and talented girls. They seemed initially like natural forwards, and that's where I played them. Both had so much potential that I naturally imagined them playing high school and college basketball. And that is where I realized that I wasn't doing them any favors by restricting them to playing forward. They may keep growing but there is a reasonable chance that neither of them would grow a lot more. While they're big for their age, they might not end up being big by major college standards.

If they were going to reach their potential and play at the major college level, they might only be able to do so at a guard or a small forward position. I began to give them a chance to handle the ball at the point guard position and shoot from the outside. While keeping them at forward may have maximized the number of victories for my team, it wasn't helping them prepare to reach their potential.

THE WEAK ATHLETE

I have a special place in my heart for the weak athlete, the flip side of the superstar. The superstar will do well (at the early level of competition) pretty much regardless of how well he is coached. It is with the weaker athlete where coaches can make the most difference. And when it comes down to it, often the game is not won or lost by the superstars, who often neutralize each other's performance. Many times winning and losing is determined by how well the weaker players perform. If my right fielder can make just one or two more plays than the other team's right fielder, it may provide the winning margin.

I have two major goals for weak athletes. First, I want to make sure that the weaker players learn some tangible skills by the end of the season. While I try to help all my players learn as much as I can, I want to make especially sure with weaker players that the fundamentals are covered. For example, in basketball I will work very hard with weaker players on defense. I want them to know how to stay with their man and between him and the basket. They may never become great shooters, but they can learn to play tenacious defense, something that gives me as a coach a tremendous sense of accomplishment. I also try to make sure they know how to position themselves so they can make full use of the backboard in shooting so that if and when they do get an easy shot, they will be more likely to make it.

Many weak players have unrealistic ideas about their own abilities and aspire to play pivotal positions such as pitcher or shortstop. I try to be as clear as I can with weaker players about what they need to do to be able to play a position that they ask to play. If they do everything I ask them to do and improve their skills, I will try my best to give them a shot at playing the position they want to play at least once during the season. I try to do it in such a way that the child himself will not be physically harmed or embarrassed. I also take care to not put him into a position where his failure will let the team down and result in his teammates becoming upset with him. A single elimination playoff game is not the time to give a weaker player the chance to pitch. But in most seasons there is at least one opportunity to let your weaker players have some fun, either because the opposition is substantially weaker or stronger than your team. Preseason games and games toward the end of the season when your team has either clinched the championship or is out of the running completely are golden opportunities for this purpose.

My second, and most important, goal with weaker players is that, more than anyone else on the team, I want them to have fun. If a weak player can have a good time on my team, I will have accomplished something worthwhile. I constantly try to encourage weaker players to think about having fun while they are trying to learn new things.

It's hard to tell what might become of a weak player. Several years ago I had a short, chubby, fourth-grade boy named Nathan on my basketball team. He had never played before but he was immensely coachable and, because of that, he improved dramatically by the end of the season, although he still would not have been mistaken for a star. Imagine my surprise a little more than two years later when, as a lean, nearly six-foot seventh-grader, he had become the star of his junior high team. So you never can tell when a weak athlete will become like the hero in the children's book *Leo the Late Bloomer*, who takes a little bit longer but eventually blooms into something quite wonderful. And, in fact, any person who can enjoy playing a sport even when he is not very good at it is already something special.

THE CHILD WITH BEHAVIOR PROBLEMS

Bart was a handful. It wasn't clear that he wanted to play basketball at all, even though he had considerable ability. At this particular practice my assistant was working with a small group that included Bart. I wasn't paying too much attention since I was working with the rest of the team. The next thing I heard was Bart's loud voice. "Oh, no, I *won't*!" I turned to see Bart storming out the door of the gymnasium into the black night with my befuddled assistant trailing vaguely after him, clueless about what to do. It turned out that he had asked Bart to do a drill that everyone else was doing and he refused. When the coach insisted, Bart resisted. The coach became angry at what he took to be insubordination and rebellion. As his temper rose, Bart became more intransigent and finally stormed out of the gym.

Now most coaches don't usually have anything as dramatic as this happen in their practices. In fact, one of the reasons coaching is more fun than teaching is that you usually get a much higher proportion of kids on a sports team than in a classroom that *want* to be there. But kids have mixed motives even about sports and every once in a while you will run across a kid with behavior problems that rise to the surface in practices and games. Every coach who has coached any length of time can tell you stories about the problem kids he's coached. It is not fun for any coach, let alone a volunteer youth coach, to find himself having to act like a policeman in a sport he loves so much.

I was fortunate early in my life to be introduced to the ideas of Rudolf Dreikurs. When I started working as a teacher's aide at the Behavioral Learning Center, I was given an intensive course in the use of Dreikurs' natural and logical consequences to respond to children with behavior problems. According to Dreikurs, a problem child is a discouraged child.

Children want desperately to belong. If all goes well and the child *maintains his courage* (emphasis added), he presents few problems. He does what the situation requires and gets a sense of belonging through his usefulness and participation. But if he has become discouraged, his sense of belonging is restricted. His interest turns from participation in the group to a desperate attempt at self-realization through others. All his attention is turned toward this end, be it through pleasant or disturbing behavior, for, one way or another, he *has* to find a place.

Earlier in Chapter 5, I discussed the idea of each child having an emotional tank that can run down. Dreikurs, in effect, identifies the behavior problem child as one whose emotional tank is habitually low.

Here I only briefly touch on Dreikurs' work. If you encounter serious behavior problems in one or more of your players, I recommend that you consider taking a positive parenting course that covers Dreikurs' ideas in more depth, or read his *Children: the Challenge*, or both. Anyone who is serious about becoming an outstanding coach or youth leader can benefit from studying these powerful ideas in more depth.

1. **The child's mistaken goals:** The misbehaving child is doing so because he has what Dreikurs calls "mistaken goals." Understanding the four mistaken goals can help you decide how to respond to the child's misbehavior. If you can accurately diagnose the child's primary mistaken goal, you can respond in a way that helps the child focus away from the mistaken goal, gain courage, and refocus toward the goal of genuine participation with others. The four mistaken goals are a desire for *undue attention*, the struggle for *power*, then for *revenge*, and a need to demonstrate *inadequacy*.

   a. *Undue attention:* A child who is constantly trying to engage you and his teammates to the point where you find yourself getting annoyed with him is probably pursuing the goal of undue attention. This is usually more of a problem with younger children who are just beginning their experience with an organized sport.

   All children appreciate attention from important adults such as coaches. The signal that a child may be seeking *undue* attention is when you find yourself constantly being distracted from what you need to do as a coach to respond to the individual needs of the same player. A player who interrupts you when you are talking to another player, or who refuses to stop bouncing the ball when you call the group together, or who takes an unusually long time to run in from the outfield, causing everyone else to have to wait for him, may be craving your attention. It is important to note that for a child like this, the attention does not need to be positive. A child who believes that he is worthwhile only if he is the center of attention usually is only marginally concerned with the *kind* of attention he gets.

A coach can channel the need for attention to good advantage. For example, if you are positive charting (see Chapter 2), you can make "paying attention in the huddle" a goal for the player seeking undue attention. Then if Pete is able to go through even a single huddle in the game without disrupting it, he will be recognized for this accomplishment the same way he would be if he grabbed a rebound or fielded a grounder. If Jeremy is constantly hassling other players in lay-up lines, his goal can be to keep his hands to himself. Then, the first time he manages to meet this goal, he receives the coach's concentrated, positive attention, perhaps in front of the entire team either at the end of the drill or the end of practice.

b. *Power:* A power-seeking child engages in some of the same behaviors as an attention seeker but with the goal of demonstrating that he is the boss. In fact, a telltale sign that you have become engaged in a power struggle with a child is when you find yourself saying or thinking, "I'll show *him* who's in charge!" Where attention seeking leads to a feeling of irritation with the child, power plays by children tend to enrage adults. The use of natural and logical consequences

discussed later in this chapter can help you disengage from power struggles without feeding a child's
unhealthy power drive.

c. *Revenge:* Revenge is the logical extension of a power
struggle in which the adult responds in kind to the
power-seeking child. In this case, the child has been
hurt to the point that, in Dreikurs' words, "he counts
only if he can hurt others as he feels hurt by them."
In most cases, a child who is in search of revenge will
probably not have the patience and self-control to
stay out for sports for long. In my years of coaching
I have seen only one or two children who clearly
seemed to have been pursuing a mistaken goal of revenge. If you find yourself with a child who may be
doing so, you will probably want to seek some specialized help.

d. *Demonstration of inadequacy:* Some children aren't interested in attention or power or revenge. They simply
want to be left alone. They have given up. They are
out to demonstrate that they are inadequate for any
task that you might ever want to ask them to perform. And they work hard, and sometimes quite
creatively, to prove to you just how incompetent
they are.

Robby was the epitome of the inadequate child.
He was a slight boy, and cultivated a frail look, as if
you might knock him over with a rough glance. He
seemed unhappy, if not miserable, most of the time.
He didn't seem to want to play baseball but, with his
dad as one of the coaches, I doubt that he felt he had
much choice. I am confident that he would have been
much happier at home reading or watching television or doing just about anything besides playing
baseball. Given that this seven-year-old couldn't tell
his father, "Look, Dad, baseball just isn't my thing
and I don't want to play," what option did he have?

Robby became obsessed with demonstrating how

absolutely incompetent he was. He couldn't catch a ball. He rarely even hit the ball off the stationary tee. He would routinely fall down running to first base. When playing catch with a tennis ball, he would treat it as a bomb that might go off if he got anywhere near it. My clue that he was pursuing a strategy of demonstrated incompetency was when I began to stop asking, or even expecting, him to do anything. I realized that he had begun to convince me that he was incompetent in even the easiest baseball drill.

Robby had given up. He didn't want attention. He didn't want power. He was beyond even wanting any kind of revenge. He just wanted to be left alone. "Don't make me play baseball!" he cried out with his behavior. "And if you do insist that I play, I won't lift a finger to try to learn anything." Robby cried an average of three times a practice. On a good day he burst into tears only once or twice. On a bad day, he might sit the entire practice on the sidelines alternating between crying and sniffling. Ironically, the one thing he was proving exceedingly competent at was demonstrating his inadequacy.

While Robby was a classic case, most coaches have players who are intimidated by one or more aspects of the game they are playing and seek to convince the coach not to even ask them to try anything that is a bit intimidating. The approach with "inadequate" kids involves a "don't" and a "do." Don't fall into the trap of feeling sorry for them. Or if you do feel sorry for them in spite of your best efforts, don't allow yourself to *act* toward them out of pity. And then do express your confidence in their ability to rise to the challenge whenever you can. For example, you might say to an inadequate child, "I can imagine it might seem hard to run around the entire field without stopping but I am confident you can do it." If he doesn't make it, you can say, "Well, you made it halfway around. Tomorrow, I bet you can make it further than you did today." In every interaction you avoid falling into the trap of pity. That is not to say that you would force a child like this to do something dangerous or scary. I would never put a kid in the position of failing at something challenging when they are not on board.

In retrospect, I believe I made a mistake by not trying to convince Robby's dad to give him an honest chance to quit the baseball team without reprisal. Given the choice, Robby might have decided he wanted to stay on the team. If he had, he probably would have responded with much greater determination to learn the game and less energy on demonstrating his inadequacy. And, if he decided to drop baseball, so much the better for him to turn his energies in a direction that he had some sincere interest in. After all, baseball isn't school. A kid shouldn't have to play baseball if he doesn't want to.

Now that I've described the problems, let's look at what Dreikurs believed was a principal tool for dealing positively with discouraged children, natural and logical consequences.

2. **Natural and logical consequences:** Dreikurs' silver bullet for helping children with mistaken goals is something he called *natural consequences*. A natural consequence is something that teaches a lesson to the child without the parent having to be involved. For example, if a child forgets to take her lunch box with her to school, the natural consequence is that she misses lunch and gets really hungry. It is not a natural consequence for a parent to drive the lunch box to school and then yell at the kid for being so forgetful and irresponsible. In the latter case, the child may have goals of undue attention and demonstrating incompetency, both of which are

fed by the parent's action. If the parent *does nothing*, the natural consequence can teach two powerful lessons: forgetting the lunch box means I go hungry until dinner, and I had better remember in the future because Mom and Dad aren't going to rescue me all the time.

Sometimes the natural consequence of an action is injury or death. A child that runs out into the street without looking may not get another chance to do so. And sometimes the natural consequences are so long-term as to be ineffective. A child who regularly fails to get his homework in on time may suffer the natural consequence of growing up to be a deadbeat who can't hold a job. In neither of these cases does the responsible parent want to let nature take its course. This is where *logical* consequences come in.

A logical consequence is one that can substitute for nature in such a way that the parent/coach does not need to get emotionally involved. For example, a logical consequence when a player refuses to stop bouncing the ball when asked is that he loses the ball. A coach can say something such as, "You are telling me that you can't control your basketball so I will help you control it. Next time if you can control it, you get to keep it." And *if* a coach can do this *without* losing his temper or raising his voice, the impact of a logical consequence approximates that of a natural consequence. It's not the coach being mean, it's simply the way the world is. If you bounce the ball when the coach is talking, the ball disappears. And this is the charm of natural and logical consequences. It gets the parent or coach out of the enforcer role. He can sit back uninvolved with his child's forgetting his lunch box, or with his player's bouncing the ball, and let nature take its course.

3. **Time-out!** But sometimes you will have a player who doesn't respond to simply losing his basketball, which brings us back to the problem of what to do with Bart, still out in that black winter evening having stomped

301

out of the gymnasium. What did I do? The first priority was to verify that Bart was in no danger. I found him outside the gym and "made" him come back to the gym. He wasn't about to be persuaded—I know because I tried—so I wrapped my arms around him and walked him back in. I did it without expressing any anger or annoyance at him. "Bart, you can't stay outside the gym. Your parents expect me to make sure that you don't get hurt, and I need to know that you are in the gym. You don't have to practice with the team but you have to stay in the gym."

After a bit of argument ("Oh, sure, I'm really going to get hurt out here!" said with dripping sarcasm), Bart understood that I meant business. I simply would do whatever I needed, including sitting on him until his parents came to pick him up at the end of practice, to keep him from leaving the gym. But I also gave him some space. He didn't have to practice; all he had to do was stay in the gym. And he did stay, although at times there was more of his body outside the gym than in. And that was acceptable because I could see that he was not in any danger.

Before leaving him to go back to the rest of the team, I told him, "You can rejoin the team whenever you're ready to do all the things that everyone else is doing." Within about 10 minutes Bart was back with the team and doing the drills.

The "time-out" principles I used with Bart can be used with any kid whose behavior disrupts the practice. If a player needs to be separated from the group, you can simply ask him to go over and stand against the wall (or sit on a chair or whatever, which then becomes the time-out place). If he refuses to go to the time-out space, you may need to walk him over there. Then you can tell him what it is that he was doing that is unacceptable and, if possible, why it is harmful to the team or the other players. Tell him that you want him to stay there and think about his behavior for as long as he needs to. He gets to decide when he is ready to rejoin the team. Sometimes the player consistently jumps back and forth to time-out (the yo-yo effect). In this case I may require that he comes back to me before he can reenter the practice. He must articulate in words that he knows why he was put into time-out, and that he is now ready to control his behavior. Otherwise, whenever he is ready to rejoin the team, he can do so.

Again, the key to making the time-out method work is the coach's attitude. If you can act as if you really aren't upset with his behavior, he will correct the behavior sooner. You present it as a choice that *he* is making. When he behaves inappropriately, he is, in effect, making the choice to go to the time-out spot. He is not hurting you by doing it. He is not hurting his teammates by doing it. He is only depriving himself of being able to participate with his team. It is not punishment time to be served. Whenever he is able to control himself, he can rejoin the team. Once he knows what his choices are, and that you are firm and don't hold a grudge, he is very likely to make choices that will make you, as well as himself, happy.

The coach who is familiar with the child's mistaken goals, and understands the principles of natural and logical consequences and the use of time-outs, will find he has tools to deal with the most common kinds of inappropriate behavior from his players. He'll be able to deal with bad behavior in an evenhanded way that will tend to decrease the behaviors rather than reinforce them as so many well-meaning but unprepared coaches inadvertently do.

THE HARD-TO-LIKE KID

As much as I like kids, every once in awhile I run across a child with whom, for some unfathomable reason, I just don't click. It isn't always related to athletic ability or even "niceness," although I would be a liar if I didn't admit to having a preference towards kids who make me look good as a coach or who treat me and others with respect and affection. However, some of the kids I don't hit it off with are good athletes. Others are quite nice. Some are even both. I don't understand it, but it happens.

But the good news is that it is possible to learn to like kids you don't like at first. The kids I worked with more than 20 years ago at the Behavioral Learning Center were either difficult to like, or if they had charm, they used it to manipulate you, which tended to undercut your liking them. Either way it was a tough place to teach. However, an amazing thing happened as the days and weeks went by.

We had a weekly "goody guy" awards assembly in which the teachers recognized children who had met their goals for the week. We were instructed by Shirley Pearl, the principal, to look for good things to recognize and to ignore, as much as possible, the things we didn't like. The good things were often small things in the beginning. With Judy, a nearly autistic little girl, it was a great achievement for her if she could stay in line on the way to the playground without hitting someone. (In retrospect I realize that it was no accident that Judy and many of her classmates were behavior problems. Most had been abused in one way or another and their acting out was tied to the trauma they had experienced.)

It will be no surprise to students of psychology that, as I began to look for positive things about each child's behavior every week, I began to *like* them. I'm not sure how much was due to my changing and how much to their becoming "nicer." But in any case, I found I began to like the most unlikeable kid when I made the right kind of effort to find positive things about him. I even began to be proud of the appropriate things that these heretofore hard-to-like kids were accomplishing.

So, if you have a player you just don't like, it can help a great deal simply to admit it to yourself. Then begin to look for things about him that you can honestly recognize him for, and then *do* it. I think you may be surprised and delighted—as I was—with the change in your perception of the child, and in his improved behavior.

THE "SOLO" CHILD

After not having played basketball myself for more than 12 years, I recently joined a basketball class in which a group of about 15 adult men meet one night a week in a local gym and play basketball for two hours. Two friends joined at the same time I did. I had some anxiety because it had been so long since I had played, but it was quite easy to go to that first session knowing that I was not going "solo"—that there would be at least two other friends there that were like me. I was not the only one who was "different."

Now I'm a reasonably responsible, mature adult who has successfully negotiated some difficult situations in my life. But I was nervous about playing basketball with a group of men on Wednesday nights! Imagine what a young girl feels when she walks out onto a baseball field with 20-some boys! Or how the only Vietnamese American boy feels playing with an otherwise white team.

When Jackie Robinson broke the color barrier in major league baseball in the late 1940s, he experienced unbelievable pressure. An athlete of immense talent, Robinson had a transcendent goal that motivated him to endure insults and humiliations he longed to lash out against. Few young solo athletes have either Robinson's skills or determination. Granted, the kind of treatment he received hopefully will not be duplicated. Nonetheless, solo athletes typically experience more stress than nonsolos, and youth coaches should do what they can to help them thrive.

When you coach a team with a solo athlete, there are several things you can do to ease the way. First, try to get another player like the solo athlete on your team. For example, if you have only one girl on your team, try to get another to join. If there is no other girl in the entire league, try to recruit one. Perhaps your player has a friend who would like to join her. Usually there will be other solos on other teams. The natural tendency seems to be to spread the solos around so that no team has more than one. Unfortunately, this is not the best approach for either the solo or the rest of the players.

The better strategy is to bunch solos for the simple reason that they then are no longer solos. Remember my adult league basketball experience? The three of us were the oldest and least talented players in the program but it didn't scare us so much because we weren't alone. In Cupertino Hoops, our co-ed basketball league, no team has less than two girls. In most cases we'll have at least three girls on a team.

In addition to providing support for the solo, it also helps the other players to see that each person is an individual. If there is only one girl on an all-boy team, it is too easy for the boys to see that girl as less than an individual. If, on the other hand there are three girls, it becomes clear that Sara is a pretty good shooter, while Jennifer can rebound, and Karen is a beginning player. They are each different.

Sometimes, however, you just can't bring another solo onto your team. Then the most important thing to do is to recognize that the solo athlete is under stress and needs your support. So . . . support him. Take special care to use the techniques in Chapter 5 to make it clear that you are *glad* he is on your team.

You can also try to enlist the help of the natural leaders of your team to make a solo athlete feel comfortable. On most teams there are one or two kids who set the tone for how the players interact with each other. Ask these kids privately if they would be willing to help the solo athlete feel more comfortable. You might ask them to suggest how they might do that. If they don't come up with anything, you might suggest things like offering to pair up with the solo athlete whenever there are drills to be done in twosomes.

A final way you can support a solo athlete is by involving the parents with the team. Make sure that the parents of the solo are introduced to the parents of the other players. If the parents feel comfortable with the other parents, that will help the player to feel comfortable with the other players.

CHILDREN WITH HANDICAPS

Children with handicaps are a particular kind of solo case. When we started Cupertino Hoops my wife suggested that we recruit some boys with Down syndrome to play basketball. Initially I was skeptical because I was overwhelmed with just getting the league up and running. But it turned out to be a wonderful idea. The two boys had a great season and a lot of fun. Each became an integral member of their team. Each scored during several of the games and in some cases both Matthew and Ross scored multiple baskets in the same game.

The other kids also benefitted. Our end-of-the-season evaluation forms came back with many unsolicited positive comments from parents about how their children had benefitted from playing with and against Matthew and Ross. I have since moved from being skeptical to being an enthusiastic booster of mainstreaming handicapped children into a league of nonhandicapped kids, a topic I address further in Chapter 17.

My experience coaching handicapped children is limited to working with children with Down syndrome. From that I have drawn some general principles, but the coach who finds herself with a child with a different kind of handicap will find that there is a world of information available if you make the effort to look, as I will cover a little further on.

When coaching a handicapped child, you want to walk a fine line. You want to make sure you treat her like any other member of the team. You also will want to make some necessary adjustments to make sure that she can become a contributing member of the team.

1. **Proper positioning:** In every sport there are some positions that are more demanding than others, such as pitching and catching in baseball, point guard in basketball, goalie in soccer, etc. The first key is finding the most appropriate position for a handicapped player.

   In soccer, a child with reduced mobility might make a good fullback, whose job it is to keep opposing players with the ball from getting close to the goal where they can kick an easy goal. In baseball the same child might be well suited for first base. A first baseman needs to be able to catch a hard-thrown ball. He needs to have some courage to try to dig out bad throws from the dirt without turning his head away. What he typically doesn't need to do is run a long distance quickly, like an outfielder. (I recognize that the ability to jump to catch high throws is also ideal but then very few things work out perfectly in this world.)

   A child who is facing the world with a handicap may well be higher in courage and determination than many nonhandicapped children. Asking a child with reduced mobility if he wants to try first base may inspire him to make great efforts to become excellent at catching throws from shortstop and third base, and digging balls out of the dirt.

2. **Telling, showing, walking through:** Using multiple modes of getting your message across is a principle of good communication and teaching for any student. For a child with Down syndrome or any kind of learning dis-

ability, it is essential. In addition to telling an athlete with a learning disability what you want him to do, show him, and then walk him through it. With Matthew on my basketball team, I diagramed the flow of our offense on paper while telling the team what we were trying to accomplish. Then we got out on the floor and walked through it. I stood with my hands on Matthew's back and guided him, showing him where to go when. I talked to him about what he was expected to do on each variation of the offense and then we ran through each step in slow motion so he could get the feel for it. In some cases I put a mark on the floor to indicate where he should line up to begin a particular play.

This past season when I did not have any handicapped children on my team, I discovered that *all* my players benefitted when I used the same kind of multiple modes of teaching that I had developed for Matthew.

3. **Special plays:** One enjoyable aspect of working with Matthew was developing a special play that we creatively called "Matthew." Matthew, the play, was a double pick that made it very likely that Matthew, the player, would get an open shot at the basket. Initially it was intended to get him open for a lay-up. However, Matthew was partial to three-point shots and he worked religiously on them in practice. So we modified the lay-up option on "Matthew" to let him shoot the long bomb off the double pick. Matthew made several long shots during the season, and he pumped up everyone's enthusiasm whenever he hit one in a game.

The ironic thing about "Matthew" is that it is now a play I use with all my teams. When we are in a crunch situation at the end of a game and we need to get our best shooter open for a last-second shot, "Matthew" is often the play. The naming of the play after a player also has become a tradition. We developed a play with our point guard taking the high post at the free throw line and having the wings crisscross past him to receive a handoff and drive to the basket. One of my wings was named Chris and thus that play became "Chris" from then on.

4. **Recruit other handicapped athletes:** As with any solo athlete, one of the best ways to help the handicapped athlete have a positive experience is to make sure that he isn't a solo. Try to recruit some other players with similar handicaps to play on other teams. For example, if several teams have a player with Down syndrome, those athletes can guard each other. I should add that if the teams are appropriately balanced (something that many youth sports leagues don't take enough care to ensure), then there should be at least one weak player on every team you play so your handicapped player can match up appropriately.

5. **Get advice and consultation:** In virtually any part of the country there should be an agency that can give you advice on how best to respond to the special needs resulting from the particular handicap of your player. *Sports and Recreation for the Disabled* by Michael J. Paciorek and Jeffery A. Jones is a terrific resource book providing information about equipment and support organizations for a multitude of sports and activities. If there is a teacher education program at a local college or university, call there to find someone with expertise in teaching people with handicaps. The local public schools also are likely to have teachers with special training who would be more than happy to share their knowledge with a coach who wanted to learn to help handicapped athletes compete successfully. Other agencies that may be of use are the Community Association for Retarded, the United Cerebral Palsy Association, and the local support group for parents of children with special needs. And, of course, the local Special Olympics can be a source of athletes for your league as well as advice.

THE SIBLING IN THE SHADOW

It's tough for a young athlete to follow a sibling who was a great athlete. It is difficult for people *not* to have expectations that Katie will be as great as Alison was before her. I have seen *very good* athletes who are perceived as failures by their coaches because they didn't measure up to the older sibling.

My advice when you have a sibling in the shadow is to shine the light to illuminate her, rather than her older sister. Typically I act as if I had never heard of the older sibling. But sometimes other kids or adults will say something that sets expectations at the superstar level. In this case, I might say something to the player to the effect that I have no expectation for her to do anything other than try her hardest and have fun with the sport. I also talk with my fellow coaches to make sure that they don't reinforce an unfair comparison with the older sibling.

THE SCAPEGOAT

One of life's repeating tragedies is the search for scapegoats. Sports teams are no strangers to scapegoating, and the longer the losing record the more compelling the need for a scapegoat becomes.

The likely candidate for a scapegoat is the kid who is different or vulnerable or both, perhaps a solo. Often a player who is the weakest athlete will become the scapegoat. Or it may be a child who is not particularly likeable. It starts when players begin to pick on the scapegoat. As they discover they can pile their frustrations on the back of the scapegoat, things can get nasty.

I've seen coaches turn a player into a scapegoat because they expected him to be better than he turned out to be when he was drafted. The player may be following in the footsteps of an older sibling who was better. Or he may have gotten lucky during the tryouts. For whatever reason, his day-to-day play just doesn't measure up to expectations. And when a coach gets down on a player, all the other players on the team sense it and begin to feel they are free to pick on the scapegoat as well.

I once supervised Wanda, a talented employee with some rough edges. Wanda was a hard driver who rubbed many people the wrong way. I was constantly hearing from other people in the organization about what she had done wrong.

Once when I was moaning about this to a friend, he surprised me by saying, "Well, why don't you get rid of her?" Without hesitation I found myself saying, "I couldn't do that. She does a great job, and I don't have anybody else who could do it." To which he responded, "Well, then, defend her!"

That was the key! I realized that in the bigger picture, Wanda was a terrific worker doing a very difficult job exceedingly well. And while she had some rough edges, they could be smoothed. As Lynn Frank used to say, "It's easier to tone 'em down than to jack 'em up." From that point on, whenever someone would come to me with a complaint about her, I would respond by telling them about the great job she was doing. Pretty soon the complaints stopped, and eventually Wanda became well-liked and recognized for the outstanding job she had *always* been doing. Perhaps she also modified some of her behaviors that irritated other people. But I believe the major factor in her improved relations with her fellow workers was my defending her. Most people had no idea of the good work she was doing. When they found out, they were more willing to give her the benefit of the doubt on other matters.

The lesson here for a coach is that the way to keep a player from being a scapegoat, or of getting him out of that role if already in it, is for the coach to stick up for the player. The players will ultimately follow the coach's lead. If some players continue to harass the scapegoat, the coach needs to deal with it as he would any inappropriate behavior, using approaches covered earlier in this chapter.

THE UNCOACHABLE KID

Coaches love the kid that takes coaching well. The players that hang on our every word and then try to do what we tell them are terrific. Then there's the athlete who seems to act as if he already knows everything and just isn't interested, thank you very much, in what you, the coach, might have to suggest.

I like the coachable kid as much as any coach does. But over the years I have come to the conclusion that the uncoachable kid has something important going for him. He owns his behavior. He takes responsibility for what he learns and refuses to learn. He may not be open to lots of things that would make him a better athlete or person, but his acceptance of responsibility can be turned to the perceptive coach's advantage. The key is the art of suggestion.

When I have a kid that is strong-willed (sometimes a synonym for uncoachable), I will *ask* her if she is open to a suggestion. "Anna, I noticed something in the game and I wondered if you are open to a suggestion." Now this is a dilemma for a girl like Anna. She really isn't all that open to a suggestion, but now she's curious. "Okay, what is it?" "Well, I noticed that several times when you shot, you turned and shot before you got set. Your feet were close together so you didn't have good balance, and you didn't square up to the basket. A couple of times you did get set first, and one of those shots went in."

And I leave it at that. Remember, Anna is a girl who takes responsibility. She will either incorporate my advice or not. Most of the time, I have noticed that she will use what I tell her when it is offered as a suggestion rather than a have-to. But not all the time. And sometimes, although it is rare, she will not even want to hear it. "Are you open to a suggestion?" "Not really." And there also I leave it alone. If I try to force her to listen at this point, she won't hear me and she certainly won't incorporate my suggestion into her behavior. But I will remember what my advice was and will save it for the next time we practice and ask her again. And it is rare that she will be able to deal with the curiosity twice in a row.

YOUR CHILD, THE COACH'S KID

My son and I were attending a soccer game that Billy, a younger friend of his, was playing in. The team was coached by Billy's father. We arrived just as the first period was ending. Billy came running off the field without seeing us. As he passed by he brushed both hands several times rapidly against the sides of his head as if he were styling his hair, and said to no one in particular, "My dad's the coach." These many years later, I still don't know if Billy was expressing pride or anxiety—perhaps it was some of both.

At the team party at the end of each year I try to give special recognition to the players whose parents helped coach the team. I tell everyone that they deserve it for putting up with their parent as coach. Regardless of how well a parent/coach and child/athlete get along with each other, there definitely is stress for both the child and the parent when the parent is the coach.

The key to doing a good job with your own kid is to never forget that your kid is *not* you. Say this to yourself 10 times every day ("My kid is not me. My kid is not me."). If she hits a home run, it is no reflection on you. She did it. If he throws a fit when he is called for a foul, it is no reflection on you. He did it.

1. **Favoritism and Uncle Clarence:** Although I hear occasional complaining among parents about coaches favoring their own children on the team, my observations are that most coaches are *too hard* on their own kids. They take everything the child does as a reflection on

314

them as a coach and as a parent and as a person. I have seen coaches who are positive and forgiving of mistakes made by other kids, but they become downright nasty when it is their son or daughter who screws up.

I have also seen situations where a coach will monitor every single action his child takes. The player cannot move without getting a direction from the coach telling him how he could have improved that step. The same coach will often be very forgiving and more hands-off of players to whom he is not related, but when there is blood relation involved, something is triggered that is not useful to the player or the team. At its most extreme, this can lead to what I call the Uncle Clarence phenomenon.

When I was a boy in North Dakota, I loved baseball more than just about anything, but it was always with some degree of trepidation that I went to our baseball games each week. The reason for my ambivalent feelings was that my Uncle Clarence often umpired the games. Clarence was determined that no one was going to be able to accuse him of favoring his nephew. The consequence was that it was virtually impossible for me to be safe at first base unless the ball was never thrown to first. If there was any play at all, I was out. I now have more understanding of the pain Uncle Clarence must have experienced at the thought of someone criticizing him for favoritism, but at the time it just seemed so unfair. We had a hard enough time winning games anyway without having perfectly good hits taken away from me.

So don't let yourself fall into the trap of acting as if you think that everyone is watching your child to see how good a coach or parent you are. There are lots of kids out there, and most parents don't pay attention to anybody's kid but their own.

If you can maintain this distance, you will be able to

be positive and supportive of your own child as well as the rest of your team. You'll also find you can have a lot more fun with your child *and* he will do better without having your fearful expectations to carry around on his back.

There clearly are situations, however, where coaches favor their children. A mediocre child of a coach will pitch while a better pitcher plays the field. Or the coach's kid seems to never sit out while other kids play only parts of games. Nothing poisons the well with parents and players alike as when a coach unfairly favors his own kid. If you as a coach are worried that you might be favoring your child (and you should at least consider that possibility), ask someone to monitor the situation for you. If you have an assistant coach, ask her to let you know if she thinks your daughter is playing more than is fair. Or ask a parent who comes to most of the games to give you a reading. Better yet, keep track, in writing, of statistics that will give you an indication. For example, keep track of playing time so you can ensure that you are not playing your own child more than other kids. Keep track of who plays what position. When positive charting, review the number of things you record about your child compared to the other players and make adjustments if you find your own child is getting most of the recognition.

2. **My son and the normal curve:** Normally my son cannot wait for practice, and he behaves himself throughout. However, one afternoon when he was in the second grade he was a real pain in the neck at basketball practice. He didn't listen to instructions. He refused to hustle back on defense. He just seemed to not care about anything. Not having the patience that many more seasons of coaching have tended to give me, I blew up at him.

Later I discussed the situation with Jeff Olson, a friend who had studied statistics in graduate school. He reminded me of the statistical concept called the normal distribution or curve. He pointed out that there is a normal curve of behavior for each child—some days the kid will be an absolute angel and others he will be a terror. Most of the time, the behavior is somewhere in the middle of the curve (if he is a "normal" child). His question to me was whether this kind of negative behavior at practice was typical. I said, "No, that's what makes it so mystifying." With the wisdom born of studying statistics and having raised five kids himself, he said, "Then I would just assume it is a random behavior and ignore and forget it. If it comes back on a regular basis, then you can worry about it. But if you dwell on it now when it appears to be an aberration, you may only be reinforcing it."

I did as he recommended. The behavior went away— to reappear about once every two years or so. Now when my son, or any kid, has a bad day, I remember the normal curve and forget about the random behavior that can seem so infuriating—until you realize it won't last.

3. **Suggestions versus have-to's:** In the section of this chapter on the uncoachable kid, I discussed the art of suggestion. This is an approach that I have found works well for coaches with their own children. I try to be clear with my son about what things *all* players have to do: he is a player, therefore he has to do them. But I am also clear on those things that I am *suggesting* to him: those things he can choose to do or not do. For example, I might say to him, "Are you open to a suggestion about your free throw shooting?" This tells him clearly that this is an area where he can decide. I am invoking neither parental authority nor the coach's authority to control him. If he says that he is *not* open to a suggestion— and sometimes he does—then I button my lip.

Because kids spend so much of their lives being told what to do by their parents, I try to minimize the amount of telling I do with my own son during practice and games. This helps both of us to remember that we are in a voluntary, fun experience together.

SPECIALIZING THE UNSPECIAL KIDS

Most kids aren't superstars, or weak players, or big kids, or hard-to-like, or solos, or handicapped, or uncoachable, or siblings-in-the-shadow, or scapegoats, or the coach's kid. Most kids are "unspecial" by most definitions. They don't excel and they don't cause much of a problem. They're there but they can go unnoticed. And that is a shame. While this chapter is focused on the special athletes, don't forget that every child is special. What makes a child special is special attention by an important adult in that child's life. *You* can be a coach that gives special attention to all of your players, those that society has designated as special, and those that are special because they don't have a special category for themselves. And when you begin to see each of them as special, each will be!

16

Ending the Season
with a Bang

> *Public ceremonies and rituals are the ingredients that crystallize per-*
> *sonal commitment. They help to bond people together and let them know*
> *that they are not alone . . . There is a family feeling about celebra-*
> *tions. While fun, they also provide a meaningful reminder about which*
> *key values are celebrated in the organization.*
> —James M. Kouzes and Barry Z. Posner
> *The Leadership Challenge*

It started months ago with high hopes. Now it is ending.
Whether your team ended up as champions or as the last
place team, the end always seems to come both sooner and
later than expected. The experience of going through a
season with a team of players is a truckload of emotional
highs and lows. A coach can end up having so many emotions that they can nearly overwhelm her. The players experience the same range of emotions. Losing seasons breed
self-doubt and frustrations. Winning seasons breed delusions of grandeur.

You have gone through a lot with a group of people—
players, coaches, and parents—and it is important to recognize that. And don't underestimate the importance of
the ceremonial aspects of commemorating the end of the
season. Completing a season is worth celebrating, so have
a party.

THE END-OF-THE-SEASON PARTY

The first requirement is to find a suitable place for an end-of-the-season party that will make it as easy as possible for everyone to focus on what you are all there for, to celebrate the completion of a meaningful event in *all* of your lives. When I first started coaching, our team party always seemed to end up being in a truly noisy pizza place where it was virtually impossible to concentrate on anything or even communicate.

After the final baseball game one season, the team parent decided to have pizzas delivered to a picnic area right next to the ball diamond. It was glorious. No video games. No blaring music. No extraneous people to worry about. Just our team members, their parents and siblings, and the coaches having a picnic in the sunny afternoon. We were able to talk to each other about the season informally while we ate. Then, when the eating was over, we were able to make the awards ceremony one of dignity without having to shout above a din.

It is especially important to end the season with a party if your season ends on a sour note, say by your team losing the last game (and at least half the teams do end on a loss). A team party gives you the chance to put the ending loss, and the entire season, into perspective.

Recognizing Your Players

A primary purpose of the end-of-the-season party is to recognize your players both for the effort and progress each player made during the season. I make a point to recognize each player individually. After most people have finished eating, but before they begin to make getting-ready-to-leave noises, I ask each player to come up in front of the entire group while I talk about their accomplishments and growth during the season. If I have done the positive charting I recommend in Chapter 2, I will have the season-long raw material I need for this so I won't end up embarrassing myself by trying to ad-lib things about each player.

There is no question that you will find it easier to remember positive contributions from some players more than others. Some players stand out. If you keep and recognize only the traditional statistics, you will find some players unrecognized. A friend once told me about a problem he had run into when he was coaching a junior high basketball team. He would announce the game statistics on the bus on the way home after each away game. His son was the best player on the team and the leader in almost all categories. Eventually some of the other players began to tease his son about being the coach's favorite. There was no question about the coach having fudged any of the statistics but it did prove embarrassing for both the son and the coach.

However, having the positive charting records will give you many positive things to share about *every* player. Some of the contributions may seem less valuable than others but everyone has made contributions and everyone gets recognized for them. It then becomes not only easy but fun to review the season before the party to identify material about what each player did in the third game or the seventh game of the season. And sharing the information about each player becomes a positive experience for all players, stars and weaker ones alike.

And believe me, it does have an impact on the players, especially younger ones. One of the first years I coached I prepared a booklet for each player with a game-by-game summary of the good things they had done. At one point after Jimmy had gotten his booklet, I heard him say to no one in particular, "Well, let's see what I did on February 16, 1986" as he paged through his booklet. And it's a good bet Jimmy still has that booklet from his second-grade basketball season.

The Problem with Most Valuable Player Awards

Often coaches will give awards that mimic the "big leagues"; for example, a Most Valuable Player or MVP award. Or they will give awards based on statistics from the season.

They often find themselves giving a couple of kids several awards while some kids don't get any. There are two situations possible with MVP-type awards, and in neither is it particularly helpful to have one. The first situation is where it is obvious to everyone who the MVP is. One player is so much better than anyone else on the team that not a single player or parent could contest it. In this case, it isn't a secret who the best player on the team is. Everyone already knows, so the award doesn't add anything in particular.

In the other situation, which I have experienced both as a player and a parent, it isn't necessarily clear who the best player is. There may be two or more players who are comparable. In this case, the selection of an MVP can be incredibly divisive, with the runners-up feeling bitter and even resentful toward the player who got the award.

But there is another way to deal with awards, and that is to make each award a special award personalized for each player who receives it.

Personalized Awards

The ideal is to create an award for each child that expresses something about their uniqueness and the specific kinds of contributions they have made during the season.

One baseball season I found a book of baseball postcards while browsing in a bookstore (see Patton in Bibliography). I picked out a particular postcard for each player that had some kind of connection with that player. One postcard had a drawing of a fielder stretching an enormous glove skyward to pull down a flyball. This card I gave to my first baseman, who happened to be named Neel, along with the *Neel the Thrill* award "for scooping up hard smashes to first base that reminded everyone of Will Clark" (of the San Francisco Giants).

Other awards (along with appropriate baseball postcards) given out that year:

- The *Play Anywhere* award for being willing to play in the outfield, the infield, behind the plate, and even on the mound without a complaint and playing all positions well.
- The *Mr. Reliable* award for consistently playing hard and well, coming through with clutch hits, and fielding plays throughout the year.
- The *Cut 'Em Down in Their Tracks* award to our catcher for keeping baserunners close to the bases and gunning them down when they tried to steal a base.
- The *Mr. Clutch* award for consistently making the clutch plays—as a pitcher, as a fielder, and as a hitter—that helped us win games and come back from what seemed like certain defeat.
- The *What Was that Big Fat Pitch that I Couldn't Hit?* award to a pitcher for having developed a wicked knuckleball that frustrated opposing batters time and again.
- The *Cardiac Arrest* award for making catches in the outfield that left the coaches in need of pacemakers.
- The *Fearless Baserunner* award for running the bases with wild abandon and scoring almost every time he got on base (14 out of 16 times).
- The *Mental Toughness* award for bouncing back time and again after being hit by pitches or bad hop grounders and always coming up ready to give it his best effort.
- The *Mr. Acrobat Defensive Plays* award for making incredible plays at third base that reminded us of circus acrobats.
- The *Can You Believe Your Eyes!!??!! Defensive Play* award for

making catches in the infield and the outfield that we still don't believe and we were there.

And finally, for a player who showed a lot of promise early in the season before he was injured:

- The *Just Wait 'til Next Year* award.

Each of the awards was tailored in some meaningful way to the individual who received the award. Everyone knew who the best players on the team were, and their awards in some way reflected that. But every player had contributed to the team during the year, and each got an award that was special for them.

The postcards were a terrific addition, but if you don't have something comparable, you might get each player a poster or trading card of a professional player who plays the same position or has something in common with each player. Then you could print the name of the award across the top of the poster or mount the trading card on a sheet of paper with the award name typed on it. With today's computer graphics technology, it's not that hard to create something that looks pretty good without great expense or time commitment. I often prepare an award page in the personal history booklet that I give each player, but some coaches buy trophies and engrave the name of the player and the award on them.

One year I bought copies of *Play Better Basketball* by Jim Pruitt for each of my players. This is a terrific self-help book for young people who want to become the best basketball players they can be. Because the book is full of great drills, exercises, and ideas to improve a young player's game, I thought it was a great gift for my players to encourage them to continue practicing basketball during the off-season. It was clear to me a year later, from the improvement I saw in a couple of instances, that the book had been put to good use.

TEACHABLE MOMENTS AFTER THE SEASON

One thing I have learned from 12 seasons of coaching is that sometimes the greatest teachable moments come at the ceremony at the end of the season. The kids are paying attention in a way that some of them haven't all year. The parents are there. The work is completed, for better or for worse.

What you have to say, and how you structure the event that celebrates the end of your season, can reinforce what you've been trying to do all year, and it can sometimes even make points that you weren't able to make effectively during the season.

When you have a child standing next to you in front of an audience of his teammates and their parents, and you are talking about *him* and what he has accomplished during the season, you can be sure of one thing: he is *listening* to you. This is a teachable moment. Sometimes it is at a moment like this that you can make the points that just didn't make it through their skulls to their minds during the season. You can also reinforce ideas with the parents, who after all, aren't with you during the season when you practice day after day.

END THE SEASON PROPERLY
EVEN WHEN YOU'RE TIRED

Sometimes you get to the end of the season and the last thing you want to do is prolong it with a party. Sometimes it was a painful season because the team lost a lot. Or maybe things went well but you are simply tired and you want to put the season behind you. Whenever I have allowed a season to end without some kind of team celebration, I have regretted it. My advice to you is to make the extra effort to end the season with a bang rather than a whimper. And you probably don't have to do it alone. If possible, enlist the support of some of the parents to organize the party. You've put so much into the season up to this point. Go ahead and end it in a way that will endorse each of the players and help them feel great about themselves and the season they just completed.

17

Moving Your League in a Positive Direction

We all think we're tops. We're exuberantly, wildly irrational about ourselves. And that has sweeping implications for organizing. Yet most organizations, we find, take a negative view of their people. They verbally berate participants for poor performance . . . They call for risk taking but punish even tiny failures. They want innovation but kill the spirit of the champion . . . they design systems that seem calculated to tear down their workers' self-image . . . The message that comes through so poignantly . . . is that we like to think of ourselves as winners. The lesson that excellent companies have to teach is that there is no reason why we can't design systems that continually reinforce this notion; most of their people are made to feel that they are winners.
—Thomas J. Peters and Robert H. Waterman, Jr.
In Search of Excellence

No matter how much you as a coach try to be a positive force with the players on your team, it won't have much impact if you are working within a structure that reinforces the worst aspects of youth sports. At some point, changes need to be made at the level of the organization or league.

In this chapter I examine why so many youth sports organizations end up putting the needs of the adults involved ahead of those of the athletes. I outline some elements of a positive youth sports organization. Finally I discuss what individual coaches and parents, working together, can do to make a positive difference in a youth sports league, using the Cupertino Hoops basketball league as a case study.

THREE KINDS OF ADULTS

Over the years as I observed many youth sports organizations, I began to realize that there are three kinds of adults who get involved with youth sports. Any league, if it is to be successful in keeping the needs of the players first, must be able to deal appropriately with each group.

The first category of adults is someone who has a positive attitude, likes kids, and cares more about the kids' development than winning. These are *members of the choir*. You don't need to convert them to a positive approach to youth sports because they already believe it. There are more people out there in this category than most youth sports skeptics would ever believe. The problem is that most youth sports leagues don't reinforce these people. In many cases, the people most able to be a positive influence in the organization get frustrated and drop out.

The second and largest category of adults contain those who are *influence-able*. Most of us respond to the norms and rules of the organizations to which we belong. We know that certain behavior is acceptable at the bowling alley but not at the workplace. Some employers care a lot about how employees dress, while others are quite relaxed. Unless the organization is unclear or noncommunicative about expectations, most people will respond to them without a lot of argument.

If a youth sports organization gives signals that it's okay to rant and rave about the calls of an umpire, most people will be tempted to do a little ranting and raving when confronted with a bad call. On the other hand, if the organization makes it clear that coaches and parents are expected to be positive, most people will become more positive in response.

The third category is very small. These are the *incorrigible*, adults who have severe problems. They may be trying to live vicariously through their children or the players they coach. They may have unresolved issues relating back to their own parents and the way they were raised. They may have been coached at some point by a negative or even abusive coach, and they may have adopted those tactics as their own. The adults in this category may respond halfheartedly to the norms and signals of a positive youth sports organization. But mostly, when they find themselves in an environment that insists that they be positive, they will leave to find another league that doesn't cramp their style. And sometimes the best that you can hope for is that incorrigible coaches and parents *will* move on.

Youth sports organizations need to signal strongly and clearly in ways that reinforce and recognize the members of the choir, that influence the influence-able to become more positive, and that encourage the incorrigible to leave if they aren't able to change.

YOUTH SPORTS ORGANIZATIONS: BY, OF, AND FOR ADULTS

Most people who are involved with youth sports organizations say they are in it for the kids, and most are sincere about it. Nonetheless, there is no question in my mind that many youth sports organizations are organized primarily by adults, for adults, with the players as raw material.

I belong to an adult service organization that relies on its members to bring service projects to the attention of the organization for a decision on which ones to pursue. Every few months we all get together to decide which projects to take on. Not all of the members who propose projects are able to attend all of the meetings. It should surprise no one to learn that the projects usually selected are ones whose sponsors are present to describe the project, answer questions about it, and generally advocate for it. Occasionally a project will get selected without the sponsor being in attendance, but not often.

This experience has a lot to say about why youth sports leagues usually are adult-centered. When most, if not all, of the decisions are made by adults with no children involved, it's not too surprising that the needs of the kids often take a back seat to those of the adults.

Several years ago I spoke with a Little League baseball manager from a nearby league who complained to me about the nonforfeiture of a game between two of his opponents. It seems that one of the teams that was locked in a tight pennant race with his team didn't have enough players, due to illness and family vacations, to play a scheduled game against a third team. The manager of the third team chose to reschedule the game rather than force the other team to forfeit. The complaining manager said that he wouldn't have forfeited if it had been his team playing the shorthanded team. I said that I thought it was ludicrous to count a forfeit as a victory when you could easily reschedule the game. When I asked him why he would have accepted the forfeit, he replied, "Because I'm fighting for the championship" (emphasis added). He knew that one game might be the difference between his team and the shorthanded team.

As I mentioned to him then, I saw this as an example of adult needs taking precedence over kids' needs. I don't think anyone had bothered to ask them, but I believed that the kids wanted to play baseball. The adult manager wanted to have a great record, win the championship, and go on to play in the tournament leading up to the Little League World Series. (To be fair to him, he also was concerned that his players have a good experience.) He argued that the kids wanted to win as much as he did. To which I could only agree. Of course they would rather win than lose. But if his players view accepting a forfeit as having the same significance as defeating the other team in a game, then something's wrong.

Fortunately in this situation, reason prevailed and the game was rescheduled rather than forfeited. But the point is that the league rules would have allowed a coach to claim the victory by forfeit, thus depriving the kids of a chance to play the game. And all too often, reason does *not* prevail. Adults tend to act in their own interests and as kids get older and more independent, more and more of them drop out of sports as they realize at some level that they're not benefitting from the system.

ELEMENTS OF A POSITIVE YOUTH SPORTS ORGANIZATION

There are five basic requirements for a youth sports league to be able to put the needs of the child above those of the adults. The league needs a board of directors that takes its responsibility seriously. It needs to develop and promote a clear set of goals that puts the child's needs first. It needs a group of positive coaches who like kids and who are committed to the goals of the league. Finally, the league needs organizational structure and rules that reinforce positive behavior by coaches, athletes, and parents.

1. **Board of directors:** This is the key to a great youth sports organization. In the nonprofit world, the board of directors *is* the organization. The board is the responsible party for decision-making, policy setting, and implementation. A league that does not have a strong board of directors is going to be in trouble over time. Often organizations will begin with a motivated individual or individuals developing a vision and getting other people excited about the organization. However, if the organization remains a product of only one or two people,

problems will ultimately keep it from fulfilling its important role.

With youth sports leagues, too often the board of directors is made up of reluctant members. Many board members would rather be involved with the kids and the sport than the organization as an entity. However, the board is where decisions get made that determine whether the kids have a good experience and learn anything about the game. The ideal situation for a youth sports league is where people on the board are excited about what the organization can do, not just about what an individual team or child can do. The ideal board is made up of people who look forward to fulfilling their board roles rather than having to be talked into being on the board.

No matter how well an organization is established, over time problems will arise that need to be dealt with. Perhaps there will be a shortage of coaches. Who is going to make sure that the league has enough coaches? Maybe the quality of officiating is poor. Who is going to deal with that problem? In both cases, and many others, it is the board of directors that needs to respond.

At the end of last year's Cupertino Hoops basketball season, the board met with the coaches to talk about the season and get input for the next season. One of the coaches warmed all of the board members' hearts by saying that he never saw a problem go longer than one week without being solved. If something went wrong on a given Saturday, there was a response from the board by the next Saturday. This was partly because the Cupertino Hoops board members were not reluctant members but committed to making the league an outstanding youth sports organization.

Ideally, your board of directors would include representatives of your ultimate customers, the kids. It is certainly an idea worth considering. If it is not feasible, there are other ways that you can make sure that the ideas and feelings of the kids are heard. You might hold an annual board meeting in which all the players are encouraged to come to talk about whatever they liked and disliked about the past season. You might accomplish the same purpose with a small "focus group" of representative players that might be less intimidating to most children.

2. **Clear and positive goals:** All great organizations begin with a clear statement of what they are trying to accomplish. A few years ago I asked a group of Little League baseball coaches what the purpose of our league was. The answers were all over the map. One coach said it was to teach the kids to be winners. Another said it was simply to win. A third said it was for the kids to have fun and learn some baseball. Another said it was to develop top athletes who would go on to play high sdhool and college baseball. The last said it was to produce one or two ballplayers over the course of a decade who would actually make it to the major leagues, like Dan Gladden, who played Little League baseball in Cupertino.

Upon reflection, I realized that the wide variation was not so surprising. Our league did not have published goals. If there were any formal goals, they certainly were not well known to the coaches. So it was natural for them to develop their own understanding of what the league was all about.

The absence of clear goals is not limited to youth sports organizations. It plagues many nonprofit organizations. Even private businesses, which at least have the advantage of an obvious goal of making a profit, all too often suffer from vague, misunderstood goals.

Fortunately the leadership of this league was interested in developing a clear set of goals, and I was assigned the task of drafting them. The Cupertino National Little

League adopted these four goals (see Appendix A):

- Create an environment in which children and adults have fun with baseball.
- Teach baseball skills, rules, and strategy to our players.
- Model and teach competitiveness with an emphasis on good sportsmanship.
- Promote increased self-esteem among our children and adults.

But just adopting the goals is not enough. If the coaches, players, and parents don't know what the goals are, or don't believe the league means business with them, they won't have an impact.

These goals were distributed to all of the managers and coaches. They were discussed in the required coaches meeting before the beginning of the season. As the minor league director that year, I referred to the goals whenever I saw an opportunity with the minor league coaches. When I saw a coach responding positively to a player after he had made a mistake, I complimented him on his positive approach and noted that it was in keeping with the league goals. When I saw a coach ragging on a player or an umpire, I reminded him about the goals and encouraged him to be positive.

As we publicized and promoted the goals, parents also began to take them seriously. At the end of the season, one parent pointed out that one of the coaches had behaved in a way that violated the spirit of the goals. Whenever a weak hitter from the other team would bat, he would yell out comments that may have encouraged his own pitcher but which also attacked the self-esteem and self-confidence of the batter. For example, he would yell, "Just throw it across the plate. He hasn't swung the bat all game." Another time his voice would carry out of the dugout with, "Don't worry. This guy hasn't gotten a hit all year." Before the beginning of the next season, we made a change to the goals document, adding section "d" to our goal on balancing competitiveness with sportsmanship:

Always treat players on other teams as members of our community first and as opponents secondarily. Refrain from actions or words that undercut the self-esteem of players on other teams.

The coach in question did not return the following season. We prominently mentioned and criticized this example, without using any names, in the training sessions for all coaches at the beginning of the season and had no similar problems that next season.

As this example illustrates, the beautiful thing about well-publicized goals is that people use them to measure other people's behavior. Other people will use an organization's goals to encourage or even force you to live up to them. If it is just a matter of someone not liking what you are doing, they may keep it to themselves. But if they believe you are violating widely understood goals, they are more likely to raise the issue. Since we all tend to slip from time to time, this is a positive position for an organization to be in.

I am convinced that these goals had a positive impact on the league. Coaches became more positive, the kids had a better experience, and, not coincidentally, the level of play also improved. My experience with a local basketball league was not so happy.

In that instance I proposed a similar set of goals to the board of the league, which immediately embraced them. However, there was virtually no follow-through. I was assured repeatedly that the goals would be distributed to all the coaches but they never were. I was asked to speak about the goals to a required meeting of all coaches, only to find when I arrived at the meeting that only about one-quarter of the coaches had even been notified of the meeting. In this case, simply adopting the goals with no follow-through had virtually no impact. Although I guess in one sense it had great impact, because it led several of us to start Cupertino Hoops (more on that to follow).

3. **Positive coaches:** It's hard to imagine how young athletes could have fun or develop increased self-esteem with coaches who yell and criticize them whenever they make a mistake. Coaches are essential to any youth sports league. Given enough time, resources, and commitment, an organization can always modify the behavior of its members. But if you start out with people who have similar values and objectives, you will get where you want to go faster.

   The first task is to assign someone the responsibility for the performance of the coaches. Most leagues I'm familiar with have people in charge of functional activities or age divisions. But if you want to assemble, develop, and keep a group of top coaches coming back year after year, you need to have someone devote time and effort to working with them.

   Recruiting coaches can be a challenge, and many leagues find themselves perennially short of coaches. The key is to beat the bushes to get more potential coaches than you think you will need. This way the league will be a buyer in a buyer's market for coaches. Robert Cialdini, in his landmark book, *Influence*, tells how a crafty seller can get the best price for a used car. He will schedule appointments for several buyers to look at the car at the same time. As the first potential buyer is kicking the tires and just beginning to point out problems that indicate that the price is too high, the second potential buyer arrives. Just a few minutes after that, the third potential buyer pulls up. The seller then heroically defends the rights of the first customer, saying, "This gentleman was here first so you will have to wait until he is through. If he decides not to purchase the car, then you will get your chance." The highly visible competition tends to cause the first buyer to give up on any real negotiation and, more often than not, pay the asking price.

If a league is in a position where it needs to beg someone to coach, it will be difficult to have much influence on that coach's behavior. On the other hand, if you can generate more coaching candidates than you have room for, they will tend to be receptive to your cues about the kind of behavior you expect from them. And if you do end up with more positive coaches than you need, you can double or even triple up coaches to work with each other. Multiple coaches, under the leadership of a head coach or manager, allow for more individual coaching and less standing around in practices. It also gives you a roster of future potential head coaches that you can observe unobtrusively in preparation for the next year's coach selection process.

There are some likely ways to increase your supply of coaches. You can advertise in the local newspaper. You can go to a local college that may have a sports or recreation program. You might ask returning coaches, who exemplify the characteristics that you'd like to see in all of your coaches, if they have any friends that might be interested in coaching. A local high school might have some students who are interested in working with younger kids or assisting an adult with a team. You might also ask the local high school coaches for the names of any recent graduates, perhaps attending community college in the area, who might be interested. Often an athlete who doesn't continue playing a sport in college misses being involved with the game and might be excited about being able to share what she has learned with young kids coming up.

Once you have identified a group of potential coaches, you can begin to help both them and you sort out whether you want to work together. You can invite prospective coaches to an orientation session at which you outline the goals and norms of your program. You can be explicit about the kinds of coaches you are interested in and what you expect from them. At this point, you actually want some prospective coaches to drop out. You should be pleased if coaches seeking a cutthroat kind of prograrn where the kids are treated like foot soldiers decide not to join your league. Individuals who sign up to coach in your league after finding out about it in the orientation will have a clear idea of what is expected. They are likely to be committed to being or becoming the kind of positive coach you want to have working with your young people.

When you have recruited and selected a good group of coaches, you need to support and recognize them for their contributions to your program. You want coaches in your program who want to continuously improve their coaching ability. Your league can help them get better by sponsoring coaching workshops presented by outstanding college and high school coaches in the area. You can help the coaches identify with your league by providing them with T-shirts or sweatshirts with the league logo. You can also hold an appreciation event at the end of the season to recognize their contributions to the success of the league and get their feedback on how it could be improved for the next year.

As important as it is to reinforce positive coaching behaviors, it is just as important to avoid the temptation to reinforce inappropriate behaviors. Many youth sports organizations have all-star teams that play in post-season tournaments. If you want to send a signal to your coaches that winning is the most important thing, there is no easier way to do that than to make the coach of the winningest team during the season the coach of the all-star team. It is hard to overestimate the insidious impact that the prestige and excitement of being the all-star coach can have on otherwise sane and positive coaches. If you want to reinforce positive coaches who have the best interests of their players in mind, there is no more powerful way than to determine the all-star coach on the basis of positive coaching throughout the season rather than on the won-lost record. To take this out of the realm of politics, you will need to design as objective a decision-making process as you can. One way would be to have the coaches in the league vote for the coach (other than themselves) that they believe best embodies the organization's goals and positive coaching values. Another way would be to appoint a panel of objective people (i.e., who have no children in the league) to make the decision after observing each coach during the season.

But there is no getting around the fact that once in awhile, in spite of your best efforts, you are going to get a coach or two who doesn't get with the program. When this happens, you need to respond or other coaches and parents will begin to lose faith that your league means what it says about its goals. Until you intervene with a coach who is a problem, you will never know if he is in the influence-able or incorrigible category. It may be that he will be open to doing things a different way. Or it may be that he is not willing to change and become more positive. If there is a problem, you need to talk openly and directly with the coach so that he can have the chance to change.

One parent mentioned that her daughter once had a terrible teacher one year in elementary school. She was happy to find out that the teacher did not return the following year. She said that she never knew whether the principal was responsible for removing the incompetent teacher or if the teacher had moved on for some reason of her own. Nonetheless, this parent was impressed and assumed that the principal was responsible for removing the teacher. When a negative coach fails to return in the next season, it can be a powerful message to parents that someone is minding the store in this league, and negative coaching will not be tolerated.

4. **League organization:** Another piece of the puzzle is how you can organize your league to reinforce the behaviors and values you want exhibited by your coaches, players, and parents. Here are four key organizational elements followed by some recommendations regarding rules.

a. *Fun for adults too:* Just because you are committed to making your league one that puts the kids' needs first doesn't mean that the adults involved can't also get a great deal of satisfaction from the experience. When Paul Solomon, Susan Solomon, Joe Bagliere, Jack Bower, Wayland Lim, and I were organizing Cupertino Hoops, we spent an incredible amount of time trying to anticipate problems so that our first year could be successful. Since we were spending so much time bringing this new league into being, we decided that it was as important that we have fun as it was to create an environment in which the players would have fun. We came up with these "operating principles":

1. *People should work on things they are interested in and/or feel strongly about to the extent possible (even if this means an unusual division of labor that looks weird).*

Many organizations develop rigid organizational charts based on some conscious or unconscious belief about the way organizations *should* be. Often people don't work as hard or as enthusiastically as they are capable of because they don't really care that much about what they are doing. We decided that we wanted to let people take the roles that they felt strongly about.

For example, Paul Solomon put an incredible amount of effort into developing an enrichment program for Cupertino Hoops players and coaches.

Paul held a special practice session for our first-time basketball players a week before the regular practices began so that they could be introduced to important ideas like pivoting, proper shooting technique, etc. He arranged for every one of our teams to play during the halftime of a local college or professional game. This past year, two of our teams played in the Oakland Coliseum at the halftime of a Golden State Warriors game. Two other teams played at the halftime of a women's game matching the defending NCAA champion, Tennessee, against the defending NIT champion, Santa Clara University. Paul arranged for players and coaches to attend a practice of the San Jose State University men's basketball team, and for Stan Morrison, SJSU's men's coach, to conduct a coaching clinic. He also arranged for clinics by two of the best high school coaches in the state, Phil Kelly of Fremont High School in nearby Sunnyvale and Guin Boggs of Washington High in Fremont. Former Stanford and Utah Jazz star, Rich Kelley, also conducted a clinic on how coaches could make practices fun so that players would want to continue playing basketball.

Imagine what our enrichment program would have been like had someone else been assigned this task who had little or no enthusiasm for it! Because Paul was so passionate about enrichment activities, he made extra efforts that resulted in exciting enrichment activities that none of us would have dreamed of

Of course, there are all kinds of tasks needing to be handled that *no one* is excited about. To the extent possible, we try to divide those tasks equitably so that no one person is stuck with only tasks they don't enjoy. And having this statement permits board members who aren't happy with what they are doing to try to restructure their responsibilities in a way that better meets their needs and desires.

2. *All board members should take responsibility for the overall success of Cupertino Hoops, even though there will be division of labor. Each of us should feel able to and responsible for making suggestions about improving all parts of the organization.*

It is too easy for organization members who are not president or chairperson to focus narrowly on their role and not speak up about problems outside their responsibility. We wanted to avoid that trap. We wanted everyone to be a generalist who looked beyond their area of responsibility to the larger picture.

3. *It's okay to make mistakes.* This is as important for adults as it is for kids.

4. *We should try to follow through on what we agree to do. We should acknowledge when we haven't done what we said we'd do, why, and what, if anything, should be done now. In any case, we should avoid having things fall through the cracks without acknowledging it.*

All of us are busy. We have jobs, families, other interests, and basic human needs for sleep and food. There will be times when we forget to do what we said we would. There will be times when we try and just don't get it done. Our commitment is not to be perfect, but to try our best, ask for help if we need it, and then to acknowledge when we have come up short. But in any case, it is critical that we not leave important tasks hanging.

5. *We all should make a point of recognizing the work that each of us is putting in to make Cupertino Hoops successful and expressing gratefulness to each other.*

Once again the principles we are trying to en-

courage our coaches to use with their players work
wonderfully with us as well.

6. *Cupertino Hoops should be a fun and fulfilling experience
for the organizers as well as the players, coaches, and referees.*
So far it seems to be happening!

b. *A community of coaches:* When I was an undergraduate
at Macalester College in St. Paul, Minnesota, I was
taken with a book by Paul Goodman, *The Community
of Scholars.* Working at the Stanford Business School,
I have been greatly influenced by John Gardner's recent work on community. In building this new basketball program from the bottom, we decided that
we wanted to create a community atmosphere in
which Cupertino Hoops coaches could become friends
and colleagues rather than seeing each other primarily as competitors.

We approached this in several ways. At the beginning of the season, we gave each coach a sweatshirt
with the Cupertino Hoops logo on it. This is not unusual for sports leagues but typically the coaches'
shirts are the same color as their teams, which reinforces the coach as a member of his team. We wanted
to reinforce the coaches as part of a community of
coaches, so we gave each coach a navy blue sweatshirt. That way each coach could be immediately recognized as a coach at the games by the sweatshirt
(and in many other places where they wear the sweatshirt as well). We ended the year with a coaches appreciation luncheon in which we treated them to
lunch and asked them for their feedback on the season and what changes we should make for the next
season.

We also started the tradition of ending the year
with a coaches game in which the players got a chance
to watch their coaches try to do what they had been

asking them to do all season. This game worked so well as a way for the coaches to get to know each other that we added a second coaches game at the *beginning* of the season. These games gave the coaches a chance to work together in a very tangible way that was fun for them as well.

Our approach has worked well. In virtually every youth sports league I have seen, there have been serious conflicts between coaches. Coaches tend to identify with their team and see opposition coaches as rivals and sometimes even as enemies. We have had few conflicts between coaches in Cupertino Hoops; in fact, the opposite has been the case. Many friendships have developed among coaches who are enthusiastic about the league and their important role in it.

c. *Evaluation and continuous improvement:* Most youth sports organizations, actually most organizations of any kind, do not take evaluation very seriously. Partly that is because it is difficult to evaluate what you are doing when you are so intimately involved with it. And partly that is because there are so many other urgent things to do that something that is merely important (if not urgent) can get overlooked. And, frankly, part of it may also be that the organization is afraid of what it might hear if it asked its customers how satisfied they were.

Several of us who started Cupertino Hoops had backgrounds in business and some familiarity with the quality movement in industry. We wanted to make sure that we continued to improve the quality of our league. On the last day of the season, we surveyed players, parents and coaches about how they felt about Cupertino Hoops. (A copy of each of the evaluation forms is contained in Appendix B.) Since we had specific goals for the league, we asked each of our constituencies how we did.

The results of the survey were heartening. Almost

all (94 percent) of our players reported that they had made new or better friends during the season. On a five-point scale (1 = *terrible*, 2 = *pretty bad*, 3 = *OK*, 4 = *pretty good*, 5 = *outstanding*), players gave a rating of 4.2 to the amount of fun they had and 3.5 to the amount of basketball learned. We asked the parents about the degree to which their children gained self-esteem and self-confidence during the season. Self-esteem was rated at 4.2 and self-confidence at 4.1. As to the quality of coaching, every parent rated their child's coach as either a 4 (*pretty good*) or a 5 (*outstanding*). Equally important, we gained insight from the evaluation responses that helped us decide to expand the league to include ninth-graders this past season as well as make other improvements. The parents of our eighth-graders wanted the program to continue to be available to their children. Testifying to our emphasis on evaluating how we were doing and making improvements, one parent this year answered the survey question, "What needs to be improved for next season?" with "Less surveys. You know what you are doing and you're doing fine!"

d. *Mainstreaming:* I grew up in small towns in North Dakota. Places like Colfax, Hickson, Wyndmere, and Mayville. There wasn't a lot of distinction between boys and girls as far as sports were concerned. There were so few kids at all that almost always our games were co-ed. And some of the best athletes were girls like my cousin Marion.

There weren't any special programs for kids with developmental disabilities. Everybody knew everybody else and everybody played with everybody else. It wasn't until years later that I realized that one of the kids I hung out with was probably mentally retarded. Had we lived in a big city, he might well have been assigned to a special education room or even to a different school. We just accepted him as "not so swift" and didn't give it much thought. He played on our baseball team and wasn't too bad a ballplayer. Nowadays there is a fancy term to describe what we took for granted. It's called "mainstreaming" and it still offers the same advantages it did in North Dakota 30 years ago. It introduces so-called normal children to children with handicaps so that each can learn about the human condition. It also gives the special needs athletes the chance to participate in a much wider set of activities than are available for people with disabilities.

The developmentally disabled: My wife, Sandra, works with developmentally disabled children and adults. When I got involved with starting Cupertino Hoops she suggested that we publicize the league among parents of developmentally disabled children to see if any of them wanted to play. I was not excited about the idea. Getting the league started was a lot of work and at that point it was not at all clear that the league was going to succeed. This seemed to be adding an additional level of complexity to an already complex operation (and I did have a job and a family and a need to sleep also).

But Sandra is nothing if not persistent. She spoke to the board, and we seriously considered her proposal. The more we all thought about it, the more it seemed like exactly the right thing to do. We were about building good people as well as good basketball players. Mainstreaming young athletes with Down syndrome into our league seemed like a great way to make a statement about the value of sports for other aspects of life. We advertised through Parents Helping Parents, a local support group for parents of children with disabilities, and Matt and Ross, two boys with Down syndrome, joined our league.

Both athletes became valued members of their teams, often holding their own against the player they guarded and occasionally scoring. In the last game of the season, Matthew, who was on my team, made two long-range baskets in a row and the entire audience including the players on both teams came unglued and cheered him as he ran back on defense, thrusting his fist into the air in triumph. In our second season, both Ross and Matthew returned, and we added a third boy with Down syndrome.

One of my favorite moments of our first season came in an early game when Ross, who stands about five feet five inches, grabbed a loose ball near his own basket and started to go up for a shot. Standing a few steps away from him was Keith, at six feet four inches, one of the strongest players in our league and a member of the other team. In addition to being big, Keith was quick and agile and only a step or two away from Ross. He had blocked many shots that season, often from players much taller than Ross. But in this case he stood immobile to let Ross take his shot (and miss, this time).

Ross's team also had a tall player who was very talented, named Todd. Over the course of the season, the two of them developed what turned out to be a very effective play. Todd would position himself under the basket while Ross set up out in three-point land. Ross is a much better shooter than you would guess at first, but nonetheless he missed quite a few from three-point range. However, with Todd near the basket, Ross became a leading assist man on the team, as Todd picked off his shot-passes and put them in the basket for an easy two points. Both Keith and Todd have gone on to excel for their respective high school teams and have bright futures as college players, but nothing they can do in the future will impress me as much as how they interacted with Ross when they were eighth-graders in Cupertino Hoops.

The overall reaction to including children with disabilities into Cupertino Hoops was more positive than any of us would have dared hope. In the evaluations at the end of the season, many parents mentioned the benefit that they had seen for their children from playing with and against Matthew and Ross. And that is what mainstreaming is supposed to be about: providing a mutual benefit that flows between the special and the "regular" athletes.

Co-educational basketball: **One** year before we started Cupertino Hoops, my team of hotshot sixth-grade boys practiced Monday nights in the same gym with a team of seventh- and eighth-grade girls. My kids had played together for several years and easily won every game they played in their league. The girls across the gym from us were even stronger relative to their competition in their all-girls league. The other coach and I decided to try scrimmaging one night and the result ultimately made Cupertino Hoops a co-ed league. This group of girls was amazing. They played my team of boys to a standstill (often beating us) week after week. Their coach told me it was the only competition they got. Their regular season games were effectively over before the end of the first quarter.

When we started Cupertino Hoops, it was only natural to make it a co-ed league. We assumed that only the top girl players would tend to come to our league for the competition with boys, with the weaker ones playing in a girls-only league, but we were wrong. In 1990-91, our first year of operation, we had 18 girls out of 108 players total. Many of the girls were top athletes but as many were not. In fact, some of them were beginners. We were worried that the weaker girl players would have a bad experience, but such was not the case, for at least three reasons.

First, as described later, we made a great effort to

balance the teams so that every team had some weak players. In some cases the weak players were girls, but just as often they were boys. In almost every case, a weak player, boy or girl, on each team was able to match up against a weak player on the other team. Second, we made sure that every team that had girls had at least two on the team. Several teams had no girls but every team that had any had at least two. This made it less likely that a lone girl would feel isolated on a team of boys. In some cases we were able to put three girls on a team, which was even better. Finally, because we had great coaches, many of the weaker players made great progress during the year. Some girls that had never played basketball before blossomed as players during the season. The mother of one girl told me that her daughter, who was an outstanding soccer player, was now hooked on basketball and couldn't wait to play high school basketball. In our second year of operation, we increased to 33 the number of girls (out of 142) and added our first woman coach. With the increased numbers, we were able to put three or more girls on most teams.

Word is starting to get around that Cupertino Hoops is the place for girls who want to play high school basketball. This past year, three girls from a nearby community signed up to play. Since we hadn't advertised in that city I asked how they had heard about us. It turned out that they had attended a Stanford women's game at which two of our co-ed teams played during halftime. Then they attended a girls basketball camp during the summer in which they were encouraged to try to get into a league where they could play against boys if they wanted to play high school basketball.

The advantage to the girls is obvious. By playing against boys, they get tougher as they get used to a rougher style of play. Big girls who could simply "out-giant" other girls are faced with having to develop some moves when they play against boys who are bigger than they are. They also see moves that boys use routinely and see no reason why they also shouldn't be able to dribble behind the back, hit three-pointers regularly, or shoot lay-ups with either hand. I am convinced that Cupertino Hoops will ultimately have a big impact on girls basketball in the Bay Area because of the experience our girls have playing against boys. And it's starting already. Two of our recent alumnae started as freshman on the Monta Vista High Schoo' team that won the 1992 Northern California Division I Championship.

I am convinced that the benefit is just as great for the boys. The boys who play with and against girls are going to have a very different view of a woman's capabilities than men of my generation who experienced sports as a male domain with girls primarily as cheerleaders. As one of the parents of a Cupertino Hoops girl remarked recently, co-ed teams give boys and girls at an awkward stage the chance to get to know each other outside the dating scene, as teammates and fellow athletes.

5. **Rules that support the goals:** In addition to the organizational structure, the specific rules of a league can either contribute to or detract from the league's ability to achive its goals. You must consider the issues of standings and championships, minimum playing time, liberal resubstitution, giving kids choices in teammates and coaches, balancing teams to avoid mismatches, grouping players by ability rather than age, and creative scheduling.

a. *Championships and standings:* Perhaps the most important decision a board can make in terms of influencing how the coaches, players, and parents in your league behave has to do with whether you will keep standings and have a championship. When people perceive that there is something important at stake, they will work hard to try to win, often sacrificing other values to do so. And many times, coaches trying to win in this situation will make decisions that have negative consequences for the players involved. For example, weaker players tend to get to play less. There is more pressure on all kids to win with players on losing teams having less fun. And even the kids on winning teams seem to have less fun.

For most sports and leagues, I believe that having a league championship brings more problems than benefits. We have operated Cupertino Hoops basketball for two years without a championship, and I have seen no lack of effort or intensity by players, teams, or coaches. Certainly the players know their team's record and comparative ability, and they get up for games against teams who will give them a tough game. The games are hard-fought and the level of basketball played is remarkably high. Many of our players have moved from our league directly on to junior varsity and even varsity basketball teams in their first year of high school.

And there are some benefits from not keeping standings or having playoffs and a championship. We have no arguments about a player's eligibility. Kids sometimes travel a long distance to play in Cupertino Hoops. Since there is no championship at stake, no one cares if they live within the boundaries (there aren't any anyway) nor if they are the correct age. We don't have to check birth certificates and photo I.D.'s. We have fewer problems with coaches not wanting certain (usually weaker) players on their team. Weaker players get more playing time. There is more emphasis on skill development than winning. And perhaps most importantly, our kids have more fun during the season.

There is a time and place for league standings, playoffs, and championships in youth sports, and I am not against them. However, I am against a youth sports system where *every* experience a child has in sports is colored by the pressure to win. Some children decide they want to become serious athletes and compete in high school, college, or even professionally, and that's terrific. But not everyone can make the high school team, and there is no reason why children who are trying to learn a sport should be prematurely pressured to become obsessed with winning. The emphasis should be on developing skills and having fun while learning to play a game they can enjoy for a lifetime. Even high school athletes who lack the talent to play on the varsity will have more fun and learn more if the emphasis is on development and enjoyment rather than winning.

Ironically, I believe that players who participate in a league that puts an emphasis on development of their skills and understanding of the game will become better players than if they are constantly sacrificing their long-term learning and development to the greedy short-term god of winning the Pennywhistle Youth Baseball Championship of 19XX.

As Peters and Waterman note at the beginning of this chapter, too often organizations seem determined to make losers out of most of their members. It is difficult for the majority of athletes to feel like winners when the system is set up so that only one team can win and the rest are losers. It *is* possible for the majority of participants in a youth sports organization to come out of the experience feeling that they are winners, and it often starts with the no standings–no championship decision.

b. *Minimum playing time:* There is nothing so disheartening to a young athlete as sitting on the bench for most or all of a game. It can be humiliating and is almost always boring. As leagues become more concerned with winning at the expense of development, it becomes less likely that an equal playing time rule would be acceptable.

Under pressure to win, the tendency of a coach is almost always to work with the players that pick things up easily and who can win games for her. Requiring a coach to play each player for a significant portion of the game forces her to devote practice time to each player, since the fortunes of the team will not ride solely on the efforts of one or two superstars.

Every youth sports league that has the goal of developing character and self-esteem in young athletes should have a minimum playing time rule. Ideally, each athlete would play an equal amount of time, but in any case, each player should be assured of playing at least half of every game.

c. *Liberal resubstitution:* Even with minimum playing time rules, many coaches don't play their weaker players as much as they might because they want to win. A rule allowing liberal substitution and resubstitution will make it easier for the coach to play his weaker players to the maximum.

For example, imagine that you are coaching a baseball game in which you are ahead by seven runs in the third inning. This may seem like a pretty significant lead, but in Little League baseball the worm can turn pretty suddenly. Every coach has seen a seven-run lead disappear in one turn at bat for the other team. The coach may be reluctant to remove his star player for a weaker player because it is often difficult or impossible to get that player back into the game again if things start to go bad.

A liberal resubstitution rule would allow the coach to replace the star players with weaker ones earlier in a blowout game, secure in the knowledge that he can bring them back in if the other team stages a comeback. I use the term "liberal" rather than "unlimited" because resubstitution should function within the minimum playing time rules.

d. *Allow kids choices in teammates and coaches:* One of the great joys of participating in a sport is being able to play with people you feel close to and like. The relationships that athletes develop with their teammates can last for decades after their playing days are finished. A player's relationship with a coach can be one of the most rewarding aspects of sports. To the extent possible, it is good to allow kids to express their preferences about who they want to play with and for. A rigid system of drafting for team selection, where player and parent preferences about teammates and coaches are intentionally disregarded, can take much of the joy out of youth sports.

I know that many people associated with youth sports leagues worry about coaches bringing in a stacked team of players so strong that they can't be beaten. And I share that concern. However, you can allow players to express their preferences for teammates and coaches while telling them and their parents that you will honor their requests *unless* it results in unbalanced teams. Very few parents will argue with this logic when presented with it up front.

e. *Balance teams to minimize mismatches:* It took me awhile to realize something pretty basic. A big reason why so many kids have bad experiences with sports is because they lose so much. And the reason they lose so much is because often they play teams whom they have no hope of beating. In spite of the best efforts of rule-based tryout and drafting systems, virtually every year in Little League the difference between the top teams and the weakest teams in the league are great. Consequently, when the top teams play the bottom teams, the games are almost always one-sided. This does not benefit the weaker team, which often gets demoralized. Nor does it really benefit the stronger team, which can get an inflated view of its abilities and develop bad habits when it doesn't have to play its best to win.

There are several ways to balance teams. I have participated in a tryout-and-draft system where coaches select players in order, like the professional leagues in the college drafts. This is a meat-market approach, and I am not in favor of it. I think it sends a bad message to the kids (that they are there to perform for and at the whim of the adults), and I have seen it enough to know that it rarely results in balanced teams, its one supposed virtue. Some coaches are better at judging the ability of players than their fellow coaches. Often there are huge talent differences in the players who are holdovers on each team. These differences often virtually guarantee unbalanced teams because the best players in the league are already unequally distributed on teams. Rarely have I seen a tryout-and-draft system result in balanced teams.

One alternative is to balance the teams blindly. You can get all or some of the coaches together to group players into teams that are balanced. The safety net here is that no coach knows which team will be his until the balancing is over. Teams are then assigned to coaches by lottery, so there is no incentive to stack one team over another.

In Cupertino Hoops, we developed a separate interview form and procedure for both new and returning players. At the end of each season, each coach is asked to rate his players. This rating is then used for any players that return the next year. The interview for returning players is then simply to ask them if they have any preferences for teammates and coaches, and if there are any times when they are not available for practice.

For new players, the procedure is a bit more complicated. Each player is interviewed by a coach to try to determine how skilled he or she is. The players are asked questions, such as "What is the most points you have ever scored in a game?" and "How often do you score 10 or more points in a game?" Coaches also ask about previous basketball experience; for example, whether they have played for their school team. The interview system is certainly not perfect, but it has worked quite well in helping us balance teams in the two years we have used it.

Ultimately, however, you can never balance all teams perfectly. There always will be players who are better than you think they will be, just as there will be those who don't measure up to their advance billing. And sometimes you will get kids who click in a way that makes the team better than the sum of the parts. And, of course, coaching always makes a difference. A great coach can sometimes coax performance from a mediocre group of athletes while a mediocre coach can dampen the abilities of even great players.

The final option is to intervene after the season starts, if it becomes clear that the teams are so far out of balance as to be a joke. This is not easy to do. The parents, players, and coaches of the dominant team will not take kindly to having their group of winners being broken up. Nonetheless, it is often better to move kids around after the beginning of the season than to force all of the kids in the league to endure a season of mismatches.

This past season in Cupertino Hoops, one team in our lower division (mostly seventh- and eighth-graders) was unbeatable. The team had several strong players, but one seventh-grader in particular was outstanding. With him on the team, it simply would not lose a game no matter how far over their heads the other teams played. After three games, with his parents' approval and after consulting with the involved coaches, we moved him up to the upper division (mostly ninth- and tenth-graders). His old team still did well, but they were no longer unbeatable. And he continued to excel in the upper division while developing more quickly as he was pushed by the bigger and more talented competition. One parent of a player on another lower division team told me how pleased she was to see that we had taken this action to rebalance the teams in midseason.

f. *Group by ability rather than age:* In most cases, ability and age track each other. Older athletes are generally better than younger ones. However, there are always exceptions. There are athletes like Damon Bailey, now playing basketball for the University of Indiana, who reportedly displayed college level abilities when he was in the eighth grade. And there always will be older kids who are smaller or less developed than their age group who could function beautifully playing with younger kids.

In Cupertino Hoops, we have successfully placed older athletes in our lower division and younger athletes in the upper division, with little fuss by players, parents, or coaches. Recently, the mother of a boy with Down syndrome told me about her dilemma about baseball. The boy was over the official age limit for the minor league but not skilled enough to play with his own age group without danger of getting hurt. He was also much too advanced to play in the local "challenger" league for severely handicapped children. He had played in the minor league in his own community for several years but now was 13, and this Little League refused to let him play with and against children of comparable ability (who happened to be younger) because Little League rules prohibited it.

Were he to play on a major league team, it would jeopardize that league's all-star team from advancing to the Tournament of Champions at the end of the season, having used an ineligible player. But for the "minor" leagues, there is no equivalent to the Little League World Series tournament as there is for the "major" leagues. This special athlete's needs were not able to be met because of affiliation with a national organization whose rules prevented it from grouping by ability and responding to individual needs.

g. *Creative scheduling:* We thought long and hard about what makes a good athletic experience for kids. The first thing we came up with was that mismatches were negative. Neither team benefits and nothing is proved when one team trounces another by 24 to 0, as recently happened in a local Little League baseball game. Learning to lose with class is worthwhile, but the most development takes place when you are facing an opponent that is beatable but challenging. We realized that despite our best efforts to balance teams, we would fail and some teams would be much stronger than others.

We came up with a heretical idea: all teams would not necessarily play each other. They would play each other only if they were comparably matched. In most cases, there is only one reason why the strongest team in your program should play the weakest: there is a championship at stake and equity requires that each team competing for the title should have a comparable schedule to eliminate any disadvantage or advantage. If your league doesn't have a championship, this becomes a nonproblem.

To find out which teams were well-suited to play

each other, we had a preseason jamboree in which each team played at least four other teams in a 15-minute "mini-game." Based on the results of the jamboree, we scheduled the first one-third of the season with teams of equal ability playing each other. Then we monitored the results of those games and used them to schedule the second third, and so on.

I believe it was this breaking of tradition—every team did *not* need to play every other team—together with our great coaches, that resulted in the incredibly positive evaluations we got from our players in the end-of-the-season surveys.

One point about so-called "competitiveness." Often people say that Cupertino Hoops is not competitive. Sometimes they say this as a compliment, meaning that it is not a win-at-all-costs environment, which is true. However, sometimes it is a put-down, meaning that we don't put enough emphasis on winning. I believe that Cupertino Hoops is *very* competitive, even more competitive than most other youth sports organizations, in a very healthy way. Because we take great care to try to balance teams and use creative scheduling, we have more closely contested games than a typical youth sports organization. We believe that players try harder and learn more when they are challenged. And nothing challenges a player or team more than playing against a team that they know they can beat but might not be able to, depending upon how well they play compared to how well the other team plays.

WHAT COACHES AND PARENTS CAN DO

But perhaps you aren't the president of your youth sports organization and aren't likely to become the president anytime soon. What can a coach or parent do to make a nega-

tive sports experience more positive for the kids in the
league? Here are some suggestions.

1. **Adopt a style of "unanxious expectation":** Many reformers turn off potential allies. They tend to assume that
   everything that has gone on before is bad. Even if they
   don't believe that, they can often come across as hyper-
   critical and put the people who are in charge of the
   league now in a defensive posture. Rarely will you find
   anyone in a position of authority in a youth sports organization who has any sort of formal preparation or
   training in running a league. Most of them are doing
   the best they can as a public service for which they are
   not getting paid.

   In Chapter 5, I used Ted Sizer's phrase, "unanxious
   expectations," referring to how coaches should relate to
   their players; but the idea has more universal practical-
   ity. You *should* have high expectations for your youth
   sports organization but you aren't there to threaten
   anyone. People who are threatened often respond by
   circling the wagons rather than changing. You want to
   identify members of the choir (you *will* find some) and
   enlist their support. You want to identify people who
   are influence-able (there will be many who share your
   concerns and values) and influence them. And you want
   to avoid giving the incorrigibles ammunition with which
   to shoot down your suggestions for improving the
   league.

2. **Link with other parents and coaches:** Talk to other
   parents and coaches about these issues. Keep talking
   until you find a group of like-minded people. It doesn't
   take a majority of parents to have an impact on most
   youth sports organizations. A group of five to 10 parents with unanxious expectations (polite and persistent)
   can have an amazing impact. Most parents aren't involved with the league administration and aren't likely
   to be. A group of five or 10 isn't a majority of the entire

parent group. However, it is likely to be close to a majority of the *active* parents. Given that there may be people already on the board or in administrative positions who agree with much of what you want to do, five or 10 reformers can be an *effective* majority.

3. **Check out the goals:** Ask league officials for a statement of the league's goals. If there is no mention of building character and self-esteem in the goals, encourage the board to incorporate these concepts into the goal statement. Ask for time at the next board meeting to discuss and propose adding them to the goals. If there is no statement of goals (don't be surprised if this is the case), ask for time at a board meeting to propose adopting a formal goal statement.

4. **Use the goals to measure league behavior:** Once you get an appropriate set of league goals that include character and self-esteem, use them. When you see behavior by a coach or player that is not consistent with the goals, point it out to the coach. Regardless of how negative a coach may be, you owe it to him to express your concerns directly to him before complaining to others or league officials. Most coaches are open to feedback from parents and even players on how they are doing as coaches. They may not want to hear what you have to say, but few coaches will fail to make adjustments when confronted by a parent. If you fail to get satisfaction, then bring it to the attention of league officials. If you are successful in adopting a style of unanxious expectations, you might find the coach remarkably open to what you are saying.

Write letters to the board. It is easier for a board member to discount a casual conversation with you after a game than a letter sent to the entire board. A letter almost demands a written response, and very few groups will allow something in writing to be sent without some thought. You want the board to think about these issues, so write a letter when it seems appropriate.

5. **Challenge the league to evaluate:** Once goals are established, any outstanding organization is going to want to know how well it is doing in achieving them. You can help create momentum for change by getting the league to evaluate how well it is meeting the needs of its players. An evaluation process can send a signal to a group that there is the possibility of change. Many people may not be happy with what they see going on but assume that there is no interest by anyone else in doing things differently. If asked, they may well respond with suggestions and constructive criticisms that can help move the league toward positive change. (Appendix B has a copy of the evaluation forms used by Cupertino Hoops, which could be adapted for whatever sport you are involved with.)

6. **Be specific:** When criticizing something, focus on specific behaviors as much as you can. It usually isn't useful to tell a coach that she is "too negative" without some more specific feedback. "Yelling at Becky after she struck out with the bases loaded was not helpful to her sense of self-esteem." "Keeping Billy on the bench the entire game while winning by 30 points is not going to help him have a positive experience this season." Coaches are more likely to be able to hear that kind of feedback and to know what they need to do to respond to your concerns.

7. **Say what you like:** In addition to pushing for changes, make a point of telling people when you see things that you like. You would be amazed at how seldom coaches hear anything positive from parents or league officials, and how seldom league officials hear positive things from anyone. You will be further amazed at how much impact some positive reinforcement from you can have with a coach or board member. Review the self-esteem building ideas in Chapter 5 and use them with adults in your league as well as with the kids.

8. **Volunteer to help:** There is an unwritten rule of volun-

tary organizations that those who do the work have the power. Many an organization will move in the direction that one or two hardworking people want to go because no one else wants to have to do all their work. If you are willing to work, sooner or later you will acquire the influence and power to move the organization in the direction you want it to go.

If there is no goal statement, for example, volunteer to develop a draft that you will bring back to the board for its approval. If there is no training of coaches in positive coaching techniques, volunteer to put together such a session. There is likely to be some positive coaching role model in your community who would be willing to speak to your organization's coaches. If you find that person and get them to agree to speak, it will be hard for the board to turn it down.

9. **Allow acceptance time:** Most people don't change on a dime, no matter how right your suggestions might be. People are creatures of habit, and it takes awhile to change a habit or a belief. An idea that may seem heretical at first blush can look better and better over time. If you doubt this, get a copy of the *Communist Manifesto* by Marx and Engels. You will be amazed at how some of these once-inflammatory ideas (e.g., "Free education for all children in public schools. Abolition of children's factory labor . . .") have become ho-hum today. Assume that it will take some time for your youth sports organization to change, and don't get discouraged by lack of early progress. Your ideas will seep like water into the cracks and crevices of people's brains, where they will ultimately have an impact.

10. **Consider going independent:** If all else fails, consider forming a brand new organization. This is a lot of work, but the advantage is that you can do it right, from the start. When I worked in the energy conservation field, there was a saying that it's easier to build a house to use little energy from the beginning than

to retrofit it to save energy later. Given how much work there is in starting a league from scratch, I don't recommend it lightly to anyone. But there is a great amount of satisfaction to be gained.

In some cases, the problems may be caused by affiliation with a national youth sports organization that has rules that can't be modified by a local league. In this case, you might not need to start all over. It may simply be a matter of dropping your ties with the national organization or even finding another national organization with more appropriate goals and rules.

I don't encourage any league to rashly decide to disengage from a national organization, but it is not an unpatriotic act to consider. And in certain situations, it might be the right thing to do. The key question that should guide the decision is what is in the best interest of the players.

GET INVOLVED, HAVE AN IMPACT

Most youth sports organizations are eager for parents and coaches to get involved with league administration. Most coaches and parents I've known look upon this at best as a burden to be borne, at worst as something to be avoided like the plague. The best coaches usually would rather work directly with kids. However, if you are enthusiastic about the ideas in this book, I encourage you to look for and take advantage of the chance to try to move your league in a positive direction. As a board member or as someone in an administrative position with the league, you can have influence that will affect the experience that *many* children have with a sport. And that makes it worth the effort.

18

Facing the Demons:
The Dark Side
of Coaching Kids

> . . . I can write a book which will employ the tools of the craft to
> create interest. Its observations will be accurate and properly documented.
> It will be orderly in design and communicate a message. In the world of
> books it may even for a season find a place. But there is another way to
> write a book. There is a book which can come out of the depths of one's
> self, so that the ordinary is transcended and one is surrendered to the
> creative force that moves through all things. If I write the first book, I
> must consider its timeliness, and how many books have been written on
> the subject, and all that is proper to weigh when one is competing in a
> competitive market. If I write the second, I do not have to be concerned
> about these things or fear that what I do will be outdated. It may be on a
> subject used a hundred times, but it will be a subject made new. The
> book will have individuality as a person has individuality.
> —Elizabeth O'Connor
> Journey Inward Journey Outward

I hadn't intended to write this chapter. In my mind this
book was going to be a how-to book for people who didn't
know as much as I did about coaching kids in a positive
fashion. It was a happy tale from someone who never lost
his cool, never got angry with a player for sulking on the
playing field, who always had the best interests of the
children (as people, not just as players) in his mind. But

the longer I coached and the more I worked on this book, I realized that I had to say something about the dark side of sports, and not as a commentary on "other" coaches but out of my own experience.

I once saw a counselor during a period of time that coincided with basketball season. Although my intention was to discuss my career and other "big" issues, almost all I ever talked about with her was basketball and my reactions to my team of third- and fourth-graders. So many issues came up in my coaching experience that there was rarely time for anything else, seldom any reason to think that other issues were more pressing.

What I discovered during the course of that season was that I had a dark, murky set of expectations about the way the world was going to work out for me in sports. When things didn't go the way I wanted them to, something mean and willing to bend the rules snuck out of me.

THE COACH AS A MIXED-MOTIVE MAMMAL

John Gardner once remarked that it used to bother him when people did the right thing for the wrong reason. However, as he has gotten older, he has found that it doesn't matter so much to him why people do the right thing, as long as they do it.

Although we may want to believe otherwise, rarely is anything that people do pure in motive. I'm not even sure that purity of motive is useful, even if it were attainable.

Last year I was asked to speak to a group of fund-raising executives on how to attract the best and the brightest young people into fund-raising for worthy, nonprofit causes. I prepared a presentation looking at the various motives people have for volunteering. Part of why people volunteer is social. They like the people they meet and work with through a particular organization. This was true for me when I served on the board of the YWCA's

Parent Education Program, and it is an important reason why those of us on the board of Cupertino Hoops are willing to spend so much time in meetings trying to make the organization better.

People also volunteer for economic reasons. The boss may expect it. In certain companies it is well known that to advance, you are expected to contribute to or volunteer on the boss's favorite charity. Networking often enters into people's decision to volunteer. People in the job market may hope to meet other people on the board of a nonprofit who might help them change companies or even careers.

Part of why people volunteer may also be because they see it as a way to develop some new skills. Women who left the job market to raise children sometimes volunteer as a way to ease back into the working world after several years absence.

And, of course, many people volunteer for noble, even altruistic reasons. Some people care deeply about a specific problem, and they want to try to solve it. They, or a loved one, may have been a victim of a particular disease, and they want to do something about it. Other people have a global sense of injustice at inequities in the world without any particular personal experience with it. They simply want to make the world a better place. The typical volunteer is motivated by her own personal constellation of these and other motives.

While I was waiting to be introduced to give my speech, the host said that the next meeting of this group was going to be a "walkaway workshop," meaning that everyone who attended would be able to take away something tangible on paper. Everyone in the audience thought the alliteration was kind of cute and laughed appreciably. While I was chuckling, a light went off in my head. When I got up to speak, my talk suddenly had an even more alliterative title: "Motivating Mixed-Motive Mammals."

My main point was that nonprofit organizations that are able to address the mixed motives of their volunteers will find themselves with a loyal band of talented people. Organizations that appeal only to a single motive will be less successful. For example, an organization may appeal to, and initially attract, volunteers solely on the basis of the altruistic value of the work they are doing. If that same organization also offers volunteers the chance to interact with other friendly, interesting people, the bond between volunteer and organization will be strengthened. If the organization can also provide training and experience working with new and useful skills, even better. And if the organization also is one that is recognized by a volunteer's employer as a worthy charity, and sends a thank-you letter to the employer for the work that the employee has done, that organization will have to beat excess volunteers away with a stick.

Coaches also have mixed motives for coaching. For many of us there is an element of pure and simple fun. We love the sport and want to continue to be involved with it. I enjoy going to basketball practices on Monday night and working with the team. It's a good time.

As coaches improve, they begin to feel good about being able to do something that they are good at, which is a motivation all by itself. And most coaches really are concerned about the kids and believe they are performing a useful service by coaching.

The social element is often there as well. A friend from out of state visited me recently and talked about how much he enjoyed going to high school basketball games. His wife said he makes the rounds at the games like a politician working a room. He has a great time visiting with people he otherwise wouldn't see much. She thinks he'll keep going to the basketball games long after their kids have graduated from high school. It reminded me of what I imagined an old-time, small-town ice cream social might have been like. It also made me realize that I felt the same way about attending Cupertino Hoops games on Saturday mornings. Unless I have another commitment, I usually stay to watch all the games, not just my own team's. There isn't anything I'd rather do than watch our kids play basketball. I get to talk to the coaches, many of whom have become friends. I enjoy yelling encouragement to the players. It's good to catch up on what's happening with the parents. It's a community and I'm part of it. It's a great feeling.

For some coaches there may be a financial motive. Many amateur coaches aspire to make a living as high school or college coaches. For me, I am not unaware that if this book sells well, I will benefit financially from my years of coaching.

It's useful for coaches to assess their own mixture of motives. There's nothing wrong with having your own personal and selfish motives for coaching as well as the more noble reasons. It's unavoidable, and in fact, most things work best when multiple (selfish and altruistic) motivations are in alignment. The combination of the two is usually much stronger than either one by itself. But sometimes there is something darker lurking beneath the surface that needs to be brought into the light of day.

WHY OTHER PEOPLE BUG ME

One day at a counseling session, I was very angry at a player on my team. Chuckie was a big kid who, during the previous week's practice, had "pretended" to be hurt and lay down on the court. I tried to talk to him to see what was wrong, but he curled up in the fetal position and refused to acknowledge that I was even there. I became enraged. I rolled him off the court and told the rest of the kids to resume playing. When I related this episode in graphic detail to my counselor, she momentarily silenced me with the question, "Why do you think it makes you so angry when an eight-year-old boy pretends to be hurt?" My anger was now directed at her. "Why do you even ask such a question? Isn't it obvious? He's not really hurt! He's just trying to get sympathy!"

But the question is reasonable. Why did I take it *personally* when Chuckie lay down. It's actually kind of funny now when I look back on it, but it wasn't then. I felt like he was out to get me, and I was determined not to let him get away with it.

I have long accepted the idea that when something about another person bugs me it is because it taps into something similar in me that I cannot tolerate. But in this concrete case, I was not prepared to accept that abstraction. I was sure that I was angry with Chuckie *only* because he was acting badly. It had *nothing* to do with me!

However, over time I began to see that indeed it was connected to some things deep within me. Chuckie's laydown triggered several reactions that I didn't want to face. One dealt with my own uneasiness about being a responsible grown-up. There was a part of me that wanted to be like Chuckie and lie down when the world got to be too much. But I couldn't let myself, and that made me angry at Chuckie. I couldn't allow myself to curl up and pretend the rest of the world no longer existed when life overwhelmed me. But he could and I resented it.

Another insight concerned my need to please others. Much of my life has seemed to be a neverending quest to please everyone, even people I've never met before and will never see again! Chuckie didn't particularly have that problem. When he laid down on the court, he wasn't concerned about whether I would be pleased or not. Chuckie had some freedom from the expectations of others that, deep down, I also wanted. I envied him.

There was another even more painful issue to face. I had some powerful unresolved issues about my own athletic career. Chuckie had a lot of potential as an athlete. He wasn't using even a fraction of the talent he had, yet he still was a pretty good ballplayer. How good might he be if he really gave it his all? I was angry at Chuckie partly because I believed that I hadn't realized my potential either. I didn't want to look at my own fears that I hadn't tried as hard as I could to become the best basketball player I could be. When Chuckie laid down, he reminded me that, at some level, I saw myself as someone who had also failed to give it his best, who had failed to live up to his fantasies.

Fantasy Number One: Greatness as a Basketball Player

I want to win. I want to be a hero. When I was a kid I was big and strong and fast for my age. I got a basketball for Christmas when I was in seventh grade. In my youthful hubris, I wrote on the ball, "West Fargo—North Dakota State Champs 1965." The year 1965 was to be my sophomore year in high school. I intended to lead my team to three consecutive state championships! Well, we never made it to the state tournament at all, except as spectators. As I got older, other kids grew more and faster than me. As a seventh-grader, I was a monster athlete. As a sophomore, I was a good athlete. As a senior, I was a little above average. When I got to Macalester College and made the freshman team, I realized that I was about the ninth man of 12 on a very weak freshman team at a weak basketball school in a weak basketball league of small liberal arts colleges in Minnesota.

During Christmas vacation, I visited my roommate and his family in Silver Bay, Minnesota. We went skiing and had a great time. I came back to campus to play in a freshman basketball game and threw out my right knee. I had been spiked on the knee playing softball the summer before, and it left me with a trick knee that I hoped would improve over time. Apparently the skiing had put some additional stress on the knee, resulting in my being carried off the basketball floor. If I hadn't been in such physical pain, I would have enjoyed the moment both because it was kind of cool to have the crowd concerned about me and because it allowed me a graceful way to quit the team.

About the same time, Macalester had a player named Gordy Cochrane who, while only about five feet eight inches, was captain and star of the team. I remember him as someone who had worked hard and made the most of his limited physical ability. Looking back, I believe that one reason I didn't reach my potential was because I became so big so quickly and then stopped growing. Basketball came easy for me in junior high school because I was bigger, quicker, and more coordinated than most other kids. I did well without ever having to try really hard. When it got tougher later on, I didn't crank up my effort level. Instead I got discouraged with basketball and ultimately quit. Could I have worked hard enough to play major college basketball? Probably not. Could I have worked hard enough to have become, like Gordy Cochrane, a good player at the small college level? That seems entirely possible. And because I believed I had never tried to become the best I could be, I had regrets.

My dreams of glory haven't gone away. They've gone underground. They stay quietly in place like a group of guerilla fighters blending into the scenery until the moment of weakness, when they strike out to do their damage. Which leads me to the next fantasy.

Fantasy Number Two: Greatness as a Coach

I am now no longer able to even imagine myself as a great basketball player, but I could still achieve greatness as a coach, couldn't I?

Yet another reason why Chuckie's behavior bothered me was that it tore at my image of myself as a great coach. I had worked successfully with severely emotionally disturbed children. I had handled kids with behavior problems the average youth sports coach wouldn't believe. And here was this kid who was making me feel and look like a monkey instead of a great coach.

In the children's book, *The Neverending Story,* a young boy begins to read a book called *The Neverending Story*. After awhile something strange happens. He discovers that he is *in* the book that he is reading about. The author uses different colored type on the printed page to let you, the reader, know when you are reading the story about the little boy and when you are reading the story that the little boy is reading.

While writing this book, I began to notice strange connections between my writing and my life. Or perhaps it is more accurate to say that I noticed strange divergences between the two. As I got closer and closer to finishing the book, my coaching behavior seemed to become more and more like that of someone who desperately needed to read the book, rather than someone who had written it.

I found myself becoming increasingly negative. I sat next to a friend and fellow coach at one of our sons' junior high school basketball games. As the game progressed, I got more and more agitated with the officiating. At one point I found myself waving my glasses at the referees to indicate that they needed them more than I did, based on their calls. He finally said, "I've never seen you like this. You're usually so calm and positive."

A few weeks later, my basketball team, playing an outstanding game, found itself 13 points ahead of a highly favored team of older and bigger kids late in the third period. In the fourth period, the other team came roaring back and took the lead by one point in the last minute. With under 10 seconds left, one of our players was fouled while shooting and went to the line to shoot two free throws. He missed both, and we ended up losing. In retrospect, the loss bothered me less and less. What began to bother me more was the fact that I hadn't reminded my free throw shooter that it was okay if he missed both free throws. In the first place, if I had remembered to do so, he might have been more relaxed and more likely to hit one or both of them. But more importantly, I was upset because I realized that I had forgotten to remind him because at that moment it *wasn't* okay to miss the free throws. I had gotten so caught up in winning that I had forgotten one of my life principles.

Later when I was writing Chapter 8 on how to make practices more fun, I noticed that the practices of the team I was coaching at the moment weren't particularly fun. As I reviewed chapters I had written months or even years before, I noted with some embarrassment that there were lots of great ideas in them that I was no longer incorporating into my own coaching.

I'm not sure I even now understand what was going on. Certainly the time pressure of having a publisher's deadline to meet, added to an already squeezed schedule, was a factor. But another factor seemed more relevant. As this book came closer and closer to fruition, I began to feel like I had to be something other than what I naturally was. If I were writing a book on coaching, didn't I have to be one of the world's best coaches? The way you demonstrated your coaching ability was by winning games. But right about this time when I was completing the last few chapters of the book, my basketball team lost five games in a row.

My teams have had losing streaks before and it never failed to bother me. But this seemed intolerable. I began to doubt my right even to write such a book. Who was I anyway to try to write a how-to book about coaching kids when my team lost five games in a row?

Fantasy Number Three: Greatness as a (Sports) Parent

There is one more sports fantasy to fall. I remember reading about Orlando Cepeda, the power-hitting first baseman for the San Francisco Giants in the 1960s. It seems that Orlando's father was a baseball player before him who had modest success as a player. He was determined to make Orlando into a great player. I suspect that this story, which I believed was true, had its influence on me. Perhaps at some level I intended for my son to be the athlete I never quite was.

When he was 12, the big year for a Little Leaguer, he decided that he didn't want to play baseball. I was to be the manager of the team, and I had big plans about how well we would do. I was going to manage them to the league championship which would make me the manager of the league's all-star team. Then I was going to lead the all-star team to a better finish than any Cupertino Little League team had ever achieved. I didn't go so far as to believe we would go all the way to Williamsport and the Little League World Series, but we'd certainly win our district and maybe even make it to San Bernardino for the Western Region championship.

Then Gabby decided he wasn't interested in working the (my) plan. I was depressed, angry, and confused. How could I be a great sports parent if my son quits baseball? I wasn't sure what my rights were in the situation. After all, baseball was supposed to be for the players and if one of them didn't want to play, how could I demand that he do so. Friends of mine who were involved with Little League advised me to force him to play. As much as that solution appealed to me in the short-term, I knew for sure that it was not the right thing to do.

I remembered telling my son about Jerry Pyle, a star basketball player from Casselton, North Dakota, who played briefly for the University of Minnesota some 20 years ago. He decided to leave the team before his eligibility had expired because, according to an interview in the newspaper, he said he'd played enough basketball in his life, and he wanted to concentrate on his studies. I had told this story in an admiring way, thinking that it communicated the message that you didn't have to do what others expected you to do if it wasn't right for you. But now I wasn't so pleased that I had shared that story with my son. This was different! This was *my* son who was making a decision to withdraw from a sport I loved (and that I was sure he *had* loved!). I felt a terrific loss. I feared I would never be able to watch him play again. He had a grace that I wanted for myself but lacked. When he fielded a hard smash at second base or shortstop, it had the beauty for me of a painting by Van Gogh or Turner.

Over time I have come to believe that my issues about sports were so strong that I began invading my son's psychological space. With me taking up so much room in his life in baseball, he may have felt squeezed out. Perhaps it was as simple as he said it was at the time: he just got tired of playing baseball. But it also may be that he was expressing his independence from me, and from my fixation with sports, by refusing to play baseball, a sport for which he possessed some talent.

SHINING A LIGHT ON THE DEMONS

While attending business school I was introduced to Joseph Luft's Johari Window, a way of thinking about what one and others may know about oneself. You can think of the Johari Window as a window divided into four panes of glass. The first pane represents the part of you that is known to all the world, including yourself. The second pane is that part of you that only you know. Often this contains things that you are keeping secret from others. The third indicates the part of you that is known by others but which you yourself do not know. And the fourth is that part of you that is unknown to all, including yourself.

When I think of coaching and the Johari Window in the same moment, I become very uncomfortable. For one thing, coaching can allow my secrets (pane two) to slip out so that others can see them. Maybe I am seen by others as a positive person who cares more about the welfare of my players than winning. But in a crucial game, people might see the supercompetitive part of me come out and begin to doubt my concern for the kids. Discomfort City.

What could be even worse, I might come to find out things about myself that others have known for a long time but which I don't want to face (pane three). Maybe it's obvious to everyone else that I'm not that positive and I'm living in a dream world. And there is always the possibility that unknown horrible things (whatever they might be) will slip out, things that I don't want to have to look at and that I certainly don't want anyone else to see (pane four).

But in general, more information and insight is almost always better than less. For example, one of the things that the whole incident with Chuckie did for me was to help exorcize the demon named "What-I-Might-Have-Done-in-Basketball."

Partly because of my new understanding of myself as a frustrated basketball player, I recently decided that I wanted to start playing basketball again. I went to a sports medicine clinic and had my knee looked at by an expert for the first time 24 years after I injured it. I was surprised to discover that I had suffered an anterior cruciate ligament (ACL) tear, a pretty serious, often career-ending injury. When the doctor told me how serious my knee injury had been, I became more forgiving of myself for dropping out of basketball in college. I realized that after the injury, I had been unable to go all out because I was constantly worried that the knee would give out under me.

The doctor advised me against getting an operation. He also suggested that I stick to running and give up basketball. I didn't take his advice at first because it was too important to me to play basketball for the first time in more than 10 years. But after awhile the experience became less of a thrill and I quit, forever this time, with no more regrets. Perhaps I have gotten past the yearning to be a great athlete. Perhaps the relief is only temporary.

What once seemed like such a simple thing, coaching kids, now seems tied in to big issues: how we coaches feel about ourselves as former athletes; how we feel about the way we were coached; how we feel about how we were raised; how we feel about how successful we are now as adults; and how we adjust to the unavoidable reality of getting older.

I have learned a lot as I have gotten older, but in spite of how mature and well-adjusted I may think I have become, it is amazing how easy it is for the old ambition to creep back in unobserved. The old dreams that I thought had died live on: *Now* I will gain the glory I had not been able to achieve when I was an athlete myself, no longer as an athlete, and perhaps not even as a coach. But maybe, just maybe, as the writer of a coaching book.

When this happens, I begin to put the old pressure on myself in new ways, and something important is lost. I lose my sense of myself as someone who is worthy in my own right, not because of anything I might do. And I also lose a sense of my own freedom, to do what I want and need to do to be what I have the potential to be.

This resurgence of ambition is a sure sign that the demons are active in me. All those horrible demonic things that "other" big-time and Little League coaches do are in me as well. They are in me, and they can rise to the surface and spill out in a nanosecond if I don't deal with them. And I have learned over the years that the way to deal with internal demons is to shine the light on them. By seeing them and accepting them as an important *part of me*, they lose their power to control me and I feel an invigorating freedom.

One thing I *can* attest to: Coaching kids has increased my understanding of myself and the world around me. Coaching has helped me see and disempower demons that were once invisible but influential. I suspect there are other revelations yet to come.

Sports have given me a lot of joy and a bit of pain. All in all, I wouldn't have anything different. Well, maybe it would have been nice to have made that tackle on Greg Lokken back in the ninth grade. And perhaps just one or two hits off Bernie Graner . . .

19

Every Kid a Coach!

This kind of coach may well gain as much satisfaction from teaching the developmentally disabled as Olympic champions . . . The best coaches and teachers are frequently found elsewhere than in the major leagues.

—Dorcas Susan Butt
Psychology of Sport

Every kid can't become a major league athlete. Few kids will be able to star for their high school team, let alone a college or professional team. And even playing on the high school team is beyond the reach of many of the players we coach. But every kid can learn to enjoy, even love, a sport throughout his lifetime. You may have read of tennis players and swimmers who retire at an early age and then never want to see another tennis racquet or swimming pool again because they didn't enjoy it. Or they once enjoyed it, but it became a job and they couldn't wait to take and shove it out of their life. Lifelong love of a sport is a gift you can help give the players you coach.

THE GOAL: MAKE EVERY KID A COACH

The most appropriate objective for a coach is not to turn his or her players into Michael Jordans but rather to give each of them the opportunity to become an effective coach themselves when they grow up.

The elements of effective coaching include communication, encouragement, teaching, developing strong relationships with people, and learning how to motivate a group of people to accomplish great things together. These are skills that are highly relevant to any career that young athletes end up pursuing. Most of the kids you will coach will themselves become parents, and the techniques of positive coaching are perfect for parents who want to support their children in their efforts to be the best people they can be.

Children who experience good coaching cannot help but pick up some of the techniques of good coaching themselves. Most of us try to replicate what is done to us, and children who are fortunate enough to experience a positive coaching style are more likely to incorporate elements of that style into their own way of doing things.

No child who comes away from a sports experience with the philosophy and tools of positive coaching will feel cheated, regardless of how well or poorly she may have performed as an athlete. The key is the coach she has, and that's where you come in. Effective coaching techniques are highly correlated with success, and you can help give your players an edge in whatever they choose to do with their lives.

MAKE THE "UNSPECIAL" KIDS FEEL SPECIAL

When I was a camp counselor for Neighborhood House at Camp Owendigo in St. Paul, Minnesota, years ago, I supervised a group of rambunctious grade-school boys. All but one of them was active and energetic. Daniel was a shy, overweight kid. Nobody paid much attention to him, and he didn't really put much energy into the activities that everyone else seemed to enjoy so much. I don't really remember doing anything special with Daniel, but nonetheless, at the end of his stay at Owendigo, his mother singled me out before she took him back home. She thanked me for the special attention I had given him. She mentioned that this was the first time he had come home each night from camp and talked excitedly about his experience.

I was pleased and quite surprised that I had had that kind of impact on Daniel. I believe lots of coaches would be similarly surprised at the impact they have on the kids they coach. The kindnesses you show kids with problems often aren't reflected in your won-lost record, but they can pay off dramatically with those kids who rarely get singled out for special attention.

THE LASTING IMPACT OF EFFECTIVE COACHING

Time and again I see people motivated by the opportunity to do something that makes an impact, that leaves a lasting mark. Many of the most successful people in this world have been motivated not by a desire to make money but rather to be remembered for having done something of lasting importance. And there is no better way to make an impact than to share what you have learned with young athletes.

Several years ago, I had a boy on my team named Michael. Michael was a hard-to-contain kid with much more energy than he was able to control. He was enthusiastic but often out of control on the basketball court or baseball field. I coached him in two sports for two years before our paths diverged. One day several years later, I ran into him. He didn't bother to even say hello before he yelled out at me, "Try hard, have fun, be a good sport."

I don't know how many times I had told the teams that Michael was a part of those three things. Before every game for sure. And several times during each practice. I believe that if you can incorporate the "big three" into whatever you do, you will be happy and successful. Here was living proof that, in at least one instance, someone had heard and remembered them.

BE THE COACH YOU WOULD'VE WANTED TO PLAY FOR

Sometimes I open coaching workshops by asking coaches to write and talk about the best coach they ever had and what made him or her so terrific. The stories that come out of this experience are wonderful and poignant. Often these adults are remembering things about coaches who are long dead. They describe coaches who were wise, encouraging, gentle, disciplined, great teachers, and wonderful human beings who cared about them as individuals, not just as athletes who could make them look good.

Unfortunately, most of them had less pleasant experiences with other coaches who failed to live up to those standards.

I recently asked Tara VanDerveer to talk to some of my MBA students about how she builds a team. Her team won the NCAA Women's Title in 1990 and just recently again in 1992 with a team that many observers felt had less talent than others. I was interested to hear her say that her goal was to "be the kind of coach I would have wanted to play for."

I now often end talks on positive coaching by challenging and inviting coaches in the audience to become the coaches they would have wanted to play for when they were young athletes.

So I end this book with two challenges and wishes for you in your great adventure as a coach of young people. First, make your goal to turn every one of your players into a coach so they can pass on to others what you are teaching them about life as well as sports. And finally, never lose sight of what it is you would have wanted in a coach when you were young, and do everything in your power to become the coach that you would have wanted to play for.

So go for it. You and your players deserve it.

Appendix A

Cupertino National Little League Goals

The goals of the Cupertino National Little League (CNLL) are to:

1. Create an environment in which children and adults can have fun with baseball.
2. Teach baseball skills, rules, and strategy to our players.
3. Model and teach competitiveness with an emphasis on good sportsmanship.
4. Promote increased self-esteem among CNLL children and adults.

THE CRUCIAL ROLE OF THE MANAGERS

The most important person in the CNLL is the manager. The players look to him for instruction, encouragement, and inspiration. Coaches and parents take their cues from him. Our goals can be met only if managers embrace them and work to achieve them.

HOW MANAGERS CAN HELP ACHIEVE CNLL GOALS

The following are some of the ways that managers can help achieve the CNLL goals.

Goal 1   Create an environment in which children and adults have fun with baseball.

a. Encourage players often. Show by behavior and words that each is an important member of the team *whether or not* they perform well. Give encouragement for effort as well as results.
b. Give every player comparable playing time. Use one-sided games as opportunities to try less-skilled players in more challenging positions.
c. Show your own enjoyment of the game to your players.

Goal 2   Teach baseball skills, rules, and strategy to our players.

a. Rely on positive reinforcement for things done correctly. Minimize negative emphasis on mistakes, which are required for learning to take place. Players can handle only so much negative feedback at a time without becoming discouraged. Players will learn more, try harder, and be more open to accepting criticism if they are praised often. Praise players in public, correct them in private.
b. Provide adequate repetition of teaching. Baseball is complicated. Lessons often need repeating before they are understood. Once players understand, they often need repeated practice before they can perform the expected behavior well.
c. Encourage players to set individual and team goals for themselves corresponding to their ability level and then work to master the skills needed to achieve them.
d. Organize practices to maximize learning and minimize standing around.

Goal 3   Model and teach competitiveness with an emphasis on good sportsmanship.

a. Teach players aggressiveness and good sportsmanship at the same time.

b. Obey the rules and show respect for the umpire even when you disagree.

c. Acknowledge good plays by the opposing team to your players.

d. Always treat players on other teams as members of our community first and as opponents secondarily. Refrain from actions or words that undercut the self-esteem of players on other teams.

Goal 4   Promote increased self-esteem among CNLL children and adults.

a. Encourage players whenever possible. *Show* by words and actions that you *like and accept them* regardless of how well they perform. Adults often assume that children can "read their minds," but children determine whether they are liked and accepted by adults by what the adults say and do.

b. Spend comparable instructional time with all players, regardless of ability.

c. Encourage and reinforce parents for being involved with the team.

Appendix B

Cupertino Hoops Evaluation Forms

Cupertino Hoops 1990-91 Season
Coaches Survey

1. How would you rate the 1990-91 Cupertino Hoops Season overall?

Terrible	Pretty Bad	OK	Pretty Good	Outstanding
1	2	3	4	5

2. How would you rate

Organization of league	1	2	3	4	5
Quality of officiating	1	2	3	4	5
Coaching clinics	1	2	3	4	5
Relationships among coaches.......	1	2	3	4	5
Behavior of players................	1	2	3	4	5
College halftime games	1	2	3	4	5
December Jamboree	1	2	3	4	5
Game site facilities	1	2	3	4	5
Practice site facilities	1	2	3	4	5
Girls playing with boys	1	2	3	4	5
How much fun *you* had	1	2	3	4	5

3. What were the best things about this season? _____

_____

_____

4. What needs to be improved for next season? _____
   _____
   _____

5. Please write the names of any coaches that set a good example (positive with players, good sportsmanship, teaching ability) _____
   _____

6. Should we expand to 9th-10th grades
   next year?   Yes   Maybe   No
7. Are you interested in coaching
   next year?   Yes   Maybe   No
8. Your name (optional) _____
9. Please use the back for any further comments.

Cupertino Hoops 1990-91 Season
Parents Survey

1. How would you rate the 1990-91 Cupertino Hoops Season overall?

Terrible	Pretty Bad	OK	Pretty Good	Outstanding
1	2	3	4	5

2. How would you rate
   Organization of league 1   2   3   4   5
   Quality of officiating 1   2   3   4   5
   Coaching clinics 1   2   3   4   5
   Your child's coaches(es) 1   2   3   4   5
   Behavior of players 1   2   3   4   5
   Behavior of coaches 1   2   3   4   5

3. The goals for our players are to have fun, learn about basketball, and develop increased self-confidence, self-esteem, and character. How would you rate

	None	Some	Lots
How much fun your child had	1	2 3 4	5
How much basketball learned......	1	2 3 4	5
Self-confidence developed	1	2 3 4	5
Self-esteem developed	1	2 3 4	5

4. What were the best things about this season?_____

_____

_____

5. What needs to be improved for next season? _____

_____

_____

6. Should we expand to 9th-10th grades
next year?   Yes Maybe No
7. What grade is your child in? _____
Boy or girl? Boy _____ Girl _____
8. What team number is he/she on? _____
9. Are you interested in volunteering with
Cupertino Hoops next year?   Yes Maybe No
10. Your name/phone number (optional) _____/_____
11. Please use the back for any further comments.

Cupertino Hoops 1990-91 Season
Players Survey

1. How would you rate the 1990-91 Cupertino Hoops
Season overall?

Terrible	Pretty Bad	OK	Pretty Good	Outstanding
1	2	3	4	5

2. How would you rate
Organization of league 1 2 3 4 5

The referees	1	2	3	4	5
Sportsmanship of the *coaches*	1	2	3	4	5
Sportsmanship of the *players*	1	2	3	4	5
Behavior of players	1	2	3	4	5
College halftime games	1	2	3	4	5
December Jamboree	1	2	3	4	5
How much *fun* you had	1	2	3	4	5
How much *basketball* you learned	1	2	3	4	5

3. What are the best things about this season? _____

_____

4. What were the worst things about this season? _____

_____

_____

5. Did you make any new or better friends
   during the season?   Yes   No

6. Do you want to play in Cupertino Hoops
   again next year?   Yes   Maybe   No

7. Your team number _____

8. What grade/school are you in?
   Grade _____ School _____

9. Please use the back if you have any further comments.

1990-91
Cupertino Hoops
Evaluation Results

5 Point Scale

Terrible	Pretty Bad	OK	Pretty Good	Outstanding
1	2	3	4	5

	Player	Parents	Coaches
Overall	4.2	4.5	4.5

Organization	4.1	4.4	4.7
Officiating	2.9	4.1	4.0
Basketball Learned	3.5	4.1	
Fun	4.2	4.6	4.6
Co-ed		4.2	
Coaching Clinics			4.4
Coaches	4.5		
Self-Confidence		4.2	
Self-Esteem	4.1		
New/Better Friends	Yes:	94%	
	No:	6%	
Play Again Next Year?	Yes:	62%	
	Maybe:	29%	
	No:	9%	

9th-10th Grade Program?	Yes	Maybe	No
All Parents	61%	31%	8%
8th Parents	73%	27%	0%
Coaches	81%	13%	6%

Coach Again Next Year?		
	Yes:	81%
	Maybe:	13%
	No:	6%

Bibliography

Ausubel, Nathan (1948), *A Treasury of Jewish Folklore*, New York: J. J. Little & Ives Company.

Bandura, Albert (1990), "Perceived Self-Efficacy in the Exercise of Personal Agency" in *The Psychologist: Bulletin of the British Psychological Society*, 10, 411-424.

Bandura, Albert (1986), *Social Foundations of Thought and Action*, Englewood Cliffs, New Jersey: Prentice-Hall.

Bissinger, H. G. (1990), *Friday Night Lights: A Town, a Team, and a Dream*, Reading, Massachusetts: Addison-Wesley Publishing Company, Inc.

Bogard, R. A., P. J. Robertson, D. L. Bradford, R. Kass, J. I. Porras, and R. Silvers (1989), *The Stanford Interpersonal Dynamics Course Support Package: Instructor's Manual*, Unpublished monograph, Stanford University.

Boswell, Thomas (1989), "99 Reasons Why Baseball is Better than Football" in *The Heart of the Order*, New York: Doubleday.

Boswell, Thomas (1991), "Macho Potatoes on the Couch," *The Economist*, January 5, 1991.

Bradley, Bill (1976), *Life on the Run*, New York: Bantam Books.

Branch, Taylor (1988), *Parting the Waters: America in the King Years 1954-63*, New York: A Touchstone Book, Simon & Shuster Inc.

Briggs, Dorothy Corkille (1970), *Your Child's Self-Esteem*, Garden City, New York: Doubleday and Company, Inc.

Brooks, Bruce (1984), *The Moves Make the Man*, New York: Harper & Row, Publishers, Inc.

Butt, Dorcas Susan (1987), *Psychology of Sport: the Behavior, Motivation, Personality and Performance of Athletes*, New York: Van Nostrand Reinhold Company.

Campbell, Ross (1977), *How to Really Love Your Child*, New York: Signet New American Library.

Cialdini, Robert (1984), *Influence*, New York: Quill.

Collins, James C. and Jerry I. Porras (1989), "Making Impossible Dreams Come True: a Guide to Demystifying Purpose, Mission, and Vision, and Putting Them to Work for You," *Stanford Business School Magazine*, Stanford, California, July 1989.

Collins, James C. and Jerry I. Porras (1991), "Organizational Vision and Visionary Organizations," *California Management Review*, Fall 1991.

Cornwell, Bill (1987), "For Jordan, the Magic is the Game," *San Jose Mercury News*, December 2, 1987.

Deci, Edward L. (1975), *Intrinsic Motivation*, New York: Plenum Press.

de Mello, Anthony (1989), *The Prayer of the Frog*, Anand, India: Gujarat Sahitya Prakash.

Dinkmeyer, Don and Gary D. McKay (1982), *The Parent's Handbook: Systematic Training for Effective Parenting*, Circle Pines, Minnesota: American Guidance Service.

Douglas, Lloyd C. (1929), *The Magnificent Obsession*, New York: Pocket Books.

Dreikurs, Rudolf, M. D. (1964), *Children: the Challenge*, New York: Hawthorne Books, Inc.

Dygard, Thomas J. (1989), *Quarterback Walk-On*, New York: Puffin Books.

Easwaran, Eknath (1978), *Gandhi the Man*, Tomales, California: Nilgiri Press.

Easwaran, Eknath (1991), *Meditation: Commonsense Directions for an Uncommon Life*, Tomales, California: Nilgiri Press.

Ende, Michael (1983), *The Neverending Story*, Garden City, New York: Doubleday.

Evans, Richard I. (1989), *Albert Bandura, the Man and His Ideas—a Dialogue*, New York: Praeger.

Ewing, Martha E. and Vern Seefeldt (1990), "American Youth and Sports Participation," available from the Athletic Footwear Association, 200 Castlewood Drive, North Palm Beach, Florida 33408.

Gardner, John W. (1981 Revised Edition), *Self-Renewal*, New York: W.W. Norton & Company.

Gardner, John W. (1990), *On Leadership*, New York: The Free Press, a Division of Macmillan, Inc.

Gardner, John W. (1968), *No Easy Victories*, New York: Harper & Row.

Gardner, John W. (1991), *Building Community*, Washington, D.C.: Independent Sector.

Goodman, Paul (1962), *The Community of Scholars*, New York: Random House.

Halberstam, David (1981), *The Breaks of the Game*, New York: Ballantine Books.

Harris, Mark (1956), *A Ticket for a Seamstitch*, Lincoln, Nebraska: University of Nebraska Press.

Hein, Piet (1969), *Grooks 2*, Garden City, New York: Doubleday & Company, Inc.

Hilfiker, David, M.D. (1987), *Healing the Wounds*, New York: Penguin.

Kanter, Rosabeth Moss and William H. Fonvielle (1987), "When to Persist and When to Give Up," *Management Review*, January 1987.

Kelly, Barbara (1987), "Self-Esteem Team's Four Local Players," *San Jose Mercury News*, September 12, 1987.

Kerr, Steven (1975), "On the Folly of Rewarding A, While Hoping for B," *Psychological Foundations of Organizational Behavior*, Edited by Barry M. Staw, Glenview, Illinois: Scott, Foresman and Company.

Kohlenberg, Leah (1992), "Little League Coach's Throat Slashed in a Fight," *New York Times*, May 21, 1992.

Kohn, Alfie (1986), *No Contest: The Case Against Competition*, Boston: Houghton Mifflin.

Kopp, Sheldon B. (1972), *If You Meet the Buddha on the Road, Kill Him!*, New York: Bantam Books.

Kouzes, James M. and Barry Z. Posner (1987), *The Leadership Challenge: How to Get Extraordinary Things Done in Organizations*, San Francisco: Jossey-Bass Publishers.

Kraus, Robert (1971), *Leo the Late Bloomer*, New York: Windmill Books.

Leboeuf, Michael (1985), *The Greatest Management Principle in the World*, New York: Putnam.

Lewis, C.S. (1960), *Out of the Silent Planet*, New York: Macmillan.

Looney, Douglas S. (1989), "A Most Unusual Man," *Sports Illustrated*, September 4, 1989, Vol. 71, No. 10.

Lord, Bette Bao (1984), *In the Year of the Boar and Jackie Robinson*, New York: Harper and Row.

Luft, Joseph (1984), *Group Processes: An Introduction to Group Dynamics* (Third Edition), Palo Alto, California: Mayfield Publishing Company.

March, James G. (1971), "The Technology of Foolishness," *Readings in Managerial Psychology*, Edited by Harold J. Leavitt, Louis R. Pondy, and David M. Boje, Chicago: The University of Chicago Press.

Marx, Karl and Friedrich Engels (1947 edition), *The Manifesto of the Communist Party*, Chicago: Charles H. Kerr.

McClelland, David C. (1966), "That Urge to Achieve," *Organizational Psychology* (Second Edition), by D. A. Kolb, I. M. Rubin, and J. M. McIntyre (eds), Prentice-Hall, 1974.

McPhee, John (1965, 1978), *A Sense of Where You Are: a Profile of Bill Bradley at Princeton*, New York: The Noonday Press, Farrar, Straus, Giroux.

Mecca, Andrew M., Neil J. Smelser, and John Vasconcellos, Eds. (1989), *The Social Importance of Self-Esteem*, Berkeley, California: University of California Press.

Mikes, Jay (1987), *Basketball FundaMENTALS: A Complete Mental Training Guide*: Champaign, Illinois: Leisure Press.

Miller, Alice (1983), *For Your Own Good: Hidden Cruelty in Child-Rearing and the Roots of Violence*, New York: Farrar, Straus, Giroux.

Miller, Alice (1981), *The Drama of the Gifted Child*, New York: Basic Books, Inc. Publishers.

Miller, Alice (1984), *Thou Shalt Not Be Aware: Society's Betrayal of the Child*, New York: New American Library.

Miller, Robert B., Stephen E. Heiman, with Tad Tuleja (1985), *Strategic Selling: The Unique Sales System Proven Successful by America's Best Companies*, New York: William Morrow and Company, Inc.

Morain, Claudia (1987), "Marathoner Tricks the Mind," *San Jose Mercury News*, May 27, 1987.

Neusner, Jacob (1991), "Make My Students American," *San Jose Mercury News*, September 4, 1991.

Nideffer, Robert (1976), *The Inner Athlete*, New York: Thomas Crowell.

O'Connor, Elizabeth (1968), *Journey Inward Journey Outward*, New York: Harper & Row.

Ozer, Elizabeth M. and Albert Bandura (1990), "Mechanisms Governing Empowerment Effects: A Self-Efficacy Analysis," *Journal of Personality and Social Psychology*, 58, 472-486.

Palmer, Parker J. (1990), *Leading from Within*, available from the

Indiana Office for Campus Ministries, 1100 West 42nd Street, Indianapolis, IN 46208.

Patton, Phil (1990), *Baseball: 30 Full-Color Cards to Keep or Send*, New York: Fawcett Columbine.

Peters, Thomas J. and Robert H. Waterman, Jr. (1982), *In Search of Excellence: Lessons from America's Best-Run Companies*, New York: Warner Books.

Pruitt, Jim (1982), *Play Better Basketball*, Chicago: Contemporary Books, Inc.

Sanders, Scott Russell (1991), *Secrets of the Universe*, Boston: Beacon Press.

Satir, Virginia (1972), *Peoplemaking*, Palo Alto, California: Science and Behavior Books.

Taylor, Shelley E. (1989), *Positive Illusions: Creative Self-Deception and the Healthy Mind*, U.S.A.: BasicBooks, a Division of HarperCollins Publishers.

Telander, Rick (1976), *Heaven is a Playground*, New York: A Fireside Book Simon & Schuster Inc.

Tolkien, J.R.R. (1937 and 1938), *The Hobbit*, New York: Ballantine Books, Inc.

Tutko, Thomas and Umberto Tosi (1976), *Sports Psyching: Playing Your Best Game All of the Time*, Los Angeles: J. P. Tarcher, Inc.

Tutko, Thomas and William Bruns (1976), *Winning is Everything and Other American Myths*, New York: MacMillan Publishing Company, Inc.

Warren, William E. (1988), *Coaching and Winning*, Englewood Cliffs, New Jersey: Prentice-Hall, Inc.

Wellman, Manly Wade (1963), *Who Fears the Devil?*, New York: Ballantine Books.

Wooden, John (1985 Revised Edition), *They Call Me Coach*, Waco, Texas: Word Books.

Yamamoto, Kaoru (1972), *The Child and His Image*, New York: Houghton Mifflin.

Topical Reference Index

Warde Publishers

for additional copies of

POSITIVE COACHING
Building Character and Self-Esteem Through Sports

Write:
Warde Publishers, Inc.
3000 Alpine Road
Portola Valley, CA 94028

Toll-free order line:
(800) 699–2733

✂ ---

ORDER FORM

Please send me _____ copy(ies) of *Positive Coaching: Building Character and Self-Esteem Through Sports* by Jim Thompson at $19.95. (Add $3.00 for first copy and $1.50 for each additional copy for packing and shipping. CA residents, add $1.65 sales tax per book ordered). Make check payable to Warde Publishers, Inc.   Total enclosed = $ _____

Name _____

Organization _____

Address _____

City _____ State _____ Zip _____

May we send information on *Positive Coaching* to a friend or associate?

Referral name _____

Organization _____

Address _____

City _____ State _____ Zip _____

Sports League and Youth Program Discount Pricing
available for purchases of more than 10 copies.
Please call our toll-free order line.

**POSITIVE
COACHING
ALLIANCE.**

Dear Reader:

In 1998 I left the Stanford Graduate School of Business to start **Positive Coaching Alliance**, a nonprofit organization based at Stanford University.

Positive Coaching Alliance is committed to transforming youth sports so sports can transform youth. We will do that in three major ways, by:

1. Changing the very nature of what it means to be a youth sports coach. We intend to replace the current model of "win-at-all-cost" coaching with the Positive Coaching Mental Model.

2. Igniting a movement of "change agents" all over this country who will provide leadership to local youth sports organizations to turn them into outstanding "educational-athletic" organizations. Our "Standards of Excellence" and toolkit will help Positive Coaching activists make this transformation beginning at the local level.

3. Providing educational experiences to coaches, parents, and youth sports leaders based on sound psychological and motivational research. Since most people involved with youth sports are volunteers with limited time, we provide workshops and other educational opportunities in "bite-size insights" that can be digested in short amounts of time.

You can find out more about **Positive Coaching Alliance** from our web site

www.positivecoach.org

or contact us at

Positive Coaching Alliance   650-725-0024
Department of Athletics   650-725-7242 (fax)
Stanford University   pca@positivecoach.org
Stanford, CA 94305-6150

If you like the ideas and tools in *Positive Coaching* or my second book, *Shooting in the Dark: Tales of Coaching and Leadership*, please join us. Together we can transform the culture of youth sports. Thank you.

All the best,

Jim Thompson